Out of the Ordinary

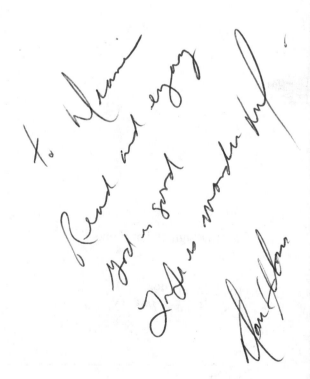

HomeFire Family Ministries
PO Box 3126
Shiremanstown, PA   17070

Cover Design by Pat Edmonds

First Edition 1996
Printed 7/96 5M LR

ISBN 0-942381-11-4

Psalm 1

How well God must like you.
You don't hang out at Sin Saloon,
You don't drink along dead-end road,
You don't go to smart mouth college.

Instead you thrill to God's Word,
You chew on scripture day and night.
You're a tree replanted in Eden,
Bearing fresh fruit every month;
Never dropping a leaf,
Always in bloom

You're not at all like the wicked
Who are mere windblown dust
Without defense in court,
Unfit for innocent people.
God charts the road you take,
The road they take is skid row.

The Message

To Judy

My wife for 38 years

My best friend

beautiful, fresh and talented

Our marriage is packed with

loving and living

Growing old together

in sickness and in health

until death do us part

Preface

Just as I was the most unlikely to ever succeed as a preacher and just as I was the most unlikely to ever succeed as a singer, I certainly am the most unlikely to ever write a book.

I will liken this challenging experience to a ride on a roller coaster with its nerve racking climb to the top or its wild plunge downward or its terrorizing upside down loop.

There were days that I could scarcely remember what happened last week let alone forty years ago. There were other days and nights when I couldn't seem to type fast enough to keep up with my thoughts. And there were those times when the whole project overwhelmed me.

I felt every emotion possible while writing my book. I poured myself into every page.

I could not have accomplished this tremendous task without the help of those who encouraged me to tell my story.

I am grateful to...

My dad and mom who have prayed for me every day of my life, thanks.

My wife, Judy, who helped me communicate my heart in an understandable way.

My three lovable daughters, Kristie, Robin, and Connie who inspired me with, "You can do it, Dad!"

My three incredible sons-in-law who gave me helpful comments and much computer instruction.

Also, my thanks to my friend Ted Terry who guided me along the way and to Ralph Bradshaw who shared his printing expertise with me.

I am grateful to Ernie "Hergie" Hergenroeder, for his delightful illustrations that add just the right touch to the book.

Ernie "Hergie" Hergenroeder
790 W. Shaw, Ste. 390
Fresno, CA 93704
Phone (209) 225-7447
Fax (209) 225-7211

Roy Dressel, Photographer, Visalia, CA.

Contents

• • •

1. If We Perish, We Perish 14

2. Good Morning, Sir, I'm Your New Paperboy 20

3. Drive, Determination And Diligence 28

4. Hit This Note, Dave 32

5. Little Is Much 44

6. Hitting The Big Time 52

7. Once A Courier, Always A Courier 60

8. The Toilet Paper Story 70

9. I Do , I Do, I Will, I Will 74

10. Diesel Smoke 88

11. Roever, Rossey, Stevens And Ward 96

12. Unforgettable Moments 110

13. The Big Boys 120

14. One More Time With Feeling 134

15. Go Ye Therefore 144

Contents

• • •

16. The Beginning Of The End 174

17. Dave Kyllonen, The Family Affair 186

18. Barbados, Here I Come 196

19. Pastoral Candidate 228

20. Wonderful Westside 234

21. On The Road Again 262

22. Father Of The Bride 282

23. Follow Your Dreams 304

24. Panama, Dios Le Bendiga (God Bless You) ... 314

25. The Enemy Attacks 324

26. And They Call Me, "Pappy" 330

27. A Prescription For A Healthy Family 336

28. You Too Can Be Successful 344

29. I Can Type 360

30. My Final Statement 362

FOREWARD

Dave Kyllonen is a man whom I have met personally. I know he walks the talk. You will know this, also, because this book is not just another autobiography dealing with tragedy and triumphs. Dave includes lessons he has learned along the way. These lessons are the basis on which his Christian principles are grounded and implemented. His story is told in a simple and humorous way so all can read and understand, and gain and execute the truth that Dave has reaped.

Dave and I have many things in common. We have both traveled around the country and seen the world, taken our families with us on the road and left them behind, preached and sang (and in my case, played the piano) in front of different audiences both young and old. So, many of the situations that Dave describes are situations to which I can relate. But the precepts he sets forth from the situations described, are precepts by which all persons can be encouraged and enriched.
For example;

- *God answers the cries of His people, and has mercy on His people when they pray a prayer of faith.*

- *Communication is to marriage as fuel is to a car.*

- *Set up stones of remembrance.*

- *An ounce of forgiveness is better than a pound of punishment.*

- *Tough decisions are never easy but are usually necessary.*

- *Your future is only as big as your dream.*

- *Friendships require an investment of your life.*

- *Satisfaction is sometimes found in the little things of life.*

- *God is bigger than your biggest problem.*

- *Money cannot buy what a family can give.*

- *Teach your family values so they will obey under any circumstances.*

- *Success is more than having money in your pocket, it is being fulfilled in your heart.*

These are just a few of the many lessons that Dave has incorporated into his book. I hope, as you read, you will allow God to speak into your heart so you will gain much from this book and, perhaps, even be encouraged as you and God face your daily situations in life.

Dave Roever

The Dave Kyllonen Family

1958
Dave & Judy Kyllonen

1959 Kristie

Gregory Hollis

Elijah
Isaiah
Alexsondra

1962 Robin

Paul Eschbach

Erica
Ellie

1964 Connie

Michael Hammer

Victoria
Tiffany

CHAPTER ONE

©HERGIE

IF WE PERISH, WE PERISH.

"GET OUT! EVERYONE GET OUT! THE BUILDING is on fire! There isn't time to take anything with you! Just run for your life!"

Edgar Hall, our neighbor, was yelling these words as he ran down the hallway of our apartment building. His voice had the fear of God in it. He knew there was great trouble for those who didn't get out of the building, immediately! His words came through the walls of our little apartment like a shot from a rifle. It landed in my five- year-old heart and sent terror through my whole body. It was early in the morning and his voice woke me out of a sound sleep. My dad had gone to work leaving, my two-year-old brother, Jonathan, my mother and me at home. I was so glad my mother was there. We were panicky, confused and disoriented. Where was our clothing and our shoes?

We never once thought of our toys and Mom didn't think of taking her money. All we could think of was getting out before it was too late!

Mom opened the door. The lights in the hallway were out and it was pitch black. The smoke got in our eyes so we couldn't open them. We were coughing and choking and struggling to breathe.

There we were, all three of us, standing two feet outside our door, not able to move one inch. Jonathan and I were screaming at the top of our lungs. Mother didn't know what to do.

Finally, she got us back into our apartment and shut the door. What were we to do now? We boys were too much for mother. Maybe she could make it out by herself, or maybe with one boy, but two of us were just too much for her. I looked into my mothers eyes and saw despair.

She sat down and began to talk to us about what we had to do to get out of the building. We had to find the stairs. She calmed us down and prepared us for our next try. When she thought we were ready, she opened the door again.

It was worse! Now there was a deafening roar. The wind and smoke were roaring. We still couldn't see and the choking began all over again. We screamed, kicked, yelled, and pulled at mother to go back. No one was there to help us. We were all alone in that hallway, knowing we couldn't find our way out.

Mother got us back into our apartment and closed the door. She took us boys by the hand and led us into our little living room. We got down on our knees and, placing her arms around us and pulling us close to her, she began to do what she did best. She prayed! She lifted her frightened voice toward heaven and prayed, "Oh, God, we need your help. We can't get out of this burning building. We are going to stay on our knees until You send help, but, if we perish, we perish."

Outside the building a crowd had gathered. Fire trucks and firemen had arrived. The fire was out of control. All six stories would be gone in a few minutes. No one was allowed near the building.

My dad was at work when he heard about the fire but rushed home to find his family. Fear gripped his heart when he arrived at the scene. It was worse than he had thought. Was his family still in there? He stood looking up at the building to where our apartment was on the fourth floor. How could he go in to get them? What about the firemen? They aren't going to let anyone go in there. Surely everyone was out!

Then came the moment! My dad made a mad dash for the building. Firemen chased him and yelled at him to not go in, but on he went.

He knew the building very well. He had been up those steps many times. Nothing could stop him. Through fire, smoke and the deafening roar, he soon reached our apartment. He crashed through the door and there we were, still on our knees, waiting for God to answer our mother's prayer.

• Success Principle 1

GOD HEARS AND ANSWERS THE CRIES OF HIS PEOPLE.

Psalm 34:17 "The righteous cry and the Lord hears and delivers them out of all their troubles." NASB

• • •

Things changed in a hurry! Dad made the difference. Just hearing his voice took away some of the fear. Dad had such authority. He assured us that we could get out of the building. He grabbed up Jonathan and told me to hold tight to my mother and not to stop for anything. Mother was to hold on to him as we made our way out. He opened our apartment door and we were on our way. We didn't cry or scream. Oh, we couldn't see and we choked on the smoke, but Dad knew the way! We inched our way along the hallway until we found the stairs.

I remember hearing someone yelling, " If any one is still in there, just keep coming. You're close to being out. Just keep on coming."

Then we were out! The crowd cheered when they saw us. We were glad to see them through our burning, blurry eyes. We hugged every one in sight.

Someone came and brought us to the side of the building where we could see our apartment window. There was fire leaping out of the window at least ten feet high. We had just been there moments before. We were taken into the house across the street to watch the fire finish it's job. The fire had gone from the basement, up through all the floors and finally only the roof was left. What a great crash came when the roof fell seven stories and landed in the basement. God had spared our lives! Somehow I knew: surely He had something special for my life.

God's mercy on my family that day has never been forgotten. We still love to talk about it. My mother and dad still cry when they relive that day. And I still remember how frightened I was as a little five year old child.

Years later, I received a package in the mail. It contained two newspapers from Monessen, Pennsylvania. It was Feb. 15 and 16, 1940. I could hardly believe my eyes. Front page headlines, a huge write up and even pictures describing the fire. It was true. It wasn't a dream. It really did happen.

- Success Principle 2

FINDING HIP POCKET HEROS.

Hip pockets are taken for granted. We use them everyday. They hold our keys, money, etc. Without them where would we put our everyday stuff?
Hip pocket heros are people who greatly impact our daily lives. Our parents, family and friends. Yet sometimes we take them for granted. They seldom are noticed, yet they are of great value. My dad qualifies as a hip pocket hero. He is an ordinary kind of person, yet I have found him to be of great value. He saved my life and those of my family. I've learned to appreciate him as a hero. We all have people who are hip pocket heroes. They helped us get where we are today. We must learn to appreciate them for that, and to realize we didn't get to this place on our

own. Others contributed along the way. Some, like my father, risked their lives. Many people blame others for their past. All they see is the negative and what others have not done for them. We need to see the positive. There's great value in finding hip pocket heros.

My mother is a hip pocket hero too! Her prayer of faith, "If we perish! we perish!" qualifies her as a hip pocket hero.

"SUCCESSFUL PEOPLE DON'T BLAME THEIR PAST, BUT ALLOW THEIR PAST TO SHAPE THEIR FUTURE."

• • •

CHAPTER TWO

GOOD MORNING, SIR, I'M YOUR NEW PAPER BOY!

OUR FAMILY GREW THROUGH THE NEXT FEW years. My only sister, Lillian, joined our family. Then two more brothers, Paul and Phillip. Now I was the oldest of five children. Dad was working hard but not making enough money to meet the demands of a growing family. I was in Jr. High and felt I needed to help Dad. One of my friends offered me his paper route. I was thrilled! I began to deliver 125 newspapers every day after school.

I really wanted to be a good newspaper boy, so I went to each house and asked, "Where do you want me to put your paper every day?" Each family was surprised to hear that I was actually willing to do that. Their paper was usually just thrown from a moving bike and landed anywhere. Well, I can tell you, it sure worked. I was an instant success.

In the fall, there was a big contest to see which paperboy could get the most new subscribers on their route. The prize was a brand new bicycle.

I knew that Mom and Dad could never afford a bicycle for any of us Kyllonen kids. I wanted to win that bike more than anything else in the world.

I went out to canvas my route and to convince all the people who were still buying their newspapers at the store that they should subscribe from me and let me deliver their papers to them.

The big day arrived and the announcement was made, "The winner of the brand new bicycle is Dave Kyllonen."

I had done it! My hard work and diligence paid off.

They even printed my picture, sitting on my new bike, on the front page of the Daily Dispatch.

My family was proud of me. Tell the truth, I was proud of myself.

On "pay your bill" day, you wouldn't believe the great tips that came my way. Christmas was even better. Gifts from my customers and lots of money made Christmas very special for my family.

I always paid my paper bill on time. I opened an account at the bank and paid it with a check. I wanted to impress my boss at the newspaper office. I did!

One day my boss called me into his office. He asked me if I would give up my present route and take a very troubled route that no one else would take. It looked like a good challenge and I said, "yes."

This may have been the first challenge I encountered in my life. Since then, the spark of my life has been when someone presented me with a challenge, especially, when they told me it couldn't be done. That turned me on! This was beginning to prepare me for the future.

I had a plan to do the same thing I had done before. What I didn't realize was that my new route would be very difficult as I was now delivering papers to the inner-city apartment buildings. Some people wanted their paper put behind the screen door, and they lived three floors up! But I did it. I put papers in safe places for people, all over my route.

- Success Principle 3

WORK HARD, DO YOUR BEST.

It's the only way to the top.
Proverbs 12:24 states
"Diligent hands will rule, but
laziness ends in slave labor."
NIV

•   •   •

Some of my clients tried my patience, especially when they dodged me on collection day. Now my number two plan was put into motion. I would not leave their paper that day. Then I would go back to the office and wait for them to call. And they would. They would ask why I had missed them. I would tell them I would be there in a few minutes, with their paper, so please have the money ready. It worked every time.

One day when I was sixteen my boss called me and said, "Dave, we want you to leave your paper route and take a job in the circulation department." I was put in charge of 50 boys. It was fun, teaching them how to be successful paper boys. I learned much about life, talking and sharing with those boys. They did not want to deliver papers my way. The boys were willing to throw the papers just some where near the porch and be done in a hurry. They couldn't pay their bill on time and didn't understand why their customers didn't want to pay them on collection day. But some of them did want to succeed and make greater strides in handling their routes. This made my job a success.

The day came when I was offered a new position in the office. It was a promotion, a step up, toward circulation manager. It seemed that I might be in the newspaper business at the New Kensington Daily Dispatch for the rest of my life.

During my last three years of high school I was on the "Work program." I attended school in the mornings and worked at the Daily Dispatch in the afternoons. It seemed that life couldn't get any better.

But as the old saying goes, "Into every life a little rain must fall."

By now I was a sophomore in high school and I had become a tall lanky six footer. Mr. Dunn, the basketball coach at New Kensington High School, approached me about playing on the team.

"Man" I thought, "this is great." I really wanted to play basketball.

On the third day of practice the coach blew the whistle and motioned for me to come. Dad was standing with Mr. Dunn and when I approached them Dad said, "David, this is a waste of your time. Get your things and come on home with me."

"Mr. Dunn", I said, " I'm sorry. I really want to play basketball but my dad won't let me."

On the way home Dad and I never said a word to each other. I was upset, frustrated and angry. I felt like I was being cheated and my dad had let me down.

I had been taking trumpet lessons and decided to join the school band. That helped fill the gap for not being able to play basketball. And dad said he would let me be in the band.

Weeks passed and it was football season. The band director announced that we would be playing during half-time.

In great excitement I hurried home to tell mom and dad what a neat thing I was going to do. I thought they would enjoy watching me march up and down the football field but dad said, "We don't believe in going to football games."

I couldn't believe what he was saying. First I couldn't play basketball and now I couldn't march with the school band.

I said, "Dad, if you don't let me play my trumpet at the football games then I can't be in the band. And if that's your decision then I'm putting my trumpet away and I will never play it again."

Dad's decision held and I regret to say I've never played the trumpet since.

Dad was wrong. He was unfair but I decided not to rebel. I would do the right thing and not fight back.

I loved my dad and had great respect for him during my teen years. It's never changed. He is 88 this year and still going strong. There isn't anything my dad won't do for me.

When I was turning seventeen a brand new Pastor, Rev. Otis Keener, and his wife, Irene, came to our church. They were special people who came into my life at just the right time. I started listening to the messages. I moved to the front row and got involved in all the services. Pastor Keener helped me find the altar of the church. At every service, it seemed, I was the last to leave. Everyone kept asking me what was wrong in my life and why was I always at the altar for so long? I finally told my family, my friends, and my pastor, that God was dealing with my heart and life and that I simply wanted to hear from Him.

As I look back at my life in the ministry I have to thank Otis Keener for his influence in my life. I've always said that I'm here because of him. He bought me my first black suit; even though I couldn't preach yet, I was beginning to look like a preacher.

A Reflection From Otis Keener

It is always a miracle watching God call and mold a man.

Dave Kyllonen was in his teens when I was called to pastor his home church in New Kensington, Pennsylvania. Physically he gained six inches in height in six months. It seemed one could stand across the church and watch his trousers grow shorter.

However, the greater joy was found in watching Dave grow spiritually. While yet in high school he cultivated a habit of responding to God's word. Many Sundays concluded with him bowed in brokeness at the altar. The Holy Spirit was shaping him to fit into God's plan. Everyone was thrilled to hear of his decision to attend Bible College and prepare for ministry. My wife and I encouraged him to enroll in Central Bible College, Springfield, Missouri. We had met and married while there and on that campus Dave was to find his lifelong helpmate. Judy has proven to be one of heaven's best gifts to Dave.

His desire to preach and his love for music combined to thrust The Couriers into singing from that campus. This talented male team ministered together the next 25 years. All across America and in many other nations, they touched lives with the love of Jesus Christ. Dave was the preacher. The men all lived what they sang and preached. God honored their faithfulness with multitudes finding Christ as their personal Savior.

Through the years I have watched Dave remain faithful to his CALL, his COMPANION and his CHILDREN. He has passed the rich spiritual inheritance received from Godly parents on to three daughters. Little wonder they all married preaching musicians. Now the whole family is on the road with HomeFire Ministries and the "song goes on."

My wife and I are thankful and honored to have had a small part in showing Dave the joy there is in serving Jesus.

A friend and fellow servant of our Lord,
Otis Keener

• Success Principle 4

LEARN TO HEAR THE VOICE OF GOD.

There are many voices that call us,
but when you recognize God's voice,
open up both ears and listen.

• • •

I'll never forget when I got the call from the newspaper office about the biggest promotion of my life.

My boss said, "Dave, we have decided to move you higher up in the circulation department. Congratulations, you can start tomorrow morning."

God had already been speaking to my heart, though, and I had decided to enter Central Bible College of the Assemblies of God to study to be a preacher. When I told my boss he couldn't believe it; but he wished me well.

I had to make quick plans and start preparing to leave for Springfield, Missouri, to enter the Fall term. That was **September, 1954.**

Little did I realize that my life would begin to move at a very rapid pace for the next 40 years.

My big news hit the church with unbelief. "Why, Dave isn't preacher material! Of all of the young people in our church, Dave is the least qualified for ministry."

You must understand that I was a tall, skinny, awkward, bashful kid that could hardly say, "hello," to my mother.

I had never been away from home and it was about 1,000 miles to Springfield, Missouri. What a major day in my life! I couldn't believe it was happening.

I looked out the window as I pulled away from the house. There was Dad, Mom, Jonathan, Lillian, Paul and Phillip, all waving good-bye.

I never thought or dreamed that I wouldn't be coming back to live with them again. For the next 40 years it would be only visits for a few hours, and then gone again!

CHAPTER THREE

DRIVE, DETERMINATION AND DILIGENCE.

I ARRIVED AT CENTRAL BIBLE COLLEGE WITH VERY little money. My family didn't have any money and things happened so fast I didn't have time to save. I would have to get a job. If I didn't find work, I would quit at the end of the first semester.

Getting a job was going to be a huge task. I prayed and asked the Lord to help. I didn't know where to begin. The Gospel Publishing House of the Assemblies of God was being talked about by many of my friends so I decided to go there and see if they would hire me.

When I got there, I was surprised. There was a long line of other students there ahead of me. I stood in line all afternoon. I thought, this is impossible! I'll never get a job here. I probably won't get a job anywhere with all these students needing work. But I stayed until 4:30 that afternoon. That was when the Personnel Director made the announcement that they were closing for the day and that the rest of us would have to come back tomorrow. I quickly took the application form and wrote one sentence, real big, at the top:

"I CAN TYPE 90 WORDS A MINUTE WITHOUT MAKING A MISTAKE."

I signed my name, David Kyllonen, handed the form to the lady at the desk and left.

The next morning, I got a call from the Personnel Director of the Gospel Publishing House. She said if I would come to her office and prove that I could type 90 words a minute without making a mistake, I would have a job!

In high school, typing had been my favorite subject. I was in a class with 30 girls and decided I would be better than them all.

The day, after the interview I got the job! I was put in a room with a group of girls. We each had a desk stacked with things to type. I went to work and typed everything in sight. The girls chatted and filed their nails while I worked.

I typed for two weeks and cleared off every desk. I had typed myself and everyone else out of a job. The director came and congratulated me on a good job, but told me there was no more work. He would call me when there was another opening. I left work that day very sad.

My diligence paid off. The very next week the Personnel Director called and said they had another job for me.

I worked at the Gospel Publishing House for four years. It paid my college bill. It gave me confidence. I was assured that God had called me and that He was going to take care of my needs.

I was the mail carrier and delivered mail to the executives and other important people of the Assemblies of God. Little did I know that the friendships I developed would last a lifetime and prove to be very important in the days to come.

- Success Principle 5

WORK YOURSELF OUT OF A JOB.

Paper Route

*I kept moving up because I exceeded the
challenges given to me.
I began to teach others how to do it
right. I was learning how to mentor,
to hand over the reigns. I was working
myself out of a job. This gave me
confidence to make the decision to go
to Bible School and be in the ministry.
This was something foreign to me and
seemingly beyond my capabilities.*

Gospel Publishing House

I worked myself right out of a job.

*A successful businessman always works himself
out of a job. He finds quality people and
mentors them to take over the business.*

*A successful pastor should work himself out of
a job. He teaches (equips) the people to do
the work of the ministry. (Ephesians 5)*

*A successful parent works himself out of a
job.*

*We teach our kids to be independent, to make
right decisions, to lead a successful life on
their own. They shouldn't always be clinging
to us. We work ourselves out of a job.*

*My life today in HomeFire Family Ministries
is still working myself out of a job by
mentoring my family to keep the ministry going
after my time is through.*

• • •

Walking into the gym at Central Bible College was an awesome
moment. I was excited about playing basketball and
getting on a team. I went to the gym for one hour everyday.
It was a great day when I sent my family the school newspaper with
pictures and write up of me making the all star team. Life does have
it's good days.

CHAPTER FOUR

HIT THIS NOTE, DAVE!

I WASN'T IN SCHOOL VERY MANY WEEKS WHEN I heard there was going to be a Gospel Concert at the Shrine Mosque featuring the Blackwood Brothers and the Statesmen quartets. I had never heard of either of these groups. Every one was going, so I decided to go see what everyone was so excited about.

When I got there, the building was already full. I bought a "standing room only" ticket and headed for the balcony.

In peanut heaven, I stood for the next three hours to hear music that would change my life forever. I listened to James Blackwood sing with all the Blackwoods backing him up. WOW! What a sound!

When I thought I had heard it all, J.D. Sumner started singing a bass solo. Now that was singing I had never heard before. What a voice! The lower he sang, the more excited I was. His voice rumbled the building. Was I impressed! I couldn't believe my ears.

I loved the Statesmen that night and especially enjoyed "Big Chief." Hovey Lister made a big hit that night also and Jake Hess sang some great songs.

Little did I know that I would some day become their friends and sing on the same stage with them. That was a great night in my life! I never missed one word that was said.

Every one was talking about the concert. I was so excited, I didn't get much sleep that night.

The very next day the campus was buzzing. Everyone was talking about starting a group. I think six or seven groups started in the next few weeks. Oh, how I wished I had learned how to sing. You see, I grew up in a non musical family. We never sang in the house, car or church. Oh, we tried but, we were all monotones. Some people call it "tin ears." I longed to sing but didn't know how or where to start.

Jim Hammil, who now sings with the Kingsmen Quartet, had come to Central Bible College for the Fall term, also. He knew all about quartets and helped organize many of the groups. Lunch line was always fun, listening to the guys that Jim had chosen to sing with him for that moment.

Jim heard me talking one afternoon and said, "You sure do talk low. Have you ever sung bass?" I told him that I had never sung and didn't know anything about singing, especially, bass singing. He asked me to go with him to the music rooms and try out my voice. He wanted to hear how low I could go. I went, only because I wanted to be in a singing group. I wanted him to say I could do it. I tried hard to get down to a low C.

Jim really got excited when I sang the notes he played on the piano. He encouraged me to start practicing every day. And I did. I didn't know what part to sing but I sang every day. Many days he would meet me and give me a lesson on how to sing bass in a quartet.

One day Jim invited me to practice with a group he was singing with. He said they needed a bass singer and maybe I could fit in. I went to the rehearsal. Jim Hammil, Ray Hundley, Dan Betzer, Dave Weston and me. I was thrilled! They were all good and sang their parts with ease. They sounded like the Blackwood Brothers. Everyone, that is, but me. I didn't know what part to sing. I was so scared my voice didn't make much sound. I couldn't sing low in front of them. I was under too much pressure.

A few days later Jim brought me the bad news. He told me they had some singing engagements and needed a bass singer that was a little further advanced. In a very disappointed voice, I said, "I understand." He hugged me and promised that he would still help me learn how to sing.

I still thank God for Jim Hammil. He believed in me when no one else did.

I was so disappointed I ran to my room as fast as I could - crying. Imagine, me, a grown man, crying. But my heart was broken. I wanted this so badly. At that moment I prayed a very sincere prayer. I said, "Oh, God, if you will help me learn to sing I will be eternally grateful."

The very next week, I decided to try out for the Revivaltime Choir, our denomination's national radio broadcast. That was real scary, too. Brother McClellan made me sing the scales for him. He seemed to be impressed. I ran to the bulletin board the next day to see who made the choir. There it was, David Kyllonen, bass section. Praise God! I was in. Maybe I would be a singer after all.

In early November, a group of fellows came to my room and asked me to sing bass with them. They were the Evangelaires Quartet. "Great," I said, "I'll do my best." What a group we were! We had so much fun trying to be like the Blackwood Brothers.

A big song at that time was, "Peace Like a River," and it featured the bass singer. That was me! I was still embarrassed to sing in front of people. When people came to our practice session, my body would tense up and all the bass notes were gone. How could I ever get over stage fright?

Gerald Ogg, Jim Payne, Dean Conklin, Jim Miller and David Kyllonen. The Evangelaires!!!

One afternoon, Gerald called me and told me some big news. He was from Nashville, Tennessee, and his pastor had invited us to sing at his church. Gerald also knew Wally Fowler, who was in charge of the All Night Gospel Singing at the Rhyman Auditorium, home of the Grand Ole Opry. He had called and asked if we could sing on the Saturday night program at the Rhyman Auditorium.

Wally Fowler got excited about a new group from a Bible College. He told Gerald to bring his group and he would fit us in for one song. I was stunned! We weren't ready for that kind of performance!

And the Grand Ole Opry stage. Do you know how long people wait to sing there? But Gerald said it was all going to happen so we packed our bags. We were going!

It was to be my first visit to Nashville. Little did I know, in the following years I would sing there many times.

Saturday night came and the building was packed! I saw the line up of groups. The Blackwood Brothers and the Statesmen were both on the program. How was I ever going to sing in front of those guys. I was shaking in my boots! We all got in a huddle and decided we needed to pray. Then they told me what song they had chosen to sing. It was, "Peace Like a River!" That was my solo! I almost fainted! How could they do this to me?

While we were waiting for our turn to sing, I sat back stage and thought over the last few months. What a change was taking place in my life. This was November. Just 100 days earlier I wasn't thinking about singing. I didn't even know I would be in Bible School. But, there I was, 19 years old, scared to death, tall, skinny, awkward, backward and looking like I hadn't reached my 15th birthday.

Wally Fowler told us that Radio Station WSM in Nashville, was going to broadcast one hour of the Saturday night program. He wanted us to sing during that hour so, get ready. We would follow the Blackwood Brothers. I had never been put under that kind of pressure in my whole life.

Suddenly I heard the announcer say, "Welcome the Evangelaires from Central Bible College in Springfield, Missouri." I tried my best to act and sing like J. D. Sumner.

When we finished, I ran off the stage as fast as I could. I was glad it was over. The crowd wouldn't quit clapping and soon they were telling me I had to sing it again. My heart was in my mouth. Somehow we finished the song again and everyone was hugging me.

It was a great feeling to leave the auditorium and head for Gerald's house. I had done the impossible, I had sung in front of J.D. Sumner.

One other neat thing happened that night. Way up in Shenandoah, Iowa, Jim Hammil was lying in bed, listening to the Wally Fowler "All night singing" from the Rhyman Auditorium in Nashville, Tennessee. He heard Wally introducing a new group known as the Evangelaires, from Central Bible College and there I was, Dave Kyllonen, singing the bass!

We talked about it years later. It was exciting that Jim had heard the broadcast.

Well, maybe I didn't sing very well, but I did sing on the Grand Ole Opry stage in Nashville, Tennesee, way back in 1954!

I've never talked about that night very much. I guess that was always intended for the book I would write some day.

- Success Principle 6

SOME THINGS ARE BEST
KEPT IN THE HEART
AND PONDERED.

"But Mary treasured up all these
things and pondered them in her
heart." (Luke 2:19) NIV
"The one who guards his mouth preserves
his life; The one who opens wide his
lips comes to ruin." (Proverbs 13:3) NASB

• • •

During my second year at Central Bible College something happened that would change my life forever. Don Baldwin and Lem

Boyles came and asked if I would consider singing with The Couriers.

The Couriers started in the early 50's. Lem had been in the group in 1954 and decided to keep the group going. It was my first time to meet Don and Lem. I couldn't believe they were asking me to be their bass singer. I said, " Yes, yes, yes!"

It was a very emotional day for me. I was going to continue singing in a group. I was on a cloud! Ed Mosher and Nick Schubert joined us. Did we have an exciting time! We sang on weekends all over Missouri, Kansas and Arkansas.

I stayed in The Couriers for the next three years of my schooling. I was having the time of my life - learning how to sing, testify, introduce a song and even preach.

We changed members many times but by 1958 we had five guys that wanted to stay together and sing full time. Don Baldwin, Duane Nicholson, Neil Enloe, Eddie Reece and Dave Kyllonen moved to Harrisburg, Pennsylvania, in 1958 and began our ministry as The Couriers.

Who would have ever guessed I would sing with The Couriers for the next 25 years! 1955 to 1980.

- Success Principle 7

YOU'VE GOT TO HAVE HEART.

I know now that things happened
to me because of my heart.
Sometimes I would say things
wrong but would get away with it
because everyone could see my
heart. At times my singing was
very poor, but it came right out
of my heart. Parents today push

*their kids to make their brains
grow; they forget that every child
has to keep his heart growing even
with his brain. I hear many testimonies
and lots of singing that have lots
of brain power but very little
heart. One of my tough decisions
was trying out for the Revivaltime
Choir. Cyril McCellan, the choir
director, may have saved
my entire singing career.*

• • •

"Homiletics" is a class where one learns the art of preparing and delivering sermons. Not only did I need to learn how to sing I needed to learn how to preach.

It was frightening just to sign my name when I enrolled in the class. I knew this class was going to require me to preach in front of people, and this was part of my schooling and I needed to get started.

The class professor was Fred Lesten. He stumbled over my name but asked, "Who is David Kyllonen?" I raised my hand to let him see me and then heard his incredible announcement.

"You will all preach from The Psalms this semester and, Dave Kyllonen, you will be first. You will preach for 20 minutes from Psalm 1 next Wednesday."

Wow! My first real sermon was going to be from the book of Psalms. I only had one week to prepare. This was my first attempt at preparing and delivering a message.

I surprised myself when I discovered that I loved getting a message together and enjoyed delivering it as well.

I was ready for my preaching debut.

I stood in front of the class and opened my Bible to Psalm 1. In my low, bass voice I read the first three verses.

"Blessed is the man who does not walk in the council of the wicked or stand in the way of sinners or sit in the seat of mockers. But his delight is in the law of the Lord, and on his law he meditates day and night. He is like a tree planted by streams of water, which yields it's fruit in season and whose leaf does not wither. Whatever he does prospers."

So, with great heart, I began.
When man is living in sin he goes from bad to worse.

1. At first, he merely <u>walks</u> in the council of the ungodly.

2. Next, he <u>stands</u> in the way of sinners.

3. Finally, he <u>sits</u> in the seat of the scornful.

The godly man lives out his life in the positive. He takes wise council and walks in the commandments of the Lord. His company is not wicked, carnal men. His footsteps are ordered by the Word of God. He stands in the rich grace of God and with the righteous. He doesn't sit with the scoffing atheists. That seat is very near the gate of Hell.

The introduction was over and I felt good and gained confidence with every statement. Now for the major points!

Greatness. It is not mere intellectual power, but moral worth. Greatness is goodness - being like God.

Happiness. It is living together with God, doing His will, in the light and joy of His love.

Prosperity. It is the soul-the true health of the soul.

The conclusion!

Five Things to teach your family.

1. Have no sympathetic relations with the wicked.
2. Be irresistibly attracted to God's Word.
3. Be fruitful in the circumstances of life.
4. Have an unfading freshness of heart.
5. Prosper in all you undertake.

I concluded my message and left the class wondering how I had done.

I got my answer the next morning while attending our daily chapel service. Rev. Fred Lesten was in charge of the service and, after a time of worship, he called on me to pray the morning prayer. Every head turned toward me. I was that tall, skinny, awkward young man that never talked.

I knew I had scored high the day before in homiletics class or Rev. Lesten would never have called on me to pray.

One day I preached my first sermon in front of my professor and the next day I prayed in front of the whole student body.

The Courier Timeline

1955.................. Dave Kyllonen
Don Baldwin
Lem Boyles
Nick Schubert
Eddie Mosher

1957.................. David Kyllonen
Don Baldwin
Duane Nicholson
Neil Enloe
Eddie Reece

1960.................. David Kyllonen
Don Baldwin
Duane Nicholson
Neil Enloe
David Young

1965.................. David Kyllonen
Duane Nicholson
Neil Enloe
Phil Enloe
Eddie Hawks

1967-1980........ Dave Kyllonen
Duane Nicholson
Neil Enloe

CHAPTER FIVE

LITTLE IS MUCH.

DON BALDWIN WAS THE ONLY MARRIED MEMBER OF
The Couriers. The other four of us were bachelors and shared a two
room apartment.

Gospel quartets had not made their way to the Northeast, as yet, so
people had nothing to compare our music to. They thought we were
great!

We sang in all the little churches. The offerings were so small that
we had to sing every night of the week and twice on Sunday. One
month, in our first year, we had sung in 25 churches and only sold
$374.00 worth of records, sheet music and pictures. Total sales for
the whole first year was $6,716.00. The offerings were all under
$50.00. But, we were busy and happy doing what we knew God had
called us to do.

As time went on some bigger churches called for us, too. Offerings went up and so did record sales.

One day we got a call from New York City. A pastor was asking
if we could come and sing at the Wendel Wilkie Memorial Auditorium. It sounded like a big night, so we booked it.

After touring the city and getting our pictures taken at a professional studio in Manhattan, it was time to find the place we were going to sing. No one seemed to know where the Wendel Wilkie Memorial Auditorium was located. We had the address, but we were
looking for this big, big building and all there was at that address
were apartment buildings, close to each other and many floors high.
We finally saw a little sign on a door, "Wendel Wilkie Memorial
Auditorium - second floor." A sign on the door stated, "seating for
212 people." The auditorium turned out to be a little room.

It was almost time for the service so we hurried to get our PA
system set up and got dressed. Thirty minutes before starting time
one person had shown up along with the pastor and his wife. We

were talking among ourselves. "What if no one shows up? What will we do?"

The pastor was out on the sidewalk asking people walking by to come up for the concert. By starting time we had 13 people. These were our friends that had driven into the city for the concert. They had heard about this date and didn't want to miss the <u>Wendel Wilkie Memorial Auditorium</u> concert in New York City! No way!

In our little huddle, we were deciding how few songs we could sing. We had a long drive home and wanted to get started as quickly as possible. The pastor said he wanted us to sing for an hour and a half. We told him we would play it by ear but, for sure, it would not be an hour and a half.

The service started. The pastor opened the hymn book and all 13 of us started singing. "I can still see it now." The pastor was acting like there were 1,000 people singing . His great big voice was loud and his hands were waving and he moved like he was handling a great crowd. He sang and sang. Then he prayed and prayed.

After a long song service, he started talking about the offering. He was asking for help for his church. He was asking God for the greatest offering ever. I kept looking around to see if any more people had come in. How much could 13 people give? This pastor was having the time of his life. We were all looking at our watches, saying to each other, "Sure, we're going to get home early."

He finally gave us one of the biggest introductions you could ever imagine. After the huge song service, prayer, announcements and introduction, I couldn't imagine how we could sing only two or three songs and then dismiss them. Two songs and it should have been over by our time schedule.

But something sweet happened that night. We started singing. The room had a great sound. It was so easy to sing. The people were acting like 1,000 were there. We started singing some new songs we had only sung in rehearsal. We sang one, then two, and before long we had sung all 10. We forgot the time. It was turning into a very long night. When it ended, no one wanted to go home.

Those special friends have supported The Couriers ministry ever since.

• Success principle 8

GIVE' EM THE WHOLE LOAD

I've never believed in cheating people or God after that service. I never cut a service short just because of the number of people. When someone talks of quitting early, something turns on in me to go the extra mile. How many people only do enough to get by? Something sweet always happens when you give your all.

GOOD ENOUGH IS THE ENEMY OF EXCELLENCE!

• • •

On the way home, we were asking each other, "Did we get paid? Weren't we on a two hundred dollar flat?" Yes, but, the preacher came with a check for $60.00. He had hoped for a better offering but didn't have any money to make up the difference. There had been two offerings that night, one at the beginning of the service for his church and one at the close for us. The pastor told us $60.00 was the total of both offerings and that we could have it all. He kept the cash and gave us a check.

Neil spoke up and said. "Hey, I gave $40.00 in the first offering for the   church, not for The Couriers. So give me my money back." We agreed, but couldn't scrape up the cash between us. The pastor had given us a check. Well, we laughed with Neil and promised to pay him back the next day.

At the office the next day we received a telegram telling us not to cash the check. No funds available. We did the date for free and gave Neil $40.00. I put the check in my desk and completely forgot about it.

Some months later, we were in bad financial difficulty and needed money. We looked every where we could for money. Looking through my desk, I found the check for $60.00. We took it to the bank and what do you know. It went through. We got our money after all. Just when we needed it!

Many years later, we sang a very special concert in New York City. This time it was Carnegie Hall. Very few people know the real story.

Mr. J.G.Whitfield, a big Gospel concert promoter from Florida, asked us to be a part of a great New York City concert at Carnegie Hall. He would be in charge. He would do all the promotion. He was bringing many groups from the South to sing in New York. He said, since we were from Pennsylvania, maybe we could bring lots of our friends from our part of the country. It sounded really great. Carnegie Hall, **WOW**!

The date was set and we went to work. We talked it up every where we went. We decided to charter buses. People made reservations to go with us for the great concert. The big day arrived. We left Harrisburg, Pennsylvania, after lunch. What a sight we were. The Courier's bus, leading the way, was full of our families. Seven charter buses followed ours, full of our friends who wanted to see and hear us sing at Carnegie Hall.

It was a fun day! We arrived about two hours before the concert. All the groups from the South had arrived. The Florida Boys, Dixie Echoes, Wally Fowler, Harvesters and, of course, The Couriers.

We brought about 300 people. They bought the cheap seats, way up in the third and fourth balconies.

At starting time, I went to see how things were going. I was in shock! The whole main floor was empty. The first and second balconies were scattered with a few dozen people. Only our people showed up. I started to laugh. This was the funniest sight I'd ever seen. Carnegie Hall, a large auditorium, and every one was sitting up at the top of the building. No one wanted to pay the big ticket prices for seating on the main floor.

The concert began and Mr. Whitfield opened with prayer. He greeted the people and tried to sing a song with the crowd, to warm things up. After the song, he decided that everyone should come down to the main floor and sit. No extra charge. The people were excited and came rushing down to those front row seats.

Then Mr. Whitfield stepped to the microphone and said, **"PLEASE WELCOME THE COURIERS FROM HARRIS-BURG, PENNSYLVANIA, TO CARNEGIE HALL!"**

What a feeling we had in our hearts! When we walked out on the stage everyone stood to their feet and gave us a great standing ovation. They wouldn't quit clapping. Every one was cheering and whistling. The groups back stage came out to see what was happening. They witnessed a group of people who loved us, believed in us, and were proud of us, making a thunderous applause. We finally got them to sit down so we could start to sing.

After every song, it was the same thing. Everyone was clapping their hands and whistling and yelling and it sounded like the building was packed. We had the time of our lives.

Every group sang their songs, but it just wasn't the same. Some of the people had left the building to see the sights of New York. The rest just sat there giving only meager applause. Nothing happened the rest of the first half. We were totally embarrassed.

After the intermission, Mr. Whitfield called a meeting. Everyone back stage was upset that the crowd had only clapped for The Couriers. None of the groups could get anything going.

Finally, it was concluded that The Couriers would be the only group singing in the second half. We would quit at eleven o'clock and everyone could go home. What a night! We smiled all the way back to Harrisburg.

A few months later we were singing with the Florida boys at a concert and noticed their new album entitled, "THE FLORIDA BOYS, LIVE, AT CARNEGIE HALL" We said, quietly to ourselves, "Now, how did they do that?"

CHAPTER SIX

HITTING THE BIG TIME.

EVERYDAY, IN OUR TWO ROOM APARTMENT, WE four bachelors got up and made record jackets for our one and only record, "Beyond The Sunset." We tried to make at least 25 a day. We were not part of a record company and we didn't have much money so we made our own record jackets. We bought cardboard, cut it to size, taped it on three sides and pasted both the cover and back on to it. They were not professional but the people bought them anyway.

If you still have the record called, "Beyond The Sunset," and the front cover keeps coming off, you'll know why. What a treasure you have!

One day we got up to make our 25 albums and discovered that we had left the lid off the glue jar. The glue had hardened and was hardly usable. We didn't have time to go and get more so we put gasoline in the glue jar and mixed it. In a few minutes we were in business.

That night, at the concert in the church, every one was smelling gasoline. The ushers were going from room to room looking for a gas leak. They were checking the stove in the church kitchen and pipes all through the church. We knew where the smell was coming from but didn't tell a soul. We needed to sell those records.

You can be assured, we never did that again! It was a great day when a record company took over making our records.

Transportation was a huge problem to us. Getting all five of us and our stuff to the church wasn't easy. We were using Eddie Reece's car. It was a big 98 Oldsmobile. The trunk looked big but after putting in the PA system, the records, pictures, and song books, there wasn't much room left for our clothes, shoes and shaving kits.

Riding in the car was trouble, too. Four big guys, and me, at six foot five inches tall. They always put me in the middle of the back seat then complained about my long legs, all day long.

One wonderful day we bought our first "Company Car." It was a 1953 Cadillac, limousine. We were able to buy it cheap from the funeral home in Wampum, Pennsylvania. The first question we asked the funeral director was, "How fast will it go?" I'll never forget his answer when he said, "Well, it will keep up with any funeral procession!"

This long, black limousine seemed to have a lot of room. My legs could stretch straight out and not touch the front seat. However, the trunk was very small. We had to jam in our equipment and our suits. You should have seen our suits when we arrived at the churches. They were so wrinkled, we killed ourselves laughing, knowing that in a few minutes we would be wearing them in front of people.

One church felt sorry for us and took up a suit offering. It totaled $135.00. Now, divided by 5 that was $27.00 per man. Nowhere in America could we find a suit for $27.00. But we graciously thanked them and went our way.

It was some time later that we were going back to that church and realized we hadn't bought a new suit. Someone told us about a cheap suit outlet in Philadelphia so off to Philadelphia we went.

"We need five suits, all alike, and we need them today. We only have $135.00, Mister. Can you help us? "

Well, some of us were easy to fit and some were hard. We could find three of a kind, but five was impossible. My 6' 5" frame was the real problem but we finally found five alike. We didn't have time for alterations, so, there I was, my jacket was too short and my pants weren't long enough. The guys said to me, "Dave, you look great! It's not perfect but the price is right and its the only one we can find."

We laid our new suits in the trunk on top of the PA system. We knew we were in trouble when the trunk lid wouldn't close. We all jumped on the lid and it finally closed.

We got to the church just in time to set up the equipment and put on our new suits. They were made of linen so you can imagine what they looked like. Squeezed all day in that hot trunk, they looked a sight. This church had given us money for new suits and we bought them so we were sure going to wear them. I didn't know how we were going to sing because we were laughing uncontrollably. But, we only paid $135.00 for all five suits. What could we expect?

Our hit song of the night was "Tis a glorious group (church) without spot or wrinkle!"

We wore those suits for a long time. We had to. The offerings were never more than fifty dollars. I do have one regret today and that is that I didn't keep that suit. What a treasure it would be.

Our big, black limousine was breaking down every week. Every church, it seemed, was getting their mechanic to work on it, usually at night. What a relief for each pastor when we left town. Pastors were asking us how our car was running. They were afraid to book us for fear we couldn't leave because of our broken down funeral car.

It was a great day when we purchased a new 1959 Chrysler Imperial. We drove it 110,000 miles in one year. But, it was too small, especially, the trunk space. And the depreciation on the car caused us to lose our money we had invested in it for only one year. Nobody wanted a car that five big guys had ridden in every day, loaded down with all of our stuff. There surely was a better way to get from one place to another besides cars.

The news was out among Gospel groups. Get a bus! Greyhound was selling many of their old buses. Talk about room, beds to sleep in, and closets to hang up our clothes. There was room underneath in the luggage bins for all our equipment and a diesel engine that would never quit running. It sounded great! But how could we ever buy a bus?

We were singing in Florida when we got our list of busses from Greyhound that were for sale. Wow! There were busses for sale all over America.

We looked under Florida and saw one for sale in Miami. It had been shined and dressed up for the Cuban market. It was everything we ever needed. The price was $5,000.

We sat inside the bus and dreamed and prayed. We asked God to help us find the money so we could have a bus, this bus. We left town and continued our work. We looked for the money everywhere. Finally, Don Baldwin's father-in-law called and said he would send a check.

We called Greyhound and said, "Save that Cuban bus for us." We were too busy to drive down to Florida, so two of our friends from Harrisburg, Pennsylvania, Jim Schambach and Howard Landis, flew to Florida and drove our bus home.

The phone rang and I heard the good news. "The bus is here!" It was parked at the Mall. We ran from our houses and dashed for the Mall. There it was, a 1947, Silversides Greyhound bus! Thirteen years old and already claiming one million miles. But it was ours! It was so exciting!

We found the key and all climbed in. We were walking up and down the aisle, talking a mile a minute about our bus. Who knew how to drive it? Where was Howard or Jim? They had already gone home. Duane jumped into the driver's seat and tried to start the engine. It wouldn't start no matter what he did.

We walked to the nearest gas station and asked for help. "How do you start a bus?" we asked. The station attendant told us we probably needed ether. What in the world is ether? We bought a can of it and headed back to the bus.

OK, so, now, where do we put it? We were learning very quickly what owning a bus was going to be like. A little squirt of ether in the right place and the engine roared. Billows and billows of black smoke filled the parking lot. The diesel smell was awful. Duane didn't know how to find first gear or how to double clutch so that the gears would change. What a first trip we had going around the block. Herky, jerky, stop and start and much grinding of the gears. I wondered how we would ever get this bus to the next church if we couldn't even get it around the block.

But we had room! We removed most of the bus seats leaving only a few up front. We were poor and couldn't refurbish our bus properly so we each set up a cot for sleeping and installed a clothes rack across the back. Wow! This was really living. My own bed and a place to actually hang my suit.

We taught each other how to drive and started off taking two hour shifts. One night we were coming home and Don was driving. His two hours were up and he looked around to see if Neil was ready for his shift. We were all in bed fast asleep. Don didn't want to yell for Neil and wake the rest of us up and he didn't want to stop the bus and waste time. The road was straight so he began to see if the bus would stay on the road without holding the steering wheel. He decided he had seven to ten seconds to get out of the driver's seat, run back to Neil's bed, shake him and tell him it was his turn to drive, then run back to the front and grab the steering wheel.

I was sound asleep, when I heard Duane say, in a loud, excited voice, "Don, what are you doing back here?" "Who's driving the bus?" We all jumped out of bed at the same time and saw Don running for the front of the bus that had no driver.

We were really upset with Don. He had scared us to death. We could have been killed! Then we started laughing about it but no one slept for the rest of the trip home. Don never did that again!

CHAPTER SEVEN

ONCE A COURIER, ALWAYS A COURIER.

I FIRST MET DON BALDWIN ON THE CAMPUS OF CBC in Springfield, Missouri. He was a delightful person, full of fun and easy to talk to. He knew so much about the things I was interested in. He was a good listener and I found myself telling Don my innermost thoughts, which was something I had never done before. After joining The Couriers, Don encouraged me to sing better. He encouraged me to start preaching. He often let me speak in the youth services. He asked me if I wanted to learn how to book some dates. Maybe I could book The Couriers for a weekend.

I gained a wealth of knowledge from Don during the ten wonderful years we spent together. When Don resigned, in 1965, he had taught me well and I became the new manager of The Couriers.

- Success principle 9

IF YOU WANT TO BE A LEADER
YOU MUST FIRST BE A FOLLOWER

*I learned this principle early on and
it gave me the experience and the
confidence to eventually lead
The Couriers. I allowed Don Baldwin
to mentor me in leadership areas of my life.
Some people resist being mentored and thus
only reach as far as their own abilities
can take them. But a person who is
teachable and allows other people into his
life to help him will increase his
potential to achieve things way beyond
himself.*

THE DIFFERENCE BETWEEN WHAT YOU ARE AND
WHAT YOU WANT TO BE IS WHAT YOU DO!

• • •

Eddie Reece was our piano player when we moved to Harrisburg, Pennsylvania. He grew up around Gospel music in Memphis, Tennessee and knew more about it than any of us. Music was his life and he was superb at the keyboard. He stayed with us for a year then left to pursue other ministries.

Duane Nicholson and Neil Enloe were two special guys. I consider them to be two of the greatest tenors in Gospel music.

Duane was from Woodward, Oklahoma. His dad was a pastor of the Assemblies of God church. Neil was from Wood River, Illinois. His dad was a barber and had his shop right next to his house.

Duane, Neil and I had a lot in common. We were raised in the same kind of homes. We grew up with the same kinds of rules and conscience. Our dads made about the same amount of money and our churches were about the same size.

No wonder the three of us stayed together in The Couriers for 25 years. That's a long time and many great things happened to us through those years.

A Letter From Duane

Dear Dave,

Thank you for allowing me to be a part of your book about your present ministry, your most interesting background and the ministry of The Couriers.

When I heard you were writing your book I "told myself" that if you put in this book some of the unusual and interesting things you told me over the 25 years we were together in ministry, and included experiences we shared together, and if you shared your experiences since taking a leap of faith with your family, it would be a "Blockbuster" book.

Volumes could be written about our experiences together, but I am leaving that up to you to portray because this is, "Your", book and the people need to hear it from you.

I am just happy to be your friend and fellow Courier. We never had many cross words in all of the 25 years together, so I have happy memories and a profound respect for everything for which you have stood. My wife, Jean Ann, and I have tried to follow yours and Judy's example in raising our two daughters. It seems to have worked because both of them have never given us a minute's trouble and both are faithfully serving the Lord. The concept of ministry that we shared together still works today. All over the country I hear good reports about HomeFire ministry. The present Couriers still hold to the same concept we shared together.

Only eternity will reveal what has been done in your ministry, Dave. That is what really counts. Keep up the good work! From the Nicholson family we say God richly bless you and your family as you faithfully continue to serve the Lord.

PS When we get to heaven there will be a great host of gospel singers. There will be several thousand Lead Singers singing together. Their will be several thousand Baritone Singers singing together. Dave, you will be the only Bass Singer and I will be the only Tenor Singer. That's all they will need. Ha!

With Gratitude and Love,
Duane Nicholson,
A Courier

Duane married Jean Ann Morton in Boston, Massachusetts.

I remember going for my tuxedo. It was so expensive I wondered how I was going to get my money's worth out of it. I put it on for the wedding and kept it on until I returned it the next day.

After the reception Duane and Jean Ann left for their honeymoon and we packed the bus for our long trip back to Harrisburg, Pennsylvania. It was my turn to drive so I jumped into the driver's seat, tuxedo and all. Everyone was asking why I didn't take it off. Man, I was going to get my money's worth. The attendant at the turnpike entrance looked at me funny but I told her I was the best dressed bus driver in the country.

My time was up for driving so Neil took over. I was tired and went to my "room." I didn't take off my tuxedo, I just pulled the covers up around my neck and went fast asleep. What great pajamas! Expensive, but who cared, I had to get my money's worth.

We pulled into a truck stop for diesel fuel. I heard everybody talking about getting something to eat. I jumped out of bed and looked at myself in the mirror. I was already dressed and ready to go, except the mirror showed I was a wrinkled mess. Everyone had gone into the restaurant so I quickly combed my hair and decided to join them, wrinkled tuxedo and all. When everyone saw me they broke into hysterical laughter. They made so much commotion the whole restaurant turned to see who was doing what. There I was in the most wrinkled tuxedo they had ever seen. We all laughed until we cried, but I was getting my money's worth! Everyone was bringing their tuxedo back on a hanger, under a plastic bag, but not me. I rolled it up in a ball and handed it back telling the clerk it was worth every dime.

We loved it when Neil was working on a new song and even happier when he said, "Well, guys, this new song might not be good enough for us to sing. If you don't like it, just say so and we'll move on to something else." If he said that, we knew he had another great song coming.

Sometimes his songs came easy, but sometimes it would take forever. Many times we would arrive at the recording studio and Neil still wouldn't have the words written to his song. But the pressure was on, so, through the night he would come up with the words, just in time.

As the emcee of The Couriers I chose which songs we would sing for the concerts. Many times, I chose all of Neil's, ten in a row. They were my favorites. I loved them all. We sang at least fifty of Neil's songs. People loved them and responded to every one .

A Letter From Neil

Dear Dave,

It was my joy to be a partner with you in ministry in The Couriers from 1958-1980. We shared rewarding and challenging times during those awesome years. My memory bank is crammed full of wonderful recollections of truly remarkable events.

I'll never forget the millions of miles in vehicles of every description from cars to busses to a funeral home limousine. We were in so many churches during those years that even now when my wife, Ruth, and I are traveling over a remote road and pass a church along the roadside, I'll turn to her and say, "We sang there umpteen years ago!" And we did. There have been many more than 10,000 such churches.

The host pastors have been some of our best friends. Their kindred spirit of servanthood and purpose certainly won a special place in our hearts.

Then there was the All Night Singin's and someone's brainstorm, the Sundown to Sunup Singin's. These outdoor summer concerts would start at about 7 pm with thousands of eager concert-goers and end at 6 am with about forty people in sleeping bags, stirring occasionally to remind us that we were obligated to sing until sunup.

But it was the churches that were our very passion. To stand in the sanctuary designated specifically for worship, and sing of the love and majesty of the God of all creation and His only begotten Son, was to encompass our total definition of the word "fulfillment." No other part of our day was to compare to that moment. To see God reward our efforts with souls at the altar every night, was to know that we were enjoying His anointing and approval.

We weren't perfect, but we always tried. I look back on the "as unto the Lord" philosophy we embraced and the standard we held and I feel that God knows we really tried.

You left The Couriers for ministry with your family. I went solo for a time and then Duane Nicholson and I reorganized The Couriers with, among others, my son, Tim, and now for the last many years, my brother, Phil. I often hear reports from those who have attended HomeFire meetings, of how your family is carrying on the tradition of ministry we established in the mid-1950's. We, too, are continuing the established philosophy set forth all those years ago. God is faithful!

Thanks for sharing the first 25 years of your ministry with The Couriers. We're better because you did. May the Lord continue to give you His strength and blessing.

In HIM,
Neil Enloe
A Courier

One night we were invited to sing at a youth rally in New Jersey. This one would be special! A huge boat was rented and 2,000 young people came to cruise up the Hudson River in New York Harbor.

It was a wonderful evening. We sang a concert in the bottom of the boat then after the concert we all went up on top deck. There were millions of lights shining in New York City. Everybody was having a great time. It was noisy with all 2,000 kids talking at the same time.

Suddenly everyone got quiet. I looked around to see why. We were gliding by that great big green lady, the Statue of Liberty. I, along with all the others, stood in awe. I squared my shoulders, lifted my head high and thanked God I was an American.

At that moment, Neil bumped my arm and said, "Dave, God just gave me a song about the Statue of Liberty." I said, "Neil we are gospel singers, where is the gospel in the Statue of Liberty? " He assured me that by the end of the week he would sing his new song for us.

When he presented it, we couldn't believe its message. It was perfect! The concept was incredible! We stood to our feet and cheered. What a song! Little did we realize it would become the number one song in Gospel Music in 1976. **It brought three Dove Awards to The Couriers.**

Everywhere we sang it, it brought the house to it,s feet. You know it's a great song when, 20 years later, people are still asking for "The Statue of Liberty."

Little David Young played the piano for The Couriers after Eddie Reece left. He really gave The Couriers a spark! We called him Little David because he was so short. He stood 5 ft. 1 in. tall and spoke with a true southern drawl. He sang a double high C and played the piano as well as anyone I have ever heard. Everyone loved Little David. He was very considerate, full of compassion and the most caring man you could ever meet. Little David made a huge hit everywhere we went. People loved the songs he wrote. He helped us out of many awkward situations with his extremely humorous wit.

One night a lady yelled out after one of our songs, "It's too loud! Do something with the PA system." Little David answered her immediately, "Madam, we can't turn it up any more, it's as high as it will go. We're turning the knobs and that is all we can do." She yelled again, **"IT'S TOO LOUD."** Little David said, "We're turning the knobs and this is as loud as we can get it." The crowd was overcome with laughter. We were laughing and everyone was having a good time. We turned the PA system down and went on with the concert. Not one of us could have handled that lady as graciously as Little David did.

Back stage, before one concert started, we were putting on our suit coats and Little David picked up my coat and put it on by mistake. I ended up with his coat and quickly put it on. Well, you can imagine what a funny sight that was! My coat, size 42 extra long, on Little David, hung to the floor and his size 39 short hit me at the waist. The sleeves on his jacket came to my elbows. We all agreed that we had to put that act into the program somehow. That night after the last song we ran off the stage and hurriedly exchanged coats and walked back out for the encore. The crowd loved it and made such a big to do about it that we exchanged coats at every concert after that.

Ever since Little David resigned from The Couriers, he and his wife, Colleen, his five children and their mates travel and sing together in a beautiful family ministry.

Eddie Hawks came to play the piano after Little David resigned. He was just a kid, fresh out of high school. He loved life and loved Gospel Music. Playing piano for The Couriers was his first job. I remember when he got his first pay check. He went to a restaurant and ordered a huge banana split. I enjoyed being around Eddie. He was a dedicated young man who put his whole heart into The Couriers. Eddie resigned after a couple of years and has become one of the greatest music ministers in the country.

Phil Enloe joined the Couriers to sing baritone when Don Baldwin left. Phil is Neil's younger brother. What a bundle of energy he was. He was up early, looking for things to do. He helped us design and lay out our promotional material. He could sing any part from bass to tenor. He was a song writer. He loved to drive the bus. There wasn't a lazy bone in Phil's body. To this day, Phil still lives with lots of energy. He is a "go getter" and will be on top of any task that needs to be done.

I spent twenty- five great years with some of the greatest guys in the world. They helped shape my life and I'll always be grateful that I had an opportunity to have my life impacted by their lives.

CHAPTER EIGHT

THE TOILET PAPER STORY.

DUANE WAS THE TALKER OF OUR GROUP. HE COULD talk all day long and still sing a full concert. Then he was off to a restaurant to talk some more. He could make friends so quick. I would sit back and admire him as he told jokes and funny stories about life with The Couriers.

We grew close through the years. Just like brothers. I knew what Duane was thinking and he knew what I was thinking. I didn't have to ask him, I just knew. Duane's high tenor voice carried The Couriers sound for years. We built our sound around his voice. When there had to be a certain clear note or sound we could always depend on Duane.

Duane laughed a lot but never on the platform. Neil and I would get a giggle fit, and even stop singing, but not Duane. Poker faced, not even a smile, he would never miss a note. The song must be sung. This would make Neil and me laugh even harder, sometimes uncontrollably. But there was one time when Duane laughed so hard even he couldn't sing.

Rev. David Lewis, a pastor in Cabins, West Virginia, had booked a tour for us in high schools across West Virginia and Maryland. We arrived at a school in Oakland, Maryland, to discover the concert would be in the gym. A small portable stage was placed at one end of the gym and folding chairs were brought in for the concert.

A small crowd gathered and we began to sing. We sang for about an hour, then took a short intermission. We all went downstairs to the men's room. It wasn't the cleanest place so we were being careful. Duane covered the toilet seat with a long piece of toilet paper. He had just sat down when we heard Rev. Lewis calling The Couriers to the platform to finish the second half of the concert.

We hurriedly ran upstairs. We had to go down the center aisle to get back on the stage. People were laughing but we didn't know why. Don announced that we were going to sing that great song that featured the bass singer, "Peace Like A River." While we were stepping up to the microphones Neil whispered to Duane that he had toilet paper on him. We all thought it was a little piece on his shoe.

When I began to sing my solo everyone else backed up. Don saw it first and yelled, out loud, "Duane, it's that long!" His hands were three feet apart, trying to illustrate to Duane that he had toilet paper hanging from his belt in back and it was touching the floor. Duane began to wind the paper up in his hand and started laughing with everybody else. Everyone in the audience could see this long piece of toilet paper getting shorter and shorter.

I was still busy singing my solo and Eddie Reece was playing the piano. We didn't know what was going on except that something sure was funny.

Finally, Don, Duane and Neil went behind a little partition that had been placed on the stage - to laugh. Their laughing got much louder and one by one they fell on the floor behind the partition.

I couldn't stand not knowing what was going on. I stopped singing and went behind the partition to find out what was so funny. Don, Duane and Neil were laughing so hard they were actually rolling on the floor. I started laughing and didn't even know what I was laughing at; they couldn't stop laughing long enough to tell me. Eddie left the piano and came back to see what was happening. He got so upset he forced me to come out to the microphone and bring the concert back under control.

I went out and tried to sing the song again but to no avail. All I could do was laugh and didn't even know why. Eddie then decided to sing the bass solo himself. That was even funnier. It was no use. The song was over.

Don finally came to the microphone to introduce our last scheduled song. "We want to sing one more song and then we'll close the concert. The last song we want to sing is, "How Long Has It Been!"

Well, every one began laughing all over again. We never would have been able to sing it anyway so we just said, "Good night, everyone."

We almost wrecked the car on the way to the preacher's house for refreshments because we couldn't stop laughing.

And, do you know, the pastor thought we had played a trick on Duane? I don't think he ever did forgive us! We never went back to Oakland, Maryland. That's one town where the song, "Peace Like A River" was never remembered and, "How Long Has It Been," was never sung.
(The Oakland, Maryland, concert made history in the Gospel singing world.)

Duane never laughed again in a church service or in a concert but, Neil and I had our moments. We saw the funniest things to laugh about and once we got started there was no way to quit. But, good ole Duane, we could always count on him to keep the song going all by himself.

Neil would say things to me during the interlude like, "James Blackwood's mother is sitting on the aisle, right side, row three." I would slowly turn my head to see row three and find the lady who was sitting on the aisle.

Now, I knew it wasn't Jame's mother but the resemblance would be so like James, I would laugh. Neil would join me and we would laugh together.

But, thank God for Duane. The mean look he gave us was usually enough to help us "get it under control" for the rest of the song.

CHAPTER NINE

I DO, I DO, I WILL, I WILL!

STANDING IN THE LUNCH LINE ONE DAY AT CENTRAL Bible College, I had my first glimpse of the girl who would change my life and eventually become my wife.

She came through the door of the school cafeteria with all of her friends. She was laughing and talking with excitement. I enjoyed watching all the fun she was making for everyone around her. She was Judy Robbins from California. I thought, "Let's see what these California girls are all about?" I wanted so much to get to know her but I was too shy to talk to her.

The whole semester went by and I only talked to her one time. I'll always remember how I felt during that brief moment. She came by the music room where The Couriers were practicing. She was with a group of girls who asked us to sing a song for them. We did and then they were gone. I wished they had stayed for a couple of more songs. I thought, "That Judy is a very special person. I wish I could date her." But I didn't have enough courage to ask.

All too soon the semester ended and we went our separate ways for the summer.

I came back to school early the next year because of my job at the Gospel Publishing House. Classes hadn't started yet so there weren't many students on campus.

One evening some of us guys were looking for something to do. One of my friends asked if I wanted to double date with him that night. I explained that I was too bashful to ask anyone but if he could get me a date I would be willing to go. A few minutes later he came back from the girl's dormitory all excited. He met Judy Robbins and had set up a date for me with her. When he said, Judy Robbins, I exploded inside! That was incredible! Of all the girls, she was my favorite!

Our first date was simply a walk through the fairgrounds across the street from our school. For a few minutes I actually found enough courage to hold her hand. I went to my room with feelings inside I never had before. I'm not sure how Judy felt. Maybe she wasn't too impressed. Maybe she thought I was too quiet. I couldn't think of much to say. However, after that, we dated several times, but there wasn't much magic in our relationship.

One evening when Judy and I were spending time together, we talked about trivial things. As usual, Judy was doing most of the talking. She asked me some big questions about my life. After a while I opened up my heart and began to talk to her. I felt so at ease that I told her everything. I told her about God's call on my life. I shared with her my dreams and goals. I told her what attracted me to her. I told her she had many qualities about her that I admired. I talked about her great energy and confidence and intelligence. I told her how I had watched her praying at the altar and her tears spoke volumes to me. I think Judy was beginning to see and hear the real Dave Kyllonen.

From then on things were different in our relationship. Judy became a big help to me. She began teaching me how to share my life with the world. She wasn't happy until I talked at the feeling level. I wanted to be around her more and more. She brought excitement to my life that no one else had ever brought. We had a great year together!

• Success Principle 10

COMMUNICATION IS TO A MARRIAGE AS FUEL IS TO A CAR.

I knew, if I couldn't share from my heart, our relationship and future marriage was in trouble.

• • •

I returned to school to finish my fourth year but Judy did not return.

That was a difficult year for me. I was coming to the end of my schooling and I didn't know much about my future. I was happy traveling with The Couriers every weekend. That kept my mind occupied and didn't allow me any time to think about dating. I wrote many letters that year telling Judy I liked her. I had promised myself I would never tell any girl that I loved her until I was sure I was going to marry her. So, "I like you," stayed in my letters and in our telephone conversations for nearly two years.

• Success Principle 11

"A WORD FITLY SPOKEN IS LIKE APPLES
OF GOLD IN SETTINGS OF SILVER."
(Proverbs 25:11) NKJV

*It's a word spoken in season. It's a
word spoken according to the circumstances.
It must be relevant, real and with clarity.
There was a time when I didn't speak
many words but I always tried to make them
count. It's a quality seldom appreciated
today. At one time, I considered it to be
a weakness, but it was really unbridled
strength in my life that needed a little training
and experience. Everyone looks to the life
of the party for leadership and wisdom, but
when the party's over you often can't find them.
The fact that I didn't shower Judy with
insincere "I love yous" while we were
dating, is unique and out of the ordinary.
"I love you" today has little meaning and
is overused. We've lost the meaning of
love.
This is a good principle to teach the*

younger generations.
In the course of my life this principle
has guided me.

Then, one day, it happened! I knew that I knew! I loved her with all my heart! I stopped at a phone booth while traveling to a service with The Couriers. When she came to the phone I said, "Judy, I always say I like you but, today, it's different. I want to say to you, Judy, I love you, I love you. I really do and will for the rest of my life." Wow! What a feeling!

Judy came to Springfield for my graduation in May. We hadn't seen each other for so long. What a great week that was!

I purchased a beautiful diamond ring and was waiting for the right moment to give it to her.

Spring had arrived. April showers had brought May flowers. The weather was warming up and I was in love.

On *THE* special night we went for a drive in the country. I stopped my old, 1951, green Plymouth and rolled down the window. A curious big white horse was standing right there along the fence. He was so close he nearly had his nose in the car. He enjoyed our conversation when I told Judy that there was a gift in the glove compartment for her.

It took her forever to find the little package I had put there. She opened the box to find the ring and hear me say, "Judy, will you marry me?" Her answer was a great big "yes, yes, yes." I will never be able to explain the feelings I had at that moment. But I was remembering the first time I had seen Judy and how I had wished she could be mine. Now it had happened, she would be mine forever. All mine!

Judy came from a broken home and I knew she would never be able to handle a husband walking out on her and the children. My promise to her that night was, "Judy, I'll be here for you as long as you are alive." We have shared a life that has bonded us together with cords that cannot be broken!

The next day Judy had a ball telling everyone about our engagement. We were busy taking care of graduation and making wedding plans and sharing about all the things that had happened during the time we were apart.

During that same week The Couriers announced their big plans. We had decided to become full time Gospel singers. We told everyone we were moving to Harrisburg, Pennsylvania, September 1, 1958. We were going to pioneer Gospel Music all over the Eastern part of the country.

Boy, did that bring up major conversation everywhere we went. Everyone was in shock! The Couriers going full time into Gospel Music.

Judy and I hoped to be married before the end of 1958. It wasn't going to be easy because she lived in Fresno, California, and The Couriers were moving to Pennsylvania, the other end of the country.

Our wedding date was set for November 28, 1958.

Judy went back to California to make plans for the wedding and I moved to Pennsylvania.

We would be separated during our whole engagement - seven long months. I began to ask myself some questions. How was I going to get to California and back again? How much time off would I have. My old, 1951, Plymouth was not able to make the trip. It needed new tires, brakes, and it was using so much oil. I knew it wouldn't get us out of the state of Pennsylvania, let alone 3,000 miles to California. Could I fly? Nope, not on the $25.00 a week I was making.

The Couriers schedule was so full that I only had nine or ten days. Three days to get out there, three days to say "I do," and, three days to get back.

Don Baldwin offered to drive me to California. He would be my best man and then visit his in-laws in Las Vegas after the wedding. OK, we got that figured out.

Now, who in my family would be able to go all the way to California for my wedding? My family was poor and no one had enough money for the trip. I really wanted my mother to be there. I talked with her and she said, "Yes, I'll go with you, no matter how we have to go. I want to be at your wedding, son."

We drove to California in the three days allotted for driving time and arrived just in time for the wedding rehearsal, the evening before the wedding. After the rehearsal, Judy and I were sitting in the car in the driveway of her mother's house. I had not seen her for seven long months so we had a lot to talk about.

It was about 11:00 p.m. when all of a sudden, Judy's mom started flashing the porch light on and off. She finally came out to the car. She wanted to make sure we were behaving ourselves. I said to Judy, "Will your mother let us get married tomorrow? Will she let us go on our honeymoon?"

Now, that's what I call parental protection!

Our wedding day arrived. As tradition would have it, I was not allowed to see Judy until the moment she came down the aisle. All I had to do was show up for the wedding, so all day long I was really bored.

Finally, a couple of the guys decided to go bowling. Maybe that would pass the time away. It did and I bowled my highest game ever, "232."

What a beautiful wedding! Judy was the prettiest bride I had ever seen. The highlight of the wedding was when we sang a love song together.

> *"I do believe that God above.*
> *Created you for me to love.*
> *He picked you out from all the rest*
> *Because He knew that I loved you best."*

It was true, we loved each other so much, and sang out of the depth of our hearts. I knew the vows we were saying were sacred and had to be kept for the rest of our lives. Little did we realize that our love for each other would help us survive the tremendous storm that was just around the corner.

The plan was that my mother would drive back to Pennsylvania with the Baldwins and Judy and I would stay in California for three days and then fly back. The first day of our honeymoon we heard the news that all the airlines had gone on strike! Our flight home was canceled! What were we going to do?

We quickly called the Baldwins, in Las Vegas, to see if they were still there and if we could possibly ride back to Pennsylvania with them? It was a long ride home. It took us three days and three nights with no stopping except for food and fuel.

Now I ask you, "Did you ever go on your honeymoon with your mother in the car?" We made it back to Pennsylvania tired and weary but excited about beginning our new life together as Mr. and Mrs. Kyllonen.

I remember saying to my mother, "Mom, I love you, I appreciate you, but it's over. I'll see you later."

Just before going to California, I purchased a 28 ft. New Moon, used mobile home from a navy man in Norfolk, Virginia. It was moved from Norfolk and placed on a lot in a trailer park in Camp

Hill, Pennsylvania. Boy, was I proud of that mobile home. I was ready to bring my bride back to Pennsylvania. I even had a NEW MOON mobile home for her to live in. All was in readiness!

We pulled the car into the trailer park and turned the corner. I stopped in front of our lot and said, "Welcome home, Mrs. David Kyllonen."

I carried Judy across the threshold (do mobile homes have thresholds?) and showed her every nook and cranny of our new home. It took about 5 minutes. We were excited about moving in and fixing our little home just the way we wanted it. We unloaded the car and piled all of our stuff in the middle of the small living room floor. We had luggage and boxes and many, many wedding gifts we hadn't even opened yet.

We were hungry but there wasn't a bite of food in the house so we left everything in the middle of the floor and headed for the grocery store. On the way out of the trailer park we stopped the fuel truck and asked for fuel to be delivered to our home. It was the first week of December and freezing cold and our mobile home had no heat in it, as yet. He agreed to fill us up so that when we returned from the grocery store it would be toasty warm.

Our first trip to the grocery store was fun. We bought everything in sight. We loaded up with food and everything we needed to set up "housekeeping." A broom, a mop, laundry detergent, a bucket, contact paper to line the drawers and shelves. Our grocery cart was full to the brim. We went way overboard. The bill was $50.00. Wow! We had spent a fortune!

At last we were alone in our cozy little home! We were so happy! Nothing could ever spoil the contentment we felt at that moment, or so we thought.

We were just beginning to open our wedding gifts when the living room heater exploded and flames shot out of the back of it and climbed the wall clear to the ceiling. The curtains caught fire and, before long, the whole living room end of our trailer was burning. We grabbed the fire extinguisher, towels, water and anything that we could to put the fire out, but to no avail. The fire was out of control. People were shouting at us to get out.

We didn't grab one possession, not even our coats. We jumped through the doorway and joined the crowd who had gathered to watch the fire. Someone had called the fire department and we could hear the wail of sirens in the distance, but by the time they arrived all they could do was pour water on the smoldering ashes!

We stood there a long time with our arms around each other. Crying until there were no more tears.

We spent the night in the Baldwin's mobile home. I never slept. I was confused and depressed. I asked myself some big questions. "Why, God? Did I deserve this? Where will we live now?" All night long I wrestled with questions I had no answers for.

- Success Principle 12

STAY CLOSE TO GOD IN THE CALM IF YOU WANT HIM CLOSE TO YOU IN THE STORM!

Sometimes we have no answers
to life's tough questions.
The song writer said it best.
"Trust and obey, for there's
no other way, to be happy in
Jesus, than to trust and obey."

●　　　●　　　●

In the morning we went back to the fire scene. Nothing was left. All of our wedding gifts - gone! All of my books and notes from four years of college were gone. Our suitcases hadn't even been opened, but the fire didn't need the key.

Then I heard the incredible news that The Couriers had a concert to perform that very afternoon. It was a high school assembly in the York, Pennsylvania, high school.

"Oh no! What will I wear?" Nobody had clothes that would fit a 6 ft. 5 in. frame, weighing only 169 lbs.

It wasn't time to be picky. Don brought me one of his suits. The pants were way too short, but didn't look too bad if I pulled them way down on my hips. The coat was too big but maybe that was good. It covered a "multitude of sins" underneath.

When I came out dressed for the concert, Judy and the guys laughed. We all laughed until there were tears in our eyes. I was quite a sight!

I was able to perform that day with God's help and wonderful moral support from Judy and The Couriers.

- Success Principle 13

A MERRY HEART DOETH GOOD LIKE A MEDICINE.

*"A cheerful heart is good medicine
but a crushed spirit dries up
the bones." (Proverbs 17:22)* NIV
*Medical research shows that
laughter has a scientifically
measurable effect on our health.
A good belly laugh causes us to
breathe deeper, releases
adrenaline, provides more oxygen
for our body and brain, improves
alertness, and releases some*

natural pain killers. We can't
control the length of our lives,
but we can control the width and
depth by the way that we respond
to life.
"He that is of a merry heart hath
a continual feast." (Proverbs 15:15)
KJV

• • •

Getting over the fire wasn't easy. I lived in a state of depression for almost six months. The insurance company refused to pay for the trailer. We had unknowingly, canceled the policy by moving the trailer out of a 200 mile radius.

We found a small furnished apartment and started all over again.

Through it all, Judy and I became best friends. True friends are loyal, trustworthy, true and steadfast. She was a great protection, source of inspiration, and solace for me. This crisis deepened our friendship. Judy gave herself unselfishly with love and devotion. Her friendship has been my life's greatest treasure. We discovered that it is friendship more than romance that holds a marriage together.

• Success Principle 14

FRIENDSHIP, MORE THAN ROMANCE,
HOLDS A MARRIAGE TOGETHER.

The kind of friend you are affects your
relationship. The Bible says "Greater
love has no one than this, that one lay
down his life for his friends."
(John 15:13) NIV
A good friend will be patient, kind,
protective, trusting and never failing in

a relationship.
Relationships grow gradually, one day at a
time. There are 168 hours in each week and
only a few are used for romance and sex.
What we do with the rest of the hours will
determine how deep our relationship will be.

• • •

We learned so much about money management that first year of marriage. We paid for three years on a trailer we only lived in for five hours.

Someday, when Judy and I retire, we hope to have a home with a fireplace but, be assured, we'll light the fire very carefully.

A Letter From Judy

To Dave, My Loving Husband,

Many years ago our love had its start in the heart of God. He knew we were meant for each other. He gave us a deep love that will never be broken. He gave us a strong faith from which we have drawn our strength in times of difficulty and our joy in times of victory. I'm so glad we found our lives in Him and thank Him for the special love we share.

Can you believe that we, two kids who really didn't stand much chance for success, started down life's pathway and have experienced the greatest life imaginable? Every dream you ever had, you have fulfilled and I have shared them all with you.

When Kristie, Robin and Connie were born, you became one great Dad! You loved our girls, protected them and, most of all, you respected them. I tried to carry out every wish you had for them and, now, look how blessed we are.

And our grandchildren.....how special they are! If even a part of you finds its way into their lives, they will be better people because of it.

You have built into all of us, your family, character. Strong, Godly character that will last forever. Thanks, sweetheart, for choosing me and sharing your extraordinary life with me.

I will always love you,

Judy

CHAPTER TEN

©HERGIE

DIESEL SMOKE.

TRAVELING WITH THE COURIERS FOR TWENTY FIVE years was the perfect life for me. I loved everything about it. All the miles, all the buses, all the records we made, all the preachers we met, many have remained my friends through the years.

I cherish the memories of the first ten years and the goal we met to minister in all 50 states. My mind is full of incredible memories of the next fifteen years when we ministered in 61.

Traveling in The Courier's bus was an experience never to be forgotten. We lived in our bus as much as we lived in our homes.

We didn't have a kitchen or a shower and no hot water. We always had to shave in the men's room of the church and shower at truck stops when we stopped for fuel. We each had our own room, 6 ft. 5 in. X 6 ft. I could lie on my bed and my head would touch one wall and my feet the other.

Our lounge area in the front of the bus contained several seats, a table and a TV.

One Sunday afternoon we were traveling from one church to another for the evening service. I was driving the bus while the rest of the guys were in their rooms getting an afternoon nap.

I stopped to get some fuel and pulled the bus up to the pump as smoothly as I could so no one would wake up. I went to the cash register, paid the bill, and started down the turnpike again.

Now, being a smooth driver was important to all of us. If you could stop at the toll booth on the turnpike, and pull away without waking anybody up, you were a good driver. I was a good driver because no one woke up, all the way to the church.

I pulled up to the front door and met the pastor. He startled me when he said, "Duane called, but don't worry, he'll be here in time for the service."

I ran back to his room on the bus and opened his door. Sure enough, he was gone. But, how? Where? I must have left him back at the fuel stop on the turnpike, over two hours ago. I never saw him leave the bus.

We waited and waited and pretty soon, here came Duane. He pulled into the church parking lot next to the bus in a rented car. I was anxious to see if he was frowning or smiling. He was laughing when he told us how he got off the bus and went to the men's room, never seeing me pay the bill. He thought he could get back before I paid the bill.

Well, the state police had to drive him to the airport so he could rent a car. Can't you hear Duane telling that policeman that his friends drove off and left him?

We started a new rule that day. Anytime you were driving and stopped the bus and started it again, it was your responsibility to check each room to see if anyone was missing. Also, if you were not driving but you got off the bus you had to find the driver and tell him not to leave without you.

Tom Baker became our bus driver in 1975. He was faithful, loyal, on time, and a hard worker. We thought he was the best in the business. He had driven those big eighteen wheeler, semi-trucks for years before becoming The Courier's bus driver.

He often said, "When I was driving truck the freight never talked back to me but, boy, the freight in this Courier bus sure talks back." He heard from all of us about shifting gears, stopping and starting.

Tom was a blessing from God! Many times he drove through the night when the rest of us were too exhausted to help. All he needed was his thermos of hot coffee and the chatter on the CB. The Courier handle (name) was "The Blue Angel."

Tom's great challenge came when we were on our West Coast tours with several other groups. The tour schedule always consisted of a concert in Oakland, California, and then on to Long Beach, California, for a concert the very next night.

After the Oakland concert all the groups would head for the restaurant and, as soon as we finished eating, we'd say "good-bye" and run for our buses. The race was on!

It was four hundred miles to Long Beach. Sometimes there would be as many as five buses racing through the night. You see, it was important to get there first in order to claim the best spot in the lobby to sell records. We would go to bed saying to Tom, "Go get'em Tom."

The final test for the bus race was driving over the mountain pass known as the Grapevine in the range of mountains just before dropping into Los Angeles. Usually we would wake up to check with Tom to see which group was ahead. Sometimes we'd all be at the top of the Grapevine at the same time. We'd yell at Tom to, "Put the pedal to the metal" and down the other side of the pass we'd fly!

We knew the way by heart. We'd fly on the Los Angeles freeways to the proper turn off and into the parking lot of the Long Beach Municipal Auditorium.

As soon as the bus stopped, we were out opening the baggage doors, grabbing our display table and record boxes. We rushed to the lobby for the best spot to set up our record table.

To win was Tom's greatest moment. There he'd be, with his empty thermos bottle, a smile on his face, bloodshot eyes and his proud voice saying, "I need to get some sleep."

We loved, Tom. He was a fine addition to The Couriers organization.

A Letter From Tom

Dear Dave,

Do you remember .... back in Gospel Tabernacle, 1230 Leishman Avenue, New Kensington, when we played trumpets in the church orchestra? You were always transposing and I was off-key or a couple of notes behind....

The Sunday afternoons when I would go home from church with you or you with me, to spend the afternoon, all we would do was play basketball and you would beat me because you were so tall. I was busy trying to get the ball --*(The good old days)*.

I don't think I will ever forget the day you called me to come drive The Courier's bus. It was Thanksgiving Day, and I was at my Mom and Dad's place in New Kensington, having Thanksgiving dinner. You guys were on the West Coast somewhere. That was a great day for me. I guess it was the Lord talking to you, because I was having trouble with my job. The company I was working for was slowly going broke. It took me a while, but I made it and it was a good move. Just look at all the good times I would have missed; all the places I have been. I wouldn't be working for the Lord today if you hadn't made that call and I hadn't made the move.

I wish you the best in what you are doing, and I know you are happy in your ministry. As long as you work for Him, you will stay happy. I love you and your family and have great respect for what you are doing. Keep up the good work till Jesus comes.

Your buddy, Tom Baker

In 25 years of traveling we only had three wrecks. One was with a car early in our ministry.

Duane was driving and fell asleep at the wheel. We were coming home from a service late at night and all of us were asleep. It wasn't a bad accident. We ran into the back of another car. No one was hurt.

That was when we established our "two hour policy." No one could drive over two hours at one time.

Our second accident happened when I was driving the old silver sides, 1947, Greyhound bus on the Pennsylvania Turnpike. It was raining and the brakes didn't work very well in rainy weather. So I was driving slowly and cautiously. We were in a tunnel and the semi-truck ahead of me stopped suddenly. I braked but nothing happened. I knew I was going to hit the truck because there wasn't anyplace to go. We were in a tunnel. I yelled, "We're going to hit. I can't stop." We hit the back of the truck going about 10 miles an hour. Our bumper was smashed and our head lights were busted.

The last wreck happened in Corning, New York, again, in the middle of the night. Duane was driving our 1963 Flexible bus. He was making a left turn and a truck, whose driver was sound asleep, hit us broadside. No one was injured but our bus was beyond repair. The next day we ordered a brand new 1968 Greyhound bus.

I thank God for safe travel through all those years.

One day, I'm sure it was an angel that stopped our bus. We were traveling on Highway 22 in New Jersey. This was not an interstate highway so every few miles we'd have to stop at a traffic light. People were driving fast and even going through yellow lights; anything to keep going.

All of us were up in the front of the bus talking and watching the traffic. Sure enough, the car in front of us decided to stop instead of going on through the yellow light. We all knew, at the same time, that there was no way we were going to get stopped in time. Without a word we all braced for the crash. Neil was driving and said, "Jesus, help us."

It was as though a big hand reached out and literally stopped our bus just six inches from the car in front. We all knew God had sent an angel to stop the bus. There just wasn't any other way it could have happened. It was a miracle right in front of our eyes.

We never forgot that day. No one ever forgets when God comes on the scene.

- Success Principle 15

SET UP STONES OF REMEMBRANCE

Never forget what God has done
in your life. God knows our
ability to forget, so He asks us
to place memory joggers all along
our path. (see Joshua 4:1-9)
Your memory of what God has done
is a powerful tool! We never
forgot that spot on highway 22.

• • •

The last bus we bought was the best. It was a 40 ft., fully automatic, 1973, MCI. No more grinding of the gears and double clutching.

We sent it to the Custom Coach Company in Columbus, Ohio, for interior work. They made four private rooms and a bath. The lounge area up front had ten seats, a dinette, TV and stereo. What a beauty she was. We called her The Blue Angel. The bill that came with that interior conversion job was $37,000. That was more than Judy and I paid for our house. She had brute strength. Many times we traveled through deep snow storms, hundreds of miles, only to find people that wouldn't drive a few blocks to church. When we stopped traveling, in 1980, seven years later, we had put over 700,000 miles on that bus.

CHAPTER ELEVEN

ROEVER, ROSSEY, STEVENS & WARD.

IT WAS ALWAYS A JOY TO INVITE PEOPLE TO TRAVEL
with us for a few days. These were always treasured moments.

One time we asked C.M. Ward to travel with us. We were honored because he was a very well known speaker. For 25 years he was
the speaker for the great radio broadcast, "Revivaltime." He agreed
to come with us for 8 days. The Couriers would sing for an hour and
C.M. Ward would preach for an hour. Every church was full and we
thought C.M. Ward was at his best.

He was fun to travel with. We gave him Neil's room and the bus
suited him fine. One time we had to travel 900 miles through the
night and arrived at the church just at service time. It never phased
C.M. Ward. He loved it!

I remember that trip well because I took lots of notes and got new
messages to preach after C.M. Ward was gone. I preached them for a
whole year. It was great.

That tour had been so successful, I called C.M. Ward and asked
him if he would like to do it again the following year. It was easy to
book the dates. Every pastor said, "Yes, come."

I was anxious because I needed to get eight new messages!

He graciously accepted our invitation and the tour was on!

Our first meeting was a two day revival in Girard, Pennsylvania,
with Pastor David Watson. The Couriers were to start the meeting
and C.M. Ward would join us for the second night.

Just as the pastor was introducing us the back door opened and in
walked C.M. Ward. He was a whole day early. I watched him walk
all the way up to the front pew.

Just after we sang our first song I stopped and began to talk to him in front of the crowd. I told him how glad we were that he came a day early and that the crowd would get a bonus message that night.

C.M. Ward stood up and in his great big voice he said, "David, I am a day early and I wanted to be in church. But I'm not going to preach. I am going to sit right here and listen to you Couriers sing and, David, you're the preacher tonight! So let's get on with the service. You just forget, I'm here."

My immediate thought was, <u>I can't preach in front of C.M. Ward. He's the world's greatest preacher. Let anyone sit on the front row to hear me preach but not C.M. Ward!</u>

I was so nervous, nothing came out right. C.M. Ward took it all in and was gracious. During the next few days he took me aside and began to teach me how to preach my message and bring the service to a close. I never forgot those helps and still use them.

The best thing he ever told me was to remember to ask God to help me with the close of every service. He said that this would be the most important moment of every service when men's hearts would be choosing God. He told me never to try it on my own. That's still my prayer before every service "Oh God, please help me with the closing."

- Success Principle 16

TAKE ADVANTAGE OF EVERY OPPORTUNITY.

C. M. Ward was a great mentor. I could
have sat and listened and done
nothing. Instead I took advantage
of the opportunity. I took out a pen
and paper and was willing to be taught.
Many men are too prideful to be an
understudy. What they don't realize

is that what a man studies, he
eventually becomes.
Paul mentored Timothy because he
would have to continue the missionary
work after his death.
"All scripture is God-breathed and is
useful for teaching, rebuking,
correcting and training in
righteousness, so that the man of God
may be thoroughly equipped for every
work." (2 Timothy 3:16,17) NIV

•   •   •

For the next eight days, we had an incredible tour. C.M. Ward knew something incredible about every subject that came up. We hardly slept during that tour. C.M. Ward was too interesting to miss.

I faithfully took my note pad to every service so I could get my eight new messages but the joke was on me. C.M. Ward preached the same eight messages he preached on the tour the year before. My note pad was empty.

Do I hear you laughing? It's a good thing he gave me a set of his books containing all of his messages. That's a lifetime of preaching material for me!

Since C.M. Ward was an ordained Assemblies of God minister, I wasn't sure if he would feel comfortable ministering in a church of another denomination. We were scheduled to be in a Methodist church. When I asked him about it he said it would probably be one of our best nights.

When we got to town we began to hear about the trouble we were causing. The Assemblies of God pastor was very upset that we hadn't called him and set the date in his church. His church had sponsored Revivaltime for years and now we were in his town but not at his church. The Methodist pastor didn't want to cause trouble and was asking us for suggestions as to what to do. C.M. Ward jumped up quickly and said, "I'll take care of this. Get me to a phone."

He talked to the Assemblies of God pastor and said that there would be another time for all of us to come to his church. He then invited him to come to the service in the Methodist church and get to know the Methodist pastor. He came that night and met the pastor and C.M. Ward.

It was a great night; C.M. was at his best. Thanks to C.M. Ward we saved a friendship with the Assemblies of God pastor, thanks to C.M. Ward. I was finding out that C.M. loved to get in the middle of a big fight! I don't suppose C.M. Ward can remember all of the churches we were in on that tour but I'm sure he never forgot that Methodist church.

Something else happened with C.M. Ward that made him very special to me. The Couriers hosted a Caribbean Cruise in 1979. We invited C.M. and his wife, Dorothy, to be our special guests along with 475 of our friends. My 44th birthday, was going to happen during the cruise.

At dinner time one night C.M. Ward quieted the chatter and said, "Folks, tomorrow is David's 44th birthday and I think we should all bring him a gift at dinner tomorrow. Now, you may purchase a gift on the island we visit tomorrow or you may purchase a gift from the ship's lovely gift shop or, if nothing pleases you, just bring cash."

Needless to say, the party was a great one! I got more gifts on that birthday than all the rest of my birthdays put together. And the cash. Wow! I had a pile of it.

And a wonderful thing happened later. I got a chance, to do the same for C.M. Ward.

Do you remember the two nights at Girard, Pennsylvania.? The second night there was C.M. Ward's birthday and I announced we would celebrate his birthday with a big party after church; everyone was invited.

He always preached hard and was usually soaked with perspiration. So we bought him a new trench coat that he could wera after preaching. He said it kept the "death dew" off his neck.

My family still laughs at me when I talk about the "death dew" on my neck. I learned a lot from C.M. Ward. He's the greatest!

A Letter From C.M. Ward

Dear Dave,

I can think of no friend with greater warmth of memory than yourself. A wonderful group of years brought profit and fellowship.

I can well remember when you were working at headquarters to pay for study and training, then came the early days of travel in the East, where your group backed my ministry. I can also remember the beginning of your television outreach. The arrangements and dress were not always as mature as today. However, the sincerity and enthusiasm more than equaled any lack of background.

We enjoyed trips into the mountain area and blessings that wealthier friends of yours afforded. We hope should Jesus tarry, you may have many more happy years of success. We will always count you among our very dearest friends.

Our love and prayers accompany this letter.

C.M. Ward

Of all the people who rode on our bus, Ron Stevens wins the prize for being with us the most. Every time we went to his church in Brampton, Ontario, Canada, we would ask him if he would like to come with us for a few days. Even in his busiest moments Ron couldn't resist and would find a way to get on the bus. It was a good time to forget his problems for a few days. Through the years we took him all across Canada, into many States and over 30 countries of the World.

Ron even traveled with us on our trip around the World that lasted 39 days.

That was an exhausting trip. We were very, very busy ministering night after night. We all felt so badly when we heard the news that Ron had a heart attack shortly after arriving home. He spent many days in the hospital recuperating.

I thought he would never want to travel with us again but not so. When he was well, and up and about, he called to ask, "When's the next trip?"

One day we were on the bus going to yet another concert and Ron was riding with us. Duane was writing in his "special book" and Ron asked him about it. He was shocked to find out that Duane had kept a record of all our dates through the years. He recorded the name of the church, the attendance, the amount of the offering and the record sales. What a book of information that was! Ron asked to see the book but we told him no one had seen that book and it was off limits to anyone but The Couriers. Our wives hadn't even seen the book.

Ron begged us to see it. He reminded us that he had been having The Couriers in his church for ten years. He also reminded us his church had given us our record offering and record sales had always been good. So, he wanted to add up all the money his church had given to the ministry of The Couriers and the book would give us the answer. We wanted to know ourselves so Duane and Ron opened the book and began adding the figures. Ron was so proud when the totals were over $30,000. To this day no one, besides The Couriers, and Ron has ever looked inside that book. Maybe that's the book I should have published.

A Reflection From Ron

Someone said, "Every man is enthusiastic at times. One man has enthusiasm for 30 minutes; another man has it for 30 days, but it is the man who has it for 30 years who makes a success of life." Truly, my friend David Kyllonen has made a success of life.

I have been privileged to have been a friend of Dave's for the past 35 years. Our friendship began at a Youth Convention in Pennsylvania when I met The Couriers. After hearing them sing, I invited them to come to sing at my church. It was not very large at the time, but they came and ministered as though there were two thousand people. It wasn't very many years until that same church was large enough to give the Couriers one of the largest offerings they ever received. Dave and I became friends from our first meeting. It was my privilege to become such a friend that when they would get tired of each other's company on an extended trip, they would call me and I would fly into an airport somewhere and travel with them for several days. Together we have been around the world touching some 38 countries. One of my most cherished possessions is the special Pewter Plate The Couriers gave to their very close friends in 1980 when they went their separate ways. Mine has the number "6" on it. June and myself spent many days with Dave and Judy on vacations or visiting them in Barbados.

Over the years, I think the thing that has impressed me the most about Dave is his honesty, spirituality and integrity. He lived what he sang about. There was never any hanky-panky but always a living testimony for the Lord Jesus Christ. He truly walked the walk and left no room for criticism.

One of the great tributes that can be given to a man is to see his children walk with the Lord. Kristie, Connie and Robin not only serve the Lord, but married preachers and now all travel together in full-time ministry. That tells me Dave fulfilled his role as the high priest of his home well with a wonderful backup in his wife Judy.

Our lives have been blessed by their friendship. June and I consider Dave and Judy to be two of our closest friends over the past thirty-five years. Our homes have always been open to each other and we pray will always be! Their love for each other and their love for God are truly an inspiration to all who know them. God bless you with continued success!

Ron and June Stevens

The Couriers were invited to be the special singers at a meeting in a town in Tennessee. It was held at the local fair grounds in an outdoor amphitheater. It was late in September and very cold. There was a good crowd and a speaker we had never heard of. We started singing but found it difficult because our teeth were chattering. I thought, these 2,000 people will never stay out in the open air tonight. Surely the speaker wouldn't dare speak over 15 minutes. The crowd was freezing. We were freezing. When our 30 minutes of music was over it seemed colder than when we started.

I rushed off the platform saying to myself, "I must get back to the bus where it's warm and stay there till the message is over." I didn't particularly care who the speaker was. All I could think about was how cold I was. I was a few steps from leaving the amphitheater when I heard someone introducing the speaker, Dave Roever. I said, "Who is he?" I soon found out.

Dave began to give his life story and from the beginning of his opening remarks I was spellbound. I was far from the platform but I took a seat as Dave continued sharing his testimony. Dave Roever was a young Viet Nam veteran who had half of his face blown off during the War. He was preparing to throw a phosphorus hand grenade into a Viet Cong bunker and just as the grenade was right next to his face a sniper's bullet hit the grenade and caused it to explode. He laid near death in hospitals for many, many months.

He has no right ear, no hair, (he wears a wig) and terrible, disfiguring burn scars on his face and over a major portion of his body.

He spoke about his experiences with such heart wrenching tenderness and yet, at times, such hilarious humor that I found myself crying and laughing at the same time.

He spoke for an hour and a half! I couldn't believe it. I had forgotten that I said, "The speaker better preach only 15 minutes and call it a night." I was so impressed with Dave I knew I had to meet this incredible man.

I made my way to the platform to talk to him. Many people had crowded around him but I pressed through. When I was face to face with him and could see the scars and disfigurement I wondered what I should say.

When I finally shook his hand I remember saying to him, "Dave, you're the most beautiful man I've ever met." We talked for awhile and I invited Dave to be our guest on The Courier's bus for a tour across America. He got all excited and we settled on dates for this to happen.

We gave him Tom's room, the back bedroom in our bus. Tom had satin sheets on his bed and one night while we were all sleeping and Tom was driving he took a curve a little too fast and Dave came sliding out on his head. I'm sure he wondered "What kind of trip is this going to be?"

But he loved everything about the tour. He was a great traveler.

Each night we sang and Dave gave his testimony! We enjoyed introducing Dave to crowds all across America. We enjoyed watching crowds respond to his testimony. Everybody loved him. Toward the end of the tour we had heard each other so much that, one day on the bus, Dave sang our songs and gave our introductions and we told his testimony, word for word.

We cried every night that we were with him and after he was gone we listened to his tape and cry again. He made a huge impact on our lives.

Dave traveled with us so many times in Pennsylvania that one night, in Harrisburg, I looked at the crowd and realized these people had heard Dave's testimony many times before. I went quietly to Dave and said, "Dave, there are so many people that have heard you many times I think it would be good to change the message and talk about your life from another angle." He argued with me but I was persistent.

That night Dave came with a whole new look at what happened in Viet Nam. He told different stories about the people and the children of that country. He shared a look at army life and told about some of the soldiers he shared life with.

Not only did we weep; Dave himself wept. He got so emotionally involved that it was the greatest night I had ever heard him speak.

I ran up to him after the service and hugged him and told him it was his greatest night. I remember what he said to me "Dave Kyllonen, I did it tonight, but don't you ever ask me to do that again." He had remembered too much and he was emotionally drained.

Thanks, Dave, for honoring my request. I think we heard a message that no other crowd has ever heard.

Every summer The Couriers operated a one week camp for teens. The year we invited Dave Roever to be our camp speaker there were over 400 kids. Camp Saginaw in Oxford, Pennsylvania, was full to capacity. Many of the regular campers brought their friends who were not church goers. Some of them were tough street kids who had no idea this was a church camp.

The first night of camp started and all the kids were told to be in the auditorium at 7:00 P.M. We opened with prayer and then The Couriers began to sing. It was then one of them yelled out, "Hey, man, this is church!" They started acting up, laughing and making all kinds of disruptive noises. It looked like the service was going to be a total failure. Those kids did not want to be there.

I was getting nervous. What had we gotten ourselves into? These were big, tough bruisers who were trying to take over.

We introduced the speaker of the evening, Dave Roever. He demanded that everyone be quiet and listen. Those kids took one look at Roever and knew they had met their match.

They quieted down and for the next hour no one moved a muscle. They were held spell-bound by Dave and his great testimony. You could hear a pin drop in the auditorium. He talked tough to them but later when the altar call was given, many came forward for Salvation. What a miracle of God!

Those tough kids ended up loving Dave Roever, loving The Couriers, but most of all, loving God.

Later, at the swimming pool, Dave was showing off his diving skills. He dived off the high board and the whole camp stood in amazement. He came up from his big dive, and, lo and behold, his false, rubber ear was missing. The whole camp jumped into the pool to find Dave's ear. He had made hundreds of new friends. That may have been our best year ever.

One day, while still traveling with Roever, we bought new suits and included Dave in the deal. We sure looked sharp for all those months we traveled together.

Dave was "destined for greater things" and went on to become the great evangelist he is today. His ministry in public High Schools is phenomenal. He talks to more high school kids in one year than most of us in a life time. I have great memories of working with Dave Roever. They are golden moments of my life.

- Success Principle 17

USE THE DESIGN GOD GAVE YOU TO YOUR ADVANTAGE.

Some people give up doing anything in life because God didn't make them six foot two and a hundred and eighty pounds with curly hair. Dave Roever is doing a mighty work for God. He didn't fit the above description. When I saw and heard little Jeff Steinberg sing, I promised that I would never complain about the way I was made. Jeff has no arms and two deformed legs and feet, but he came to many Courier concerts and sang his way into the hearts of everyone.

"I will give thanks to Thee, for I am fearfully and wonderfully made..."
(Psalm 139:14) NASB
"Before I formed you in the womb I knew you, and before you were born I consecrated you, I have appointed you..." (Jer. 1:5) NASB

• • •

Another friend who would travel with us from time to time was a business man from Pennsylvania. Ted Rossey was in the used car business. He bought and sold cars at the Manheim auction in Manheim, Pennsylvania. I nicknamed him Tedford.

Occasionally, Tedford would call and ask us where we were going and if he could ride along just for the day. He loved to drive the bus and it was a nice change of pace for us. Actually, I'm not sure if he wanted to be with us or if he came just to drive our bus. He called our bus his sanctuary. His greatest joy was to buy the fuel for the bus. All 140 gallons.

One year Tedford took a 40 day trip with us to the West Coast. He insisted that he buy the fuel for all 40 days. I remember, he ran out of money and had to call home for Lorraine, his wife, to send him more.

He kept a sharp watch on our tires, too. When they were all worn and we needed new ones he suggested we buy Michelins. We said, "Tedford, they're too expensive." But the next day we had eight new Michelins, thanks to Ted! We guarded those tires and watched as they ran 200,000 miles. Ted was so happy and got such a blessing out of buying those tires, he decided to buy tires for us from then on. By the time I left The Couriers in 1980, Tedford had bought 42 tires. That was a major blessing for The Couriers ministry.

A Letter From Tedford

Just a note to tell you, Loraine and I are enjoying retirement. We're busy with flowers and lawn work and all the other things associated with home owning.

I have plenty of time for memories and a whole lot of nostalgia. I remember the times with the Couriers, your inspiration and the influence you've had in my life. The love you've taught your family and mine shall always be remembered.

Dave, I would like you to know that I serve on the deacon board of our Baptist church and am always drawing from experiences I had with you. We're praying for your safe travel, your family, your ministry and your well being.

Love and prayers, Ted Rossey

CHAPTER TWELVE

UNFORGETTABLE MOMENTS.

AFTER A SERVICE ONE NIGHT THE PASTOR INVITED US to his house for a snack. He said, "Follow my car and I'll lead the way." We were making our way through traffic turning left then right then left again. We found ourselves in heavy conversation and didn't pay too much attention to what we were doing. Just follow that car, we told Tom, and he did.

After awhile we began to remark that the preacher lived pretty far out in the country. We were going this way and then that. After we went over a big bridge and turned left down a narrow road we all started watching close and really wondered where the pastor lived.

Finally, we saw the car pull into a road that led to a lot of big buildings and then into a driveway. It was spooky dark. The pastor sure lived in an unusual place. The car we were following came to a stop and a man got out. Oh boy, he wasn't the pastor! We followed the wrong car.

The man was frightened. He ran up to our bus and said, "This is the Catholic Monastery, what do you want? Why did you follow me? I can't believe you brought this big bus in here. What is happening?" We started laughing. This was hilarious! The Monk didn't think so until we told him who we were and that we followed the wrong car. He finally smiled and we backed our bus out of his driveway.

Now, where is that preacher? What kind of car was he driving? Sure, this would be a quick stop. Just a few minutes to the house, a light snack and then straight home.

Judy capped off the whole night when she met me at the bus and asked the question. "What took you so long? Why are you so late? Didn't you say you were going to be home early tonight?"

A terrible thing happened the night we had a concert in Allentown, Pennsylvania with The Happy Goodman Family.

Singing with the Goodmans always made a great night. We all loved the Lord together and the Spirit of God was so precious in the songs we sang. This night was to be no different.

After we sang our songs we introduced The Goodmans. I decided to sit in the audience while they sang instead of backstage. I wanted to see the faces and expressions of the singers. In the middle of their program something very scary happened. Vestal was talking and everyone was listening intently. A family, sitting in the balcony, was caught up with what Vestal was saying and not paying attention to their baby boy who was crawling around under their feet.

Suddenly, he crawled over to the wall and fell through an opening to the first floor. We all heard the heart stopping thud and knew immediately that something or someone had fallen from the balcony. Someone yelled that a baby had fallen.

Vestal immediately began to pray. I sat in my seat stunned. I couldn't move. I knew that I should be running that way but my body wouldn't go. I didn't want to see the baby. I just knew he was dead. I wasn't sure if I could handle what was happening.

I finally got a grip on myself and started for the baby. They carried him to a special room off the foyer. Someone was calling an ambulance. I looked at the baby and saw that he was alive. I couldn't see anything wrong with him. I knew it had to be internal injuries. It was a long fall and the baby landed on hardwood flooring. There wasn't any carpet. How could he live?

After the ambulance came and took the baby and the family to the hospital I went back into the auditorium to see what was going on. The crowd was still praying for the baby. I never heard a crowd pray like that before. Everyone prayed as though the baby was theirs.

After the concert was over I called the hospital. They still didn't know much and needed more time. We left for home and prayed through the night for that family. The next morning we called the hospital again and talked with the parents. They gave us an incredible report. Absolutely nothing was wrong with their baby. He was kept over night just to watch him. Now they were leaving the hospital to go home. Their little baby was perfect, not one thing wrong. I knew we had gotten a hold of God and that He had answered our prayers.

One night we were singing in the deep South with many groups. We had always talked about rigging up a microphone backstage and singing along with a group without them knowing it. At the end of their song, just as they were ready to quit, we'd grab a big breath and sing the last note with them. We would be ready to hold on for a long time but they wouldn't. We didn't know how it would work, but we decided, to see the expression on everyone's faces would be worth the try.

Well, the night was right, the mood was right, and the microphone was easy to rig backstage without anyone seeing it. So, we tried it.

The Florida Boys were singing and Duane, Neil and I got together back stage and prepared for the experiment. We got around the microphone and when the Florida Boys got to their last note we took a giant breath and sang the last word with them. They were trying to stop singing but heard each other holding out the ending note. Their faces were getting red and they were looking at one another trying to stop but, man, the sound was still there.

The band heard voices and kept their instruments going. Finally, the singers ran out of breath and had to stop. But here we were, behind the curtain, keeping the sound going. They all took a breath and jumped in again one at a time. The crowd couldn't understand what was happening and neither could the Florida Boys. We had fooled them.

They did a very smart thing. They started the song again. We wanted to do the same thing at the end of the song but we couldn't. We were laughing too hard. What great guys they were. They ended up laughing as hard as we did. They said they would get us back someday but never did.

A few weeks later in Boston, Mass., we were singing with the Keystone Quartet. They were young and aggressive. They were having themselves a great night.

We decided to hide the microphone backstage and do the same to them as we did to the Florida Boys. It worked perfectly. We started singing on the last note of their song. They, too, tried to stop but heard everyone still singing and got red in the face and almost collapsed on the floor. When they turned around to see what had happened we stepped out from the curtain and showed the crowd what we had done. Everyone had a good laugh. We were proud of ourselves. We had done it again.

After the intermission The Couriers were introduced again for the second half of the concert. After our first song, the massive curtain suddenly started closing in front of us. The Keystone Quartet was pulling on the ropes and bringing our stand to a screeching halt.

They were killing themselves with laughter. They had paid us back! What a night! What memories!

My most embarrassing moment happened in Bryson City, North Carolina. I haven't told this story to very many people.

The Inspirations Quartet held a yearly concert right in the middle of the Great Smoky Mountains. The Couriers waited many years for an invitation to be a part. We were finally booked and couldn't wait for the day to arrive.

What a great trip we had getting there. They named those mountains right. I was looking for the smoke in those hills and sure enough I wasn't disappointed. The tops of those mountains had a blue haze surrounding them and looked like smoke from a thousand camp fires down below.

There was a great crowd there that night. All the groups had arrived. The concert was outdoors and the people were sitting in their lawn chairs.

People were saying, "Boy, Dave, it sure took you guys a long time to get here. We know you are going to have a great night."

I noticed that as the groups began to sing people were doing funny things. At the end of some of the songs people would run through the crowd and on out to the field next to the concert grounds. They would wave their hands, wildly, as they ran across the field as fast as they could go. I have seen people get excited about Gospel Music but this beat anything I had ever seen. It seemed like the faster the song the more they would run. I felt the groups were singing loud, fast songs to get the people to run to the field.

Then it was our turn. We were a little nervous but I liked it that way because we always sang better if we were nervous.

We got a great introduction and walked out to sing our first song. We were Northerners, brand new to this part of the country and to this crowd.

As usual, we began our stand with slow, easy songs. The harmonies were just melting together. It was that unexplainable feeling that comes into your heart that's called the sweet anointing of God. Others felt it, too, when we began singing that wonderful old hymn, "Whispering Hope", accapella.

During the song two men started dancing around in front of the platform. Several people began to shout and clap their hands. They were calling out to the two dancing men and egging them on. It seemed so inappropriate for the quiet sweetness of the song.

When the song ended I stepped to the microphone and asked, very nicely, if the two men would be seated. I thought I would stop them now before things got worse. I told them that they were distracting the people from hearing the message of the song.

The two men took their seats and the audience became so quiet you could hear a pin drop.

I knew I had offended the whole crowd when, at the end of our next song, there was no response whatsoever. The crowd just sat stone silent, and glared at us. We went on with our program and finished every song with the same response.

Even our big number one song, "The Statue Of Liberty", laid dead. We had sung that song for many years and always had a standing ovation when it was over.

We were making some kind of history. We walked off the stage in silence wondering what had happened.

I quickly walked to the bus and sat stunned while the next group started singing. I kept asking myself, "Had I done the wrong thing? Why didn't I just let it go?"

Duane, Neil and I sat in our bus just staring at each other. I had made a huge mistake and now that whole crowd hated us. I knew they were thinking, "Who did these Yankee boys from the North think they were, coming down here to the South and telling us what we cannot do."

Not a soul came by our record table during intermission. Not one soul!

The Inspirations were upset, to say the least. They called me into their office during the intermission and told me the two men I had asked to sit down were very important people and were everyone's friends. These two men had been coming to this Gospel Singing for a long time and they had become spiritual giants in the eyes of everyone. I had offended the whole crowd because I hadn't accepted their way of worshiping God.

They couldn't believe that we had turned a great night into such a disaster. They were disappointed and angry. They said we would never be invited back and, furthermore, we would not even be singing on the second half of the program.

They handed me our check but I was reluctant to take it. I was so embarrassed and felt so bad that my body was shaking on the inside. All I could do was hang my head and stand there. I thought, <u>I've been singing for over 20 years. I have dedicated myself to living right and I don't have a mean bone in my body. And I am a preacher. How have I have gotten myself and The Couriers into this situation?</u>

I went back to the bus to face Duane and Neil. I apologized for letting them down and told them I was sorry. They were gracious and told me it wasn't the end of the world. We had learned a big lesson.

As we were packing up to leave, The Inspirations sent word that we would be allowed to sing for fifteen minutes during the second half, after all.

I prayed, "Oh God, please help me now." I knew what I had to do to make things right.

We were introduced and I immediately went to the front of the stage. I quieted the crowd by asking for the two men to come to the front of the stage.

My heart was pounding and my brain was asking, "Will they or won't they come?"

They came and the crowd was on the edge of their seats. When they got to the stage I jumped down and met them. I said, "Gentlemen, I owe you an apology for what I said to you earlier in the evening. I hope you'll forgive me and let me leave the Smoky Mountain Singing without making any enemies. Will you forgive me?"

They grabbed me around my neck in a great big hug and said, "Yes." I asked them if they wanted to say anything to the crowd and they both gave a brief testimony as to what the Lord meant to them. It was a special moment as they went back to their seats and the crowd cheered.

Then I addressed the crowd. I said, "I won't sing another song until you, too, accept my apology and forgive me for offending each of you."

There was a long silence that seemed to last for eternity. Then a man yelled from the crowd, "It takes a pretty big man to do what this man has done. I think we should forgive him." Someone else called out, "That's true."

Then several people ran to the stage and hugged me. The people kept coming to the stage. Everyone started clapping their hands and we started singing. Duane and Neil ended up singing a duet while I shook hands and hugged. I never felt so good, trying to hug 2,000 people.

We ended the night with a huge record sale and hundreds of new friends.

But, the Inspirations kept their word. They never invited us back.

After that night, you could dance the jitter bug on stage and it wouldn't phase us in the least!

• Success Principle 18

AN OUNCE OF FORGIVENESS IS BETTER THAN A POUND OF PUNISHMENT.

*I shutter to think what would have
happened to me if I had never
asked the crowd for forgiveness.
I would be living this day with
torment. Thank God they forgave
me and I left the concert with
peace in my heart.*

*"A brother offended is harder to
win than a strong city, and
contentions are like the bars
of a castle." (Proverbs 18:19)* NKJV

• • •

CHAPTER THIRTEEN

THE
BIG BOYS.

I ALWAYS LOVED IT WHEN WE BOOKED A TEN DAY tour with only one other group, especially if it was a big-name group.

I'll never forget one such tour. It was with the Oak Ridge Boys before they turned "Country."

The tour started in Western Canada. The great Jubilee Auditoriums in Calgary, Edmonton and Vancouver always were filled with thousands of people. They were great auditoriums with great sound! Just walking out on stage gave us goose bumps.

We always met with the promoter before a concert to see when we would be singing.

On this particular night, he said, "Couriers, you will be first and your time will be one hour. Then we will have an intermission and the rest of the evening will be for the Oak Ridge Boys. Is that OK?"

Wow! We were excited! We quickly went to our dressing room and began to talk about the great evening we were going to have. It's not good to go first, usually, but this would be different.

We couldn't believe it. We were going to have an intermission before the crowd even heard the Oak Ridge Boys. Maybe we had a chance to sell some records!

We prayed and headed for the stage. We had one hour to sing and minister to the crowd.

I don't think anyone expected much from us. It was really an Oak Ridge Boys' crowd.

But we started singing, putting every ounce of energy we could find into it. After the first song it was like we had scored a big touchdown. We could hardly wait to sing the second song and then the third. What a night we were having.

By the time we got to our last song, we knew we were going to finish with a bang. Our new song, "The Statue Of Liberty," written by Neil Enloe, was making a big hit everywhere we sang it even in Canada. Many Canadians had been to New York and had visited that big, green lady that stands so tall in the New York Harbor.

Everyone understood the first verse which talks about liberty and freedom.

> *In New York Harbor stands a lady*
> *with a torch raised to the sky.*
> *And all who see her, know she stands*
> *for, Liberty for you and me.*

When the second verse started, people began to raise their hands as they heard us sing about Mt. Calvary.

> *On lonely Golgotha stood a cross*
> *with my Lord raised to the sky.*
> *And all who kneel there, live forever*
> *as all the saved can testify.*

When we got to the last chorus the words said,

> *"Oh, the cross is my Statue of Liberty.*
> *It was there that my soul was set free.*
> *Unashamed, I'll proclaim that the rugged cross*
> *is my Statue of Liberty."*

Now the crowd was on it's feet and they stayed standing until the song ended and the thunderous applause was over.

We barely beat the crowd to The Courier's record table in the lobby. What a night! One of our best record sales ever!

Well, the second night of the tour we expected things would be different. We were sure that the Oak Ridge Boys would sing before the intermission. But the promoter gave us the same schedule as the first night. The Couriers before intermission, the Oaks after intermission. It happened that same way the entire tour.

When the tour was over and we were saying, "Good-bye" to the Oak Ridge Boys we said, "Let's do it again next year." They said, "Couriers, we don't want to see you again for a long time. When your stand was over the concert was over. The crowd knew it and we knew it. There was nothing we could do. This was the toughest tour we've had in a long time. Good-bye, Couriers, you're on your own."

When I think of the Oak Ridge Boys I also think of another interesting incident.

When I resigned from the Couriers, in 1980, I received a telephone call from Joe Bonsall, the tenor for the Oak Ridge Boys. He wanted to thank me for helping him get started in Gospel Music many years before. We talked about the "Faith Four Quartet," and the "Keystone Quartet." These were groups Joe had sung with before joining the Oak Ridge Boys. He told me he was sorry I was leaving Gospel Music but knew I was doing what God had asked me to do.

Just before we hung up I said, "Joe, before you hang up I want to say one thing to you." There was a long, silent pause. I think Joe was thinking, "Oh, no, here comes the sermon." But instead, I said, "Joe, thanks for your call. And thanks for wishing me God's best, but I thought you were calling me to replace Richard Sterban and sing the bass for the Oak Ridge Boys." We both laughed and said our good-byes.

I had no contact with the Oaks after that for about a dozen years. I was busy pastoring Westside Assembly of God Church in Davenport, Iowa.

One Sunday, evening my son-in-law Gregory who was also my associate, told me the Oak Ridge Boys were in town. He suggested I shorten my sermon so that he and I could go see them after church.

Gregory kept asking me, "Do you really know them? Did you really sing with them? Do they know who you are?" I said, "Yes, Yes, Yes. and I'll prove it to you."

We drove to the auditorium where the Oaks were in concert and parked the car. We walked up to their two buses like we knew what we were doing and their bus driver approached us wanting know who we were and what we were doing. I said we were friends of the Oaks, and just wanted to say, "Hi" He told us that the concert was almost over but if we hurried maybe we could catch their last song. Then he added, "Let me show you where to stand so you can see them when the concert is over. After their last song they will go out the stage door in the alley. The police will escort them to their bus and, if they know you, they may invite you to come into the bus."

"If they know you," was said in a tone of disbelief and gave us the feeling that not many people got to go in their bus.

Gregory and I hurried to the balcony just as they were introducing their last song, "Elvira." I was all eyes and ears. There were my friends, Joe Bonsall, Duane Allen and Richard Sterban.

As the crowd stood to their feet, clapping, whistling and yelling for them to sing, "Elvira," again, I couldn't help but remember the many nights we shared the message of the Gospel in song.

Then it was over. I grabbed Greg and we took the steps, two at a time to the main floor. Out the door and up the sidewalk we rushed. We met the bus driver and got to our place.

The stage door opened and, sure enough, the police came out first and then The Oak Ridge Boys.

There were lots of people swarming them and their bus; lots of noise with people yelling. I began to understand why the police escort was needed. By the time they got to their bus, hundreds of people were crowding around us.

The moment of truth was near. Would they remember me? About 15 feet from the bus door I caught Joe Bonsall's eye and yelled, "Hi Joe." They all saw me and came over and invited me into their bus. I said that my son-in-law was with me and wanted to come, too. "Sure," they said, "He can come in, too."

I smiled at the bus driver on my way into the bus. That was a great victory for me. I did know them just like I said. We had to be good friends to be invited on their bus.

We had a great conversation, remembering some good old times, and before we left I invited them to sing at our church the next time they came to town. There would be just one hitch. After they sang they had to stay and listen to me preach. They agreed to it all.

I gave them a big hug and we said our good-byes.

On the way home Gregory and I had a neat conversation about how we would tell our congregation that the Oak Ridge Boys were coming to our church. By now people knew the Oak Ridge Boys only as Country Singers but in days gone by our church had hosted a concert featuring Johnny Cash and 16,000 people attended the service.

It never happened. We resigned as pastors from the church that year to join Homefire Family Ministries so I missed my only chance to sing a song with the Oak Ridge Boys in church.

Another great group we toured with was The Imperials. They drew a different crowd than the Oak Ridge Boys.

We loved the way they dressed so much that we bought suits to look like them. We were always eager to see what they would be wearing.

I remember a certain concert in Long Beach, California featuring The Couriers and The Imperials. Armond Morales, their bass singer, came to me in the dressing room of the Long Beach Municipal Auditorium and said, "Dave, there is something different about the way you look. I can't figure out what it is. I think it might be your hair. Are you doing something different?"

I said, "Armond, I'll tell you a secret. I quit using that shiny, sticky hair cream. I shampoo my hair, dry it with a hair dryer and spray it with hair spray."

Armond said, "That's it, Dave. You don't have that slicked back look anymore. Your hair is fluffy now and looks like you have more of it."

You must remember, back in 1963, men didn't use hair dryers and they were just beginning to use hair spray. In fact when Don Baldwin brought his first can of hair spray on our bus I thought, not me, never me.

But I liked what it did to my hair so I ended up buying my own can of spray and my own hair dryer.

What a great turn of events that was for me. I was the king of the "Little dab will do ya."

Boy, did we laugh when the Imperials hit the stage later that evening. They all had fluffy, sprayed hair.

Armond had shown me how to sing a smooth bass part with my voice, and I showed him how to comb a smooth hair part on his head.

We thoroughly enjoyed touring with Andrae Crouch and The Disciples. They had a brand new sound that we knew nothing about. Wow! What singing! They poured more energy into their singing than any group we had ever heard. They tore the house down each evening!

They had a huge dilemma on that tour. The records they ordered for the tour never arrived. Can you imagine? Big crowds and all wanting to buy, but no records. I noticed that Andrae just stood around and scratched his head a lot during intermission.

However, this was good for us because the people ended up at our table buying everything in sight. We loved that tour and thanked Andrae every night for not bringing his records and tapes.

Big John Hall did a tour with The Couriers in Canada.

John is fun to travel with. He has a lot of great stories. He traveled with the Stamps Quartet and the famous Blackwood Brothers Quartet. He is a great bass singer and makes friends everywhere he goes.

John loves to play the card game Rook. We played more Rook with John Hall than anyone else in the world. When it was time to bid, he would always say, "Well, guys, since there isn't any money on it, I bid 200." John loved to take the bid and he loved to win.

The first night of our tour we were in London, Ontario. While we were setting up the PA system, John and I were talking. I jokingly told him we were hot in Canada. John began to tell me how much Canada loved him. The conversation ended with both of us saying, "Let's talk again during the intermission and see who did the best."

John sang first and after 35 minutes of singing the crowd stood to it's feet and cheered John with a great standing ovation. He came off the stage with the biggest grin, saying, "I told you so." But I said, "John, it took you 35 minutes to get the crowd on it's feet. Just watch us, John, the crowd will stand during our first song."

We walked out on the stage and started singing, "Oh, Canada," the Canadian National Anthem. Immediately, the crowd got to it's feet and started singing their song with us. I looked off stage to see John's expression. He was shaking his fists at us. We had won the contest.

I know that Big John Hall is still singing. I wonder if he ever learned the Canadian National Anthem?

A highlight for any Gospel group was to attend the National Quartet Convention. It was fun meeting all the groups and watching each group take it's turn at winning the crowd. Some groups were under great pressure to be booked by the promoters who sat in the audience watching and listening. It was amazing what some groups did to get the crowd on it's feet.

When all the quartet's buses started rolling in for the week it was really exciting. Who had the biggest? The newest? Whose bus was painted the sharpest?

One year The Couriers rolled into the National Quartet Convention with a brand new bus. We were really proud of our rig. We knew we had the sharpest bus because we had designed a lighted, neon sign to run the length of 10 feet on both sides of the bus. You could stand a block away and see, **THE COURIERS**, in lights.

I remember, we didn't get to sing on the program until 2 am, but our bus was lighted up on the street outside. Some things really mattered!

Let me tell you about an incredible, once in a life time, experience I had concerning the National Quartet Convention.

My phone rang one day and when I said, "Hello," a voice, so low, rumbled in my ear. I sat stunned for a moment when I realized this was J.D. Sumner of the famous Blackwood Brothers Quartet.

My mind went back to the first night I ever heard J.D. sing in Springfield, Missouri. He moved me that night and now he was moving me 20 years later on the phone.

I was shocked when he invited The Couriers to sing for the Sunday morning service and would I, Dave Kyllonen, preach the message? I said, "J. D., is this a joke? Are you really for true?"

Then he said, "Don't you know, Dave, that you are the velvet throated orator of Gospel Music and we need you on Sunday morning?" I had a hard time believing what he said but I was thinking, "Wow, we've gone from last place to first place in just one phone call."

All the dreams of being heard by all the groups at the same time were coming true. I said, "J.D. the answer is yes. I don't have to ask God or Judy. It will be a great honor to be a part of the National Quartet Convention's Sunday Morning Service."

I could hardly wait to tell the great news to Duane and Neil. I told them, "We've been asked to sing and preach for the Sunday morning service at the National Quartet Convention! Can you believe it?" Some days everything goes right! This was beyond my wildest dreams. This was twenty years of waiting in the wings, just doing my best everytime it was my turn.

Of all the people to be asked, I had to be at the bottom of the list. But when God sees your heart and it's pure, He puts you in places you just can't believe.

I was scared on Sunday morning when I got up to speak. All the music groups were sitting in front of me. Rev. Hovey Lister had preached this service for years and it had become a highlight of the Quartet Convention.

He wasn't available so they had chosen me. God had given me a message and after a few moments I relaxed and preached up a storm.

What a change came over all the groups concerning us. Guys began to come quietly to our bus and ask for prayer for themselves and their families. All the years of being called the "Holy Joe's" was coming to an end. We had gained their respect and had a marvelous time ministering to them one on one. They wanted what we had in our hearts and some of them wanted to know how to get the anointing on their singing.

Everytime there was a knock on the door of our bus we knew it was another opportunity to make a difference in someone's life. God called us to be the salt in the field of Gospel Music and we never dared lose our savor.

- Success Principle 19

DO YOUR BEST IN THE SMALL THINGS
AND GOD WILL LET YOU DO THE BIG
THINGS, TOO.

*Never give up on your dreams, their
fulfillment could be just around the corner.
I always wanted to speak to our peers,
the quartet crowd and all of their friends.
After twenty years of waiting, I got my opportunity.*

•　　•　　•

We sang and preached the Sunday morning service at the National Quartet Convention for two years in a row. I'll cherish the two audio tapes of those services for as long as I live.

We were privileged to be a part of a weekly television program called The Gospel Singing Jubilee. Every month we, along with The Florida Boys, The Happy Goodman Family and the Dixie Echoes, traveled to Nashville, Tennessee, to tape programs for the following month.

It was a long haul from Harrisburg, Pennsylvania, to Nashville, Tennessee, but it was worth it because we were getting a lot of exposure.

One morning Joel Hemphill called and said, "We are going to open a Gospel Music Hall of Fame in Nashville and we are asking many of the singers to have their heads "done" in bronze for the Hall of Fame. Would you be willing to have your head "done?" I said, "Well, sure! I'd like to have my head in bronze on display in the Gospel Music Hall Of Fame!"

So arrangements were made and on the next trip to Nashville I was put on the schedule to have my head "done."

I had to go to an old part of town in an old building early in the morning when no one was up and about. Once inside the old building, I got on an old elevator and rode to the top floor. I stepped out of the elevator and walked the dimly lit halls until I found the door I wanted. I knocked and was relieved when it opened.

I was ushered into a small room and asked to sit in an odd looking chair. There were three men talking among themselves. This was going to be all business and no small talk for sure.

They just asked me to lie back and close my eyes. They poured a cold mixture of water and a flour like substance on my face. They said, "Put a smile on your face and don't move or change your face for the next twenty minutes."

Thank God for two little nose holes. At least I was able to breathe. I couldn't see or talk. I just had to keep that same smile on my face.

It was then that I got frightened. Here I lay in a spooky room, on the top floor of a spooky building, in a spooky part of town, with three spooky guys making spooky sounds and I couldn't open my eyes.

My mind began to play tricks on me. I imagined the worst. At one time, I told myself they were making a movie and I was dumb enough to accept their invitation to come to this place and be their victim. From time to time they would laugh loudly and I was even more frightened.

Then it was over. Off came the cold flour and water mixture that had hardened on my face. They told me I would be able to see the finished product in a few months.

The moral of the story is this. If you ever have your head made into a bronze bust take a good friend with you.

I got to thinking how nice it would be to have my bronze head in my home so I called Joel and asked him if I could get a second one done for myself. He said they would make an extra one for me but that it would cost $300.00. Duane and Neil wanted to have a bust of themselves, too, and so did our promotional manager, Paul Wislocky.

So, on our next trip to Nashville we arrived at the same old building after driving all night to make our early appointment.

Tom Baker, our bus driver, was sleeping, but the rest of the guys were excited to get started. I asked the man in charge if there was enough time to do our bus driver too. He said, "Sure, bring him in before the next appointment arrives."

I woke Tom out of a deep sleep with the news that he could get his head "done" too. He wasn't quite ready that was for sure, but we only had a short time.

We hurried him to the odd chair. He wanted to wash his face but we said, "There's no time for that, Tom. Just lie down and smile for the next 20 minutes."

Today, when you see Tom's bronze head, you want to say, "Wake up, Tom."

One night in a church in New Jersey a lady came and asked me if her eleven year old daughter could sing a song in the service. I said we would try to work it in.

The little girl came to the platform and sang her song. She was remarkable! She sang like a grown up at age eleven. Her name was Evie Tornquist.

The crowd loved her and, needless-to-say, The Couriers were impressed.

Any time we sang in New Jersey and Evie was there we invited her to sing a song. I remember saying to the crowd the first time I heard her sing, "This girl is going to make it big some day."

One of the great nights I will always remember is the night The Couriers and Evie sang at the General Council of the Assemblies of God in Oklahoma City, Oklahoma.

Years had gone by and Evie was now twenty-one, grown up and famous. The audience was not aware that we had sung together, ten years before, in a little church in New Jersey.

CHAPTER FOURTEEN

ONE MORE TIME WITH FEELING.

THE HARDEST TASK FOR ME AS A MEMBER OF THE Couriers was recording our albums. We tried to make two records per year. Even though I was in over forty studios, it never got any easier.

I always seemed to have the hardest part. The baritone part usually had some big octave jumps to an odd chord that I just couldn't hear. After singing one line for a dozen takes and missing it every time it got to be embarrassing.

Hearing myself on tape was always discouraging. I would record my part thinking I had done pretty well. Then the engineer would play it back in the studio and it wouldn't be good at all. I remember many times wanting to quit.

Duane and Neil would sing their solos once or twice and everyone would say, "That was great, let's move on." But after I had sung my part nine or ten times, and thought it was finally good, they would say, "Dave, could you do it one more time and put just a little more feeling into it?"

What simply rolled out of Duane and Neil always had to be chiseled out of me. When everyone would say, "Dave, that was great, let's move on," were golden moments for me.

My favorite record of all was called "Town and Country." A big band sound on one side and a country sound on the other.

Jesse Peterson came up with the idea. He was the president of Tempo Records affiliated with The Lillenas Music Company in Kansas City, Missouri. He helped us get a recording contract with Tempo Records and we made our last eleven albums with them.

It was Jesse who arranged for all the music, the sound tracks, the photographer, the studio, the write ups and all the rest that goes along with making a record.

He would send us the sound tracks and music about 3 months prior to recording. We would rehearse and get ready for the scheduled date to record.

Most of the time we were ready but, when we weren't, Jesse would really get up tight with us. After all, there was a lot of money involved in recording an album.

We decided that our friends would enjoy a sing- along album. We entitled it, "Sing With Us."

The recording date was set in a studio in Southern California. This would work well because we were hosting a tour to Hawaii with many of our friends. On the way home from Hawaii we were stopping to tour Southern California and cross the border into Mexico for a day. On one of those days The Couriers would record while our wives hosted the tour to Mexico.

Weeks before the trip we were calling Jesse about the sound tracks. He had sent the sheet music but no sound tracks. We were leaving for Hawaii and needed them badly. Well, they didn't come so we left on our trip without them. He promised to send them to Hawaii but we never got them.

When we arrived in California the first thing we did was call Jesse; but we couldn't reach him. We were recording the next morning. We decided to be at the studio on time so that we would live up to our part of the contract.

What a surprise when we arrived! Jesse, the engineers, the arranger and the sound tracks were there. Everybody was ready to go but us.

Jesse said, "Hi, guys, welcome. I hope you brought your voices with you because today we are recording your new album." We yelled together, "Never! we haven't even heard the sound tracks yet."

It would take many pages to write the whole conversation that morning but Jesse finally won and we began to record, one segment at a time. We would learn the verse and record it. Then we would learn the chorus and record that. We did that for sixteen hours and, believe it or not, we finished recording the album that day.

I treasure that album above all the rest. I love to tell people about the recording day before they even hear it. I guess when the same guys sing together for twenty five years you can sometimes do the impossible.

If you have the album, "Nothing But The Gospel Truth", you have a real prize. There were only a few made and you might be interested in it's story.

Long before we met Jesse, we made records on our own label, called "Hymntone." We had only recorded six or seven records when we decided to make an album with a full orchestra.

We scheduled our recording date at the RCA studio in Nashville. Brock and Ben Speer of the Speer Family made some of the arrangements for us and also played their instruments.

We were young and fairly new to Gospel Music and needed something to catch the attention of the Gospel Music World. Most groups were using three or four instruments for recording so we were moving ahead of our time to use a full orchestra. We had rehearsed for hours, making sure we were ready. This album was costing a lot of money.

It was an exciting day for us. We walked into the studio and heard the orchestra members warming up their instruments. Questions were flying about the session. "Who were the singers? Who was paying for all this? Who ever heard of using a full orchestra for "back up" on a Gospel album?"

You should have heard us talking, too. "Wow! Look at all those violin players. Is that an oboe? Boy, those trumpets are going to sound great. Are they going to use all those drums?"

The musicians were ready, we were ready. It was time to record our first song. The red light came on. I was trembling inside. The conductor raised his baton and gave a wave of his hand with a one, two, three, and four.

The sound was absolutely unbelievable. We were overwhelmed. The introduction was over and we were to start singing but all we could do was laugh. When something is so good, and beyond what you expected, the greatest reaction is to laugh.

It didn't take us long to get serious and we enjoyed ourselves to the hilt all day long. "Joshua Fit The Battle Of Jericho" never sounded better. "Sweet Jesus," now that was a song. The wailing of those violins turned us on and we sang at a level we had never sung before.

I was intrigued by those professional musicians. They never made mistakes. And if we had to work on a part they would put their instruments down and pick up the books they had brought along. When we were ready to sing again they put down their books, picked up their instruments, and on the count of three start playing, as though they had never stopped. I thought, <u>maybe I should have learned to play an instrument instead of trying to sing</u>.

We walked out of the RCA Studios that day with a brand new master tape. Our hearts were as light as feathers and our feet were walking on a cloud. We had made a fantastic album!

Now we needed a sharp record jacket to match it. We needed a "knock out" picture of ourselves and a great layout and design. Then we would be on our way. Surely, now, we would get some attention from the right people.

A couple of weeks later we pulled up to an auditorium and saw the Speer Family bus parked there with all the others. What a surprise! We didn't remember them being on the program. As we walked into the auditorium and stood at the back, we couldn't believe our ears. All the singers had gathered on the stage; Brock and Ben Speer were playing our new album for them. When everyone saw us they raved about how much they loved the album. Brock said, "The album is so good, we got a copy from the studio and have been playing it every night before the concert. Everybody loves it. Couriers, you have made a hit record!"

However, I must tell you the rest of the story.

Warner Brothers called and had heard so much about the album that they wanted us to sign a recording contract. They were willing to buy the tape from us, pay all the costs and promote our records in stores all over the nation. We were flabbergasted, to say the least.

We signed the contract and smiled at each other for days. Can you believe it? We were recording artists for Warner Brothers.

The first shipment of albums came in a few weeks. We hadn't seen a proof of anything. We had only sent them our picture and they had designed the jacket, front and back, on their own.

This was better than opening a Christmas present. Duane pulled three records out of the cardboard box and handed one to each of us. We all looked at the same time.

I said, "Yuck! It's orange! It's ugly! Why did they use bright orange? It's worldly! It's not Gospel! They actually put the title in purple! Nothing matches!"

The back of the jacket wasn't anything I thought it should be. The write up was in large print and took up the whole back. Senior citizens didn't need their glasses to read that back liner. It all looked so wrong at the time, but there wasn't a thing we could do about it.

We got one thousand records with the first order. Everyone loved the bright jacket and our new sound tracks. The Couriers never sounded better and everyone wanted the new album.

We remarked later that not only was the music ahead of it's time but so was the bright orange jacket with purple lettering.

There was a lot of pressure being on a major label. Warner Brothers called often to see how our record sales were going. Every time they called we ordered one thousand more records whether we needed them or not. We wanted to impress them with our sales. After a period of time we had accumulated over five thousand albums in Neil's basement. Just the Warner Brothers album. Going to Neil's basement was an overwhelming experience. Record boxes were stacked high, everywhere, with little aisles to walk through. If we'd had a fire or flood we would have been out of business.

We were asked to make our second Warner Brothers album which we called, "We Gotta Sing." Now we had two records coming from Warner Brothers.

That same year Don Baldwin and Little David Young resigned from The Couriers. It was June of 1965 and I was the new manager.

One of my first calls was from Warner Brothers. I don't remember the agent's name but I remember the conversation. He said, "David, I hear you've made some changes in The Couriers and that you are the new manager. Just in case you didn't know, I'm calling to inform you that your account is long over due. We need a check from you, today, for $17,000!"

You can imagine how I felt. Managing The Couriers wasn't going to be easy. I had a tough decision to make.

- Success Principle 20

TOUGH DECISIONS ARE NEVER EASY BUT ARE USUALLY NECESSARY.

Truth always pays off.

• • •

I made the dreaded, humiliating, embarrassing call to Warner Brothers and said, "We are unable to pay for the records we ordered. We have over five thousand albums here in our basement and tomorrow we would like to ship them back to you. We are very sorry! We did wrong and need you to forgive us for what we have done."

They did forgive us and accepted the thousands of albums back and canceled our debt and contract. We were never able to purchase anymore albums from them.

We tried for years to make another album just like it, but it never happened. "Nothing But The Gospel Truth" was truly one of a kind. Only a few people ever bought "We Gotta Sing."

If you have either one, or both, get them out and play them. You'll enjoy listening to them again, especially now, that you know the real story.

The most exciting album we ever recorded is the one called, "Ovation." It was exciting because it was recorded live in front of a sold out crowd in the Masonic Temple in Toledo, Ohio.

Jesse Petersen brought a sound truck and parked it behind the building. The sound tracks were piped into the building from the truck. Jesse told us to just do a normal program and he would take the best of the evening and record an album from it. We were to fit all of our new songs into the program.

The concert began with electrifying enthusiasm. The Cathedrals and The Jerry Goff Singers thrilled the crowd and then it was our turn.

The crowd cheered as the music came through the house speakers, loud and clear. The Couriers were "live" in Toledo! From the first note of, "I Sing the Mighty Power of God," we were ready. Our new songs were a hit.

Even our wives, Jean Ann, Ruthie, Judy and our bus driver's wife, Naomi, joined us for a song. The crowd loved them, too!

Jesse was outside in the sound truck listening to every note. It was a powerful night! The Cathedrals, The Goffs and The Couriers joined together for the grand finale, "How Great Thou Art." It was a great ending!

After it was over Jesse came running, all excited, to the stage saying, "It was all so good I'm not going to cut any of it out. We'll make a double jacket album and keep the whole evening. We'll keep all the songs, all the comments, all the laughing, all the clapping and even your preaching, Dave."

One little incident that our wives were not too happy about, was the newspaper article that stated, "The Courier's wives sang with their husbands but they had the ability to turn a golden note into lead." You can be sure that we teased them often about that.

The Ovation album won the coveted Dove award as the Inspirational album of the year. I keep the Dove next to my Bronze head. I guess I'm too proud. Each record has a special place in my heart. I can recall every recording session, every studio in every town, and the joy we felt as we were recording. The Courier's music still ministers to me and brings me a lot of comfort.

CHAPTER FIFTEEN

GO YE
THEREFORE!

THE COURIERS HAD LEFT CENTRAL BIBLE COLLEGE IN Springfield, Missouri, with a huge dream in our hearts.

We established a dream to sing in all fifty states. We knew this included Alaska, Hawaii, Florida, California, Washington, Maine and every state in between.

This fabulous dream was accomplished during the next ten years.

Then a new dream was birthed in our hearts. We wanted to sing in fifty foreign countries. So, for the next 15 years we worked to fulfill that dream.

That dream changed our lives! It kept us together and helped us fulfill the mandate of every Christian believer. (Matthew 28:19) "Therefore go and make disciples of all nations, baptizing them in the name of the Father and of the Son and of the Holy Spirit, and teaching them to obey everything I have commanded you."

- Success Principle 21

YOUR FUTURE IS ONLY AS BIG AS YOUR DREAM..

*Our dreams were huge. I don't think we
ever thought that we would fulfill any
of them, but those dreams kept me in
The Couriers for 25 years. A dream
keeps husbands and wives together
through the years. A dream keeps family
members in the family. Dream something
bigger than yourself and watch God work
it out for your benefit.*
*"When the Lord brought back the captive
ones of Zion, we were like those who
dream." (Psalm 126:1) NASB*

So a dream was born of giving one month every year to missions. I could write a story from each nation but I'll give you a few of the highlights.

Paul Olson, an evangelist from Minneapolis, Minnesota, booked our first missions tour. He encouraged us to start small and go to some place close. The West Indies were easy to get to and not too expensive. He made all the contacts and booked us for three weeks in Jamaica, Barbados, St. Lucia, West Indies and Guyana, South America.

I met Holmes Williams for the first time on that tour. He was the pastor of The Peoples Cathedral in Bridgetown, Barbados. However, the meeting was held at the Garrison, a part of the Barbados military base. That was February of 1968.

Holmes invited us back to Barbados for an open air crusade in February, 1969. He said, "Couriers, bring all your songs, and Dave, you do the preaching. We'll have a great crusade in the Queens Park. People will come from all over the island and God will use you fellows to bless our nation."

This was our first overseas crusade where The Couriers were totally in charge. I was already feeling the pressure of preaching a ten-day crusade.

February of 1969 came quickly. Barbados, here we come! We were excited!

Holmes picked us up at the airport. Driving from the airport to his home was an experience never to be forgotten. He was driving on the left; it was very narrow and filled with people walking along both sides. He was dodging bicycles and donkey carts, weaving in and out of traffic like an expert. He made it look easy; but I wasn't anxious to get behind the wheel, that was for sure.

Soon we pulled into the yard of a very, tiny house. It was a typical one room Barbados shack, actually. No paint on it's weathered boards, a rusted tin roof hanging every which way. A goat and several chickens picking around the yard and a big, brown cow, calmly chewing her cud, looking at us.

A typical little Bajan woman in bare feet, with her hair tied up in a scarf, came to the door to see who was coming. To our surprise, Holmes called out, "Rosie, we're here." She smiled, real big, and waved.

Well, you can just imagine what was going through my mind. "It's only one room. Where would we all sleep? Boy, I never thought Holme's wife would look like this."

When Holmes saw the look of shock on all our faces he burst into laughter and backed the car out into the traffic again, waved to the Bajan lady, and continued on to the real William's residence.

We were all laughing so hard at one point we nearly had to stop the car to keep from having an accident!

We started a friendship with Holmes Williams that has lasted all these years and, today we are best friends.

Everywhere we looked we saw posters of the crusade. Every telephone pole seemed to have a big picture of The Couriers hanging on it.

Holmes had printed thousands of leaflets announcing the crusade. We started dropping them out of the windows of our car. People ran from everywhere to pick them up. You would have thought that we were dropping money out of the windows.

Holmes had installed a loud speaker on the roof of his car and was playing our music and making announcements of the crusade to be held at the Queens Park. This was great! We could hardly wait for the first service.

We moved in with Holmes and Rosie and their three boys, Peter, Paul and David. Duane, Neil and I took over one bedroom that had three single beds. Not too bad! Rosie called us for lunch and we got our first taste of a true Bajan meal, flying fish, peas and rice and hot Bajan pepper sauce. Umm! It was so good.

The beach was close by so we took our first sea bath. Swimming in the warm waters of the Caribbean was absolutely wonderful. The waves were big and we body surfed until we were exhausted.

Soon it was service time and Holmes was yelling, "First four, let's go." The first four that were ready needed to get going. That's all the car would hold. The second trip would carry four more. We arrived at the Queens Park after a hectic ride into town. Every street was crowded with people walking to the crusade. Hundreds of people everywhere.

The Queens Park was really just a large open field where cricket matches were held. People were packed into the park, all standing. "Hey, where are the chairs? I asked. A high wooden platform had been built and a fence had been put up to save room for an altar area. The people would have to stand for the entire evening. I never heard one complaint from anyone. The Bajan people are the sweetest people in the world.

The service started; I will never forget what I felt when that crowd began to sing. The Bajan's love to sing, and when it's their turn they turn the volume to "high" and lift their voices to the heavens. They clap on the off beat, calypso style, which adds to the unique style of their singing. I had never heard anything like it.

Then it was our turn. Our music was new to the people and they loved it from the very beginning. Every song became their favorite and they wanted to hear them over and over again.

Soon it was time for the message. I walked up to the homemade pulpit at the front of the platform. I looked out at that massive crowd standing quietly waiting for God's message. I couldn't see them all because it was dark and they were dark and the few lights didn't cover the whole park. But I knew they could see and hear me.

There is no thrill in the world like preaching the Gospel on foreign soil. It was exhilarating! The adrenaline flowed, the anointing came, and compassion and love flowed out of my innermost being. I found myself weeping as I preached. I felt so honored that God was using me and to think that just a few years before I was that tall, skinny, shy, backward kid from New Kensington, Pennsylvania. Many accepted Christ as their personal Savior that night. God had honored His word.

I phoned Judy immediately and told her all about Barbados and the crusade. I knew we couldn't afford it but I told her to borrow the money and get a baby-sitter for the girls and make arrangements to fly to Barbados as quickly as possible. She needed to be a part of what God was doing in our ministry.

I couldn't believe it, but she came the next day and, together, our lives were changed concerning missions.

A few nights into the crusade I asked Holmes, "What really gets the Bajan's attention?" He said that "FIRE" was number one on the list. I decided that I should get a sermon about fire. I had been in two fires so that gave me my introduction right away.

I found a man in the church that knew about propane. I asked him if he could rig up a torch. One that would shoot flames three or four feet.

He put together a bottle of propane and a thirty foot line that would tie into the handheld metal torch. He brought it to the house one morning just to show me how it worked. I held the long piece of metal in my hand and he struck the match. Fire shot out so big it scared him and me but, after some adjustments, we had it working perfectly. This was just what I needed.

That night, at the meeting, I announced that the following night I would be preaching the most unusual message they had ever heard. I said to the crowd, "Bring a friend and don't miss this unusual message."

The next night we had a big crowd. It was exciting. I knew the message would be exciting especially when I saw the propane equipment and the torch at the edge of the platform. I checked to see just how far away I could walk from the platform while preaching the message.

I was ready! The song service was enthusiastic and enjoyed by everyone. No one wanted to quit singing. And when there are several thousand Bajan's singing, there is nothing quite like it.

Then it was our turn and The Couriers sang our songs with all our might. This was life at it's best.

Everybody knows, you can't have church without taking an offering. So it was announced, "Please give your offering to the men wearing black arm bands only!" Since there was no seating the ushers just moved among the crowd with offering containers. We had heard that the night before some individuals were taking their own private offering. In fact, some churches were bringing their own offering bags!

I was introduced as the evening speaker and quickly went to the pulpit with my Bible. I told the crowd that they were about to witness a message that they would never forget.

After reading my text, I asked for every head to be bowed for prayer. While I was praying I felt the torch being slipped into my hand and as I said amen two things happened at the same time.

Someone turned all the lights out in the Queen's Park while another struck a match that lighted the torch. Fire leaped into the air as I held the torch far above my head.

Thousands of people silenced themselves.

For the next hour I ran all over that platform preaching at the top of my voice, waving the torch in every direction. I definitely had the attention of every person there.

Holmes was right. I decided that I needed to preach about fire more often. That was one of the greatest nights of my preaching career.

We held a crusade in Barbados every year for the next eleven years. We planned our schedule so that, we were able to visit sixty other countries of the world.

Thanks, Holmes, for believing in us. You inspired us to a great life of missions.

- Success Principle 22

DON'T BE AFRAID TO DO SOMETHING FOR GOD FOR FREE.

We would get back from a month of missions and be totally broke, but everytime, the next month would be an outstanding month in our finances. We always enjoyed the first month home after a missions tour.

• • •

I remember an open air crusade in St. Lucia, West Indies. The Canadian missionary, Rev. Leroy Lebeck, found a soccer field that would be a great place to have the crusade and had everything ready when we arrived. The field was very close to the airport and the main street of the city had to cross over the runway so, when a plane took off or landed, the street was closed and the traffic backed up.

Leroy took us to see the crusade grounds and cautioned me to have my message and altar call over by 9:15 p.m. because at 9:15 p.m. the huge plane arrived from America and, as it landed and reversed its engines, the noise would be so deafening it would stop anything we were doing at that time.

That night, at the crusade, The Couriers were introduced and we started singing. I knew we were in for a great crusade. The people hung on to every word. Our sound system was loud you could hear us many blocks away. We could see the traffic slowing down to see what was going on.

Suddenly, we heard a big crash as two cars collided.

Immediately, the crowd ran to the accident. I don't mean a few people, I mean most of the crowd took off. Several hundred people ran across the field right in the middle of our song.

After the song was finished, I turned to see where Leroy was sitting. He was grinning from ear to ear and yelled, "Just hold on for a few minutes, they'll be back. They can't stand it, they have to go see what happened."

After a few minutes they all came running back to their place's. Leroy shouted, "OK, Couriers, you can go on with your singing." What an interruption! But, that's what outdoor crusades are all about.

It was finally time for the message and I was preaching away, having the time of my life.

I was so caught up in the message that I didn't see the huge, jet airplane coming in for a landing. The high pitched whine of the engines started softly. I didn't recognize what it was until the plane was a few feet from touching down.

Suddenly, it felt and sounded like the earth was exploding! The noise was frighteningly loud and scared me so badly my whole body shook uncontrollably.

At that point, I still didn't know what it was but I was sure it was going to crash on the platform where I was preaching. Then the engines went into reverse and the whole world exploded in my ears. What was happening? It sounded like the end of the world.

I just stood there stunned, unable to speak. I looked down at my watch and it read, 9:15. I was too embarrassed to look back at Leroy, but I noticed that Duane's and Neil's faces were as white as a sheet, just like mine. The plane had caught them off guard, too.

You better believe that all my messages and altar calls, for the rest of the crusade, were over by that 9:15 curtain call.

While I'm talking about that hour, let me insert another incident here.

While preaching a tent crusade in Ontario, Canada, near the Thousand Island Bridge, I was cautioned to be finished with the service before 9:15 p.m. because that was when the mosquitoes would arrive and the service would be over whether we wanted it to be or not.

Of course, I forgot the time and, late into my message, I began to see the people waving their hands in front of their faces. They were getting up out of their seats and everyone was slapping their arms and legs. Suddenly, I found myself doing the same thing. It was 9:15 and I was swatting more mosquitoes than I had ever seen. They were all over the tent and they brought mass confusion with them. In one minute the service was over and people were running for their cars. No altar call and no one to buy our records! The next night the service was over before........!

• A Success Principle I never learned

THE MIND CAN ONLY ABSORB AS MUCH AS THE SEAT CAN ENDURE

I've been preaching a long time and still can't quit on time.

•   •   •

Now, back to the crusade in St. Lucia.

I noticed one lady, in particular, who was coming each evening and enjoying the services more than anyone else. She came to me one night after the service and asked me to pray for her husband. He had told her she could not come to any more services. This was possibly her last night.

The next night I looked to see if she was there and, sure enough, she was in her place enjoying the service. I talked to her again and she said that her husband had hidden all of her clothes. She had to borrow clothes from a friend to come to the service that night. She was afraid to go home and wasn't sure if we would see her the following night.

When she got home her husband was waiting for her. He was furious! He had a knife in his hand and chased her around their second floor apartment. In his rage he was yelling, "I'm going to kill you! You'll never go to that crusade again!"

She knew she was in great danger. He was out of his mind. When she reached the last room and knew he was just a few feet away from grabbing her, she jumped from the window and leaped to the pavement, two stories below. The crowd on the street rushed to her body that lay on the concrete sidewalk. She was taken to the hospital and no one knew whether she was dead or alive.

She survived the fall but had many broken bones and bruises. She would be in the hospital for a long time.

The next morning she asked for the singing evangelists. We got a call from the hospital telling us of the accident and asked if we could come to see her.

We found her in a huge ward with many other people. We could tell immediately which bed was hers. Her two broken legs were hanging high off the bed in traction equipment. Her arms were in casts and you could tell she was in great pain by the look on her face. But she was alive and when she saw us she managed to smile the best she could.

She was so glad we had come to visit her. We sang a few songs and prayed for her. All the other patients in the ward were hearing every word and asked us to have special prayer with them. We stopped at each bed and prayed. That was a hospital visit never to be forgotten!

We found out later that week that the husband was sorry for what he had done and asked for forgiveness. He even promised to go to church with her after she got out of the hospital.

When something like that happens, and it involves you, you never forget it.

We were beginning to love the West Indies and some of our friends were talking about going with us for our next crusade. We decided to host a cruise to the West Indies. We'd visit five or six islands, touring during the day and holding meetings, in the evenings. We would return to the ship after church for the ship to leave port and travel through the night to the next Island.

This was our first Missionary Cruise and 320 of our friends joined us. Our friends were from several states and Canada. We arranged to fly to Puerto Rico and meet on a certain day at a certain time.

Excitement was running high as we all boarded our buses that would take us from the airport down to the harbor where we would board our cruise ship.

There they were...... huge, glistening white ships, several of them, all lined up along the dock.

Our buses pulled up to the first one in line and we all said, "WOW." But, our buses didn't stop! They drove on past the first ship, the second ship, the third ship, and finally stopped at the last ship. It was only half the size of the others!

We didn't see any other passengers boarding and soon discovered our group of 320 would be the only passengers.

After we left port and were out to sea we began to feel privileged. We felt like we were sailing on our own private yacht. The ship's crew only had our group to care for.

The crew admitted later that we were the most unusual group they had ever cared for. The dance band members had nothing to do and they even shut down the ship's bars because no one drank.

I suppose every island in the West Indies offers it's own special story. But my first glimpse of Dominica is definitely unforgettable.

Cruise ships rarely visit Dominica because the island has few hotels and shops. The beaches don't look inviting because it is a volcanic island and the sand is gray instead of white like the other islands. It's a mountainous island with high peaks and the roads are narrow and winding and filled with deep pot holes. Driving is difficult for cars and walking is difficult for the people.

Our boat came over the horizon about 7:00 a.m. and dropped anchor out in the harbor, a ways from the shore. The shoreline was lined with people waving hundreds of white hankies. We could hear them singing and playing their tambourines. They couldn't believe that a big cruise ship filled with Christians was coming to their island to give them a service. They wanted to give us the best welcome they knew how.

We all got in the shuttle boats and headed for the shore. What a welcome! The people were so sweet. They kept singing and waving their hankies until all were on the shore.

Seven churches were involved with our one day in Dominica. Our plans was to split up into seven groups and visit all seven churches at the same time. A short service was planned with testimonies from our group and a brief message. Then in the afternoon we all gathered at the big church near the harbor. One giant rally was scheduled for the afternoon and then back to the ship for our 5:00 p.m. departure.

In each of the churches there were wonderful meetings. The people turned their cars into taxicabs and carried us to their little churches. When the final "Amen" was said, leaving was difficult. We had made friendships that would last forever. We waved good-bye and sailed off into the sunset.

Somehow, I knew I would visit them again. Several years later, I did.

Don and Janice Scheske, the Canadian missionaries in charge of all the churches in Dominica, invited The Couriers to participate in the dedication services of one of their new churches. Special services had been going on for several days before we arrived.

When we were met at the airport we heard of the terrible tragedy that had struck this little Island of Dominica only a few days earlier.

A dump truck filled with 32 people was making it's way to a church service. The roads were narrow and without guard rails. Coming down one of the steep hills the truck lost it's brakes and picked up speed. On a hairpin turn the driver lost control and couldn't make the turn. The truck went straight out over the cliff and fell 500 feet down the steep mountain.

Bodies were thrown in every direction. It was already dark and it happened where not many people lived.

The news reached the church and Don Scheske went out to help. He discovered that everyone was afraid to go over the cliff in the dark so he put on ropes and was the first person lowered down the steep mountain side.

Thirty one people died. Only one person survived. The man who had been riding "shotgun" inside the truck cab.

The church, where the dedication was held had 16 members die in that accident. The mass funeral service was held in the new church building. Caskets were built during the night and made ready for the funeral the next day. They were simple pine boxes that the bodies were put into for burial before the sun went down. Blood dripped from the simple caskets that stained the floor of the church. It was hard to imagine 16 caskets lined up in the front of that church. Family and friends could do nothing but weep.

The whole island of Dominica mourned over the loss of so many people. The congregation in the church was devastated. The pastor was so despondent he said he never wanted to preach again. That little nation was asking questions about the good of the crusade services. Why did this happen to God's people? Maybe serving God wasn't such a good thing after all.

Our plane landed right in the middle of all this confusion and despair. We wondered why God had chosen us for this special time but when we sang our first song that night, I knew why. God had brought us to soothe this pastor and his congregation with music and sing them back to the place where they were willing to go on with life. We sang and sang and sang, for seven nights. People just sat and soaked up every word.

It was a great moment when the pastor stepped to the microphone and announced that he was ready to preach again. Then, one by one, the congregation followed with their testimonies that they were ready to be a church again. There wasn't a dry eye in the church that night. We realized that some songs we had learned years before were meant just for the congregation of "The Streams of Living Water Church" in Dominica.

Both of my visits there have been precious and are captured in my heart forever.

On one of our trips to Africa we stopped in Liberia, West Africa to work with our missionary friends, Jerry and Maxine Falley. They kept us busy from morning till night singing in the churches and in the Bible School.

On the last day of our visit Jerry came to us and said, "You have three choices for things to do today before you go home tomorrow.

1. You can sleep all day or rest around the house.
2. We can all go to the ocean for a swim.
3. You can visit a primitive village where
   we have started a new church. The trip includes
   a five mile walk thru the jungle."

We wanted to see primitive Africa so we chose number three.

- Success Principle 23

ADVENTURE AWAITS THOSE WHO CHOOSE IT.

Adventure rarely comes to you. You must
pursue it. On every detour there's
opportunity for adventure. Sometimes
it's good to take the hard road.
Getting to choose is the key.
We all have many choices to make. It's
up to us.

•   •   •

We drove 35 miles out of the city, parked the car at the edge of the road and headed for the bush.

We hadn't walked very far when we came to a small river. Now, how were we going to get across this? Jerry didn't tell us our walk also included a swim! He smiled real big and walked down to the water's edge. He pulled from behind the tall weeds his homemade raft.

"What? we have to cross the river on that? How safe is it? Can we all ride at the same time?" We were all talking at the same time.

Jerry finally reached into the brush and pulled out two long poles. He said, "These poles will reach the bottom of the river and they will help us push to the other side."

After a shaky start we made it across the river, safe and sound.

Now the long five mile walk. Jerry shared with us his dreams and goals. During his four year term he wanted to do more than just teach in the Bible School and preach in the church. He wanted to find villages that had never heard the Gospel and build a church and congregation. The village we were visiting today was one of those villages.

The villagers had accepted Christ and now there was a church already established. Jerry was so excited that we were coming to see the new church. He tried to prepare us for what was ahead but you had to be there to get the full impact of our special visit that day.

We climbed the last hill where we could finally see an opening in the dense jungle. Then we could see their small homes. Little huts with thatched roofs.

We walked to the edge of the village looking for life but it looked deserted. Not one person was in sight. Jerry told us the people were very timid and probably hiding.

Then, as we looked closer, we saw some of them peeking out from within their homes. They didn't know who we were and they were afraid. Jerry stepped forward and walked into the center of the main area. When they recognized him they came out of hiding and ran to hug his neck and hold his hand. What a sight that was! The whole village encircled Jerry. It was clear that these people loved this man.

Jerry introduced us. We, too, were welcomed to their little village. Once we were friends they wanted to show us everything. Their little homes were without modern conveniences. A perpetual fire was burning in the yard of each hut. Supper was in the big black pot. Chickens, goats and dogs seemed to come from everywhere.

After we walked through the village, Jerry asked them to ring the bell so that we could have a short service in the church. When they heard the bell they got all excited and ran for their homes.

"Jerry, where did they go and will they come for church in the middle of the day?" "Oh, yes!" he said. "They went back to their homes to get their clothes on."

He had already taught them to wear clothes when they came to church.

When they arrived for the service they were a sight to behold. They were wearing clothes from their heads to their toes!

I wouldn't have missed that service for anything. We sang and gave our testimonies while they beamed from ear to ear.

After we were through, Jerry asked them to stand and sing for us. They sang an authentic African song, sung as only they could sing it.

Then Jerry had a surprise for us. He asked his new congregation to sing for us the new song he had taught them. They stood to their feet and with their faces beaming they sang, in English, a chorus we all knew so well.

> "Allelujah, Jesus loves me!
> Allelujah, Jesus loves me!
> Allelujah, Jesus Loves me!
> Allelujah, Jesus Loves me!"

Before they got to the third line tears were running down my cheeks. I sat stunned at what these precious people were singing.

Here I was, sitting in an old dirty hut with a dirt floor and home-made pews. The pulpit was a prize. It was a crooked stick that had been pounded into the ground with a small board placed on top held on by some kind of twine. It was probably the poorest church building I had ever been in; but I felt the Spirit of God like never before.

That service will always be in my memory; forever etched on my heart.

• Success Principle 24

ANYWHERE YOU GO CAN BECOME A
HOLY PLACE WHERE GOD CAN
TOUCH YOUR LIFE.

•   •   •

We had our Polaroid camera with us so after the service we gathered the people for a picture. That was the best thing that we could have done. We took two pictures and let the people watch them develop right before their eyes. When they saw themselves in the picture, they became ecstatic. They laughed and laughed at each other.

Then they all begged for their own picture. We came up with a great idea. We took one picture of the whole group standing together in front of the church. It turned out great and, after everyone had looked at it, we placed it on the wall of the church as a gift. We made a hit! They would surely be our friends for life.

They gathered at the top of the hill as we were leaving. Waving good-bye took a long time because they kept waving till we were out of sight. We walked down the long hill backwards, our arms waving good-bye. Finally we backed into the dense jungle and out of sight.

And to think we almost went to the beach instead.

• Success Principle 25

FULFILLMENT IS ATTAINED BY DOING
THE EXTRA IN LIFE.

The extra things always provide excitement.

•   •   •

Missionaries, Jim and Louella Hance, invited us to sing in their part of the world, the South Pacific! Western Samoa, American Samoa, Fiji and Tonga were all on the schedule.

We arrived in Tonga in a small plane. As we landed on a grass runway, I said, "This is going to be another one of those special adventures."

We were met by Dwain and Jean Jones, our hosts. They had just arrived in Tonga as new missionaries. We went to their home and found it empty. None of their stuff had arrived. But it was fun and we all made it together for a few days.

It was very important, according to Dwain Jones, that we visit the palace and explain to the King why we were in his nation. Maybe we would be able to sing a song for him. His approval would go a long way to make our stay in Tonga successful. Dwain made the call and came with the news. "Couriers, you have an audience with the King tomorrow at 1:00 p.m." "WOW!"

Dwain had never been there himself, so he couldn't tell us anything concerning our visit. He was filling out the required forms with our names and positions in ministry. Howard Landis, our long time friend from Harrisburg, Pennsylvania, was traveling with us and it looked like he wouldn't be able to go to the palace because he had no position in the Couriers. So we invented one for him, "Minister of Luggage." It was worth the try.

When the formal invitation came there were five names on the paper. David Kyllonen, Duane Nicholson, Neil Enloe, Dwain Jones and Howard Landis. Howard made it and we all rejoiced together.

- Success Principle 26

SOMETIMES IN LIFE YOU MUST IMPROVISE!

•   •   •

The next day we were excited about our visit to the palace. We jumped into Dwain's car and drove through town like important people. We were ushered through the gate and into the guest parking place.

I looked around at the whole setting and thought, <u>this doesn't look like a palace to me</u>. It was just a big house. Maybe the biggest house in Tonga.

Then I saw the King's private car. It was a black, 1953 Cadillac limousine. Just like the one we had bought from the funeral director in Wampum, Pennsylvania.

Servants welcomed us into the palace and seated us in a small room with a table and chairs. We were told that the King was ill and maybe we wouldn't be able to see him after all.

While we were waiting we were served a cool drink. We smiled at each other when five different kinds of glasses were brought. They were not an elegant set like you would expect to find in a palace but a conglomeration of leftover glasses. They poured our drink and, after taking our first sip, we concluded that it was "Kool Aid."

After a short wait, we were told the King was getting out of bed and would see us in the throne room. In a few minutes we heard slow, heavy foot steps descending the stairs. Dwain whispered to us, "From the sound of those footsteps, he must be a very large King."

We discovered later that he became the King because of his size. He was the largest man on the island weighing nearly 400 pounds.

We were ushered into the throne room to stand before a King.

Here we were, young Gospel Singers who didn't know anything about protocol. Were we to bow? Should we salute? Could we speak?

Only The Couriers, Duane, Neil and I, had been allowed to enter the throne room. We were on our own. We stood looking at this huge man sitting on his huge throne. He was the King!

But he was short of breath, wheezing and coughing and we knew, right then, the song we would sing for him would be, "He Touched Me."

Without the help of instruments we blended our voices together with harmony that filled the throne room. There was a special feeling that touched both us and the King as he quietly settled himself. It was an awesome, golden moment in my life.

(Proverbs 18:16) "A gift opens the way for the giver and ushers him into the presence of the great!

Our conversation with the King was surprising. You won't believe what we talked about. The American cheeseburger!

He had traveled to America and tasted our cheeseburgers. We guessed, by his size, that he tasted more than one! Would you believe, this was the very thing that endeared the missionary, Dwain Jones, to him.

We explained to the King that we were here as guests of this new missionary to Tonga. He was hoping that the King would grant him permission to build churches and be granted freedom to work among the Tonganese. We mentioned that Dwain Jones was with us and was waiting for us in another room.

The King thanked us for coming and asked to speak to the missionary. We were taken back to the room and given more Kool Aid while we waited for Dwain.

Later, with great excitement, Dwain shared his conversation with the King. He had promised the King that his wife, Jean, would fry up a batch of cheeseburgers every Friday, and bring them to the palace.

There was an instant friendship between the King and the missionary. I was happy to be a part of helping Dwain get started in Tonga.

I'm reminded of other special times when The Couriers were invited to be with dignitaries of other nations.

One of those was in Israel in the little town of Bethlehem. Our tour bus brought us to the entrance of the Church of the Nativity. I couldn't believe I was actually at the spot where Jesus first came to this earth. I was all eyes and ears and my heart was bursting with a great tenderness. All I could do was cry - just to view the place, feel the fabric, and understand where the Holy Scriptures came from and where our faith was born. I was living the spiritual experience of a life time.

After leaving the church our whole group walked across the town square to the little souvenir shops. One young man invited us into his shop where "mother of pearl" items were sold. Our group was in a spending mood so business was good for him that day.

We told him we were Gospel singers from America and that some time, on a future tour to Israel, we would like to sing a concert in the Bethlehem square.

He told us about Pat Boone's great concert in the square the previous year. He had sung to a great crowd and maybe we would be able to do the same.

Then he said, "My father is the mayor of Bethlehem. I think he could arrange something for you." Of all the shops we had chosen to visit we had picked the right one.

Later that day, when we returned to the hotel, we received a special invitation from Mr. Friege, the Mayor of Bethlehem. The Couriers, our wives and evangelist, Paul Olson, were invited to dine with the Mayor and his family in their home for dinner the following evening. What an awesome privilege!

It would be a short twelve miles from our hotel in Jerusalem to Bethlehem. "Ollie," who was Paul Olson's personal tour guide, drove us in his red Mercedes.

We were fascinated with Ollie, a short man, middle aged, with graying hair. His eyes were red rimmed and bloodshot. His rough gravelly voice, along with his Palestinian accent, made him hard to understand. He looked tired and from the smell of his breath we thought he had had one too many drinks.

When we arrived at the Mayor's home in Bethlehem, Ollie was invited to eat with us. A typical Israeli dinner was served. It was delightful.

Our conversation consisted mostly of Mr. Friege's work as Mayor of Bethlehem and our work as The Couriers. The conversation grew quite lengthy and, much to our chagrin, our friend, Ollie, laid his head right down on the table and fell fast asleep. We hadn't noticed until he began to snore. I don't think he worried much about protocol.

Mr. Friege was not only the Mayor but he was in the business of making mother of pearl items for his souvenir shop. He suggested we purchase mother of pearl crosses on a chain to sell to our many friends in America.

Immediately we recognized an opportunity for "a deal." The three of us put our heads together and decided to splurge. Surely Mr. Friege would give us a great deal on 3,000 crosses. Probably no one else had ever bought so many. We thought Mr. Friege would be overwhelmed by such a big order. But it was our turn to be overwhelmed when he told us that the Rev. Robert Schuller, from the

Crystal Cathedral in California, had just ordered 100,000 crosses. Boy, was I embarrassed. I felt about an inch high.

The deal was sealed. We thanked the Frieges for a wonderful evening, woke up Ollie, and drove back to Jerusalem.

On the drive back we all had a good laugh about Ollie falling asleep on the Mayor's dinner table.

We had such a great desire, while in Jerusalem, to actually walk on the top of Golgotha's hill, the place where Jesus was crucified. But entry up to Golgotha's hill was totally unattainable. It is now a Jewish cemetery and unlawful to enter it's gates.

In our conversation with Ollie we mentioned this. And he said to us, "Don't you know to whom you are talking? My best friend is the gate keeper and, for the right price, I can get you in."

Now, here was the deal. We must go in the middle of the night while the town slept. We set the time for 3 a.m.

Taxicabs had to be ordered to transport our group from the hotel. And Ollie would need $2.00 per person for making the arrangements. We told Ollie there probably wouldn't be that many from our group interested in going since it was set for 3 a.m.

At suppertime I asked, "How many in our group of 120 people would be interested in going?" All 120 raised their hands.

Now, what would we do? We were faced with a major undertaking! Enough taxicabs to transport 120 people at 3 a.m. to make an illegal visit. Ollie told us, not to worry.

I awoke in the dark of early morning with great anticipation. I knew we were about to experience something very few people had done.

I entered the hotel lobby half expecting to see no people, no cabs, no Ollie and no key to the cemetery gate.

The lobby was alive with people, noise, excitement, and Ollie, standing in the middle of it all, with a smile on his face and the key in his hand.

We were given strict instructions to be absolutely quiet when we arrived at the gate to the cemetery. It was important not to draw attention to what we were doing.

We climbed into our caravan of taxicabs and snaked our way through the dark streets of Jerusalem. It was quiet, oh, so quiet.

It was a very difficult task to make our way over rocks, around the tombstones and through the thorn bushes, to reach the top of the hill. There was no path to follow. I felt sorry for the older people, some even in their eighties, who were struggling so we each helped the other. It would have been so much easier in daylight.

Here I was, standing on the top of this hill called, Golgotha. Me, Dave Kyllonen, actually standing in the place where God's son, Jesus, was crucified on a cross for me. Out of my heart came such thankfulness that Jesus loved me so much that he died for me. Running through my mind was the song I had sung so many times,

> *"I believe that the*
> *Christ,*
> *who was slain on*
> *the cross,*
> *Has the power to*
> *change lives today.*
> *For He changed me*
> *completely,*
> *A new life He gave,*
> *That is why,*
> *at the cross, I will stay.*

*I believe in a hill
called Mt. Calvary.
I believe whatever
the cost,
And when time has
surrendered,
And the earth is no
more,
I'll still cling to
the old rugged cross."*

I felt it appropriate for our entire group to sing that old hymn of the church, "The Old Rugged Cross." I cautioned them to sing as quietly as they could. So in barely audible voices we sang with much gusto.

One by one people dropped to their knees in an act of humility to God. Our friend, Larry, stood holding his shoes in his hand. He said, "We are standing on holy ground."

I felt compelled to pray for anyone who wanted to receive Jesus Christ. Several in our group responded. So as the sun was peeking over the horizon, we united in prayer for all of our family members who had never knelt at Calvary to ask forgiveness. It was an incredible moment.

At that moment, Ollie came running, wildly waving his arms, motioning for us to come down quickly. If we were caught in the cemetery by the authorities it could mean prison for all of us.

Our main concern now was coming down Golgotha's hill and getting outside the gate. It wasn't any easier coming down than it was going up.

When we were all out and Ollie locked the gate behind us, I breathed a huge sigh of relief.

Ollie was quick to reprimand me for staying too long. He had told us to take one hour but we lost track of the time and had taken more.

In all my experiences of eight trips to Israel this one is the most outstanding!

Before closing this chapter I must tell you about one more experience in the Holy Land.

I found myself standing in front of the Wailing Wall praying and observing those around me who were also praying. I stood for many minutes and watched people put their prayers on little pieces of paper and cram them in between the cracks in the massive rocks. There were thousands of rolled up pieces of paper jammed into the cracks. Each one containing someone's prayer request.

As the old saying goes, "Curiosity killed the cat" and my curiosity nearly killed me. When I thought no one was watching I dug out an old piece of paper that had been there, perhaps for years and put it in my pocket.

I turned and walked a few feet away from the wall when a short, Jewish Rabbi tapped me on the shoulder and whispered in my ear that no one was allowed to take a prayer paper from the wall and that I should put it back.

Sheepishly, I walked back to the wall and returned the prayer request to it's crevice.

In the meantime, tour buses dropped their passengers and hundreds of tourists crowded in around me.

I thought, "That little Rabbi can't see me now" so I slipped another prayer request from the wall and put it in my pocket.

I was almost out of the court yard when he loudly shouted, "I told you not to take those prayer requests from the wall. Now, please bring that one in your pocket back and leave it there." I knew he was shouting at me.

People were staring at me and I felt like I had committed an unpardonable sin. Needless to say, I was embarrassed and in my several return trips to the Holy Land and to The Wailing Wall I never touched another prayer request.

CHAPTER SIXTEEN

©HERGIE

THE BEGINNING
OF THE END.

THE COURIERS GET READY TO CELEBRATE 25 years! Our silver anniversary year! The time of celebration was set. October, 1980.

We talked of buying silver tuxedos. Our new album, already in the process of being made, would be our silver anniversary album. The year was packed with special concerts. I was sure this would be our greatest year. Financially, we would do better and make more money than ever before. The talk was encouraging among the pastors. Everyone wanted to make a great night in their church to help us celebrate. It would be the easiest year to book.

The girls who worked in our office, Delores Smith, Connie Sweigart and Donna Metzler, were ready for action. Paul Wislocky, our promotions coordinator, was having one success after another and couldn't wait to put some of his ideas together for our Silver Anniversary Year.

The previous years of 1978 and 1979 were good years for The Couriers but during those years we had to deal with a major problem.

Neil went to the doctor and came home with the news that he had to have an operation on his vocal chords. A nodule, or a callous, had formed on one of his vocal chords and had to be surgically removed. This meant Neil wouldn't be able to sing for at least 6 weeks. He would have to whisper or write what he wanted to say on paper. Who would be available to replace him?

Our friend from Staten Island, New York, Phil Armenia, was traveling and singing with his wife Marie. Phil had followed The Couriers for many years and always wanted to sing with us so he had prepared himself just in case we ever called. He bought all of our records and tapes and knew all of our songs by heart. He learned to play the piano like Neil and sang Neil's lead and solo parts without missing a note or word. Unknown to us, God was preparing him.

He was very excited when our call and invitation came. He gave an immediate, "yes." He promised to come the day after Neil's operation and stay with us for six weeks.

I remember our first day with Phil. We decided to leave early so there would be enough time for rehearsal. Phil assured us that he didn't need a long rehearsal and that he knew all our songs and would be able to play and sing any song we wanted.

It was amazing! All the songs I asked Phil to play and sing came without hesitation. We only rehearsed for about 30 minutes and couldn't believe how much Phil sounded like Neil. We were ready for a concert with a brand new member after just a few minute's practice. This was phenomenal!

We told Phil that Neil's room on the bus was his. He asked us what he should wear. I told him to look in the closet and see if any of Neil's suits were there. Sure enough, Neil's new suit was still hanging in the closet and it fit Phil to a T.

I said, "Phil, you might as well try on Neil's shoes because everything else is fitting." Yes, they fit too.

What a night! For all the people coming for the first time to hear the Couriers we could have introduced Phil as Neil and no one would have known the difference.

We were scheduled for a whole week of meetings at the Milford Park Camp. We always enjoyed going to this cozy campground nestled in the trees along Rt.100 just a few miles south of Allentown, Pennsylvania. Known for it's quaint cabins and large tabernacle, it was not far from the highway.

The dining room always served our favorite snack, "Pirogies." A pirogi is a small pastry turnover, filled with potatoes, then deep-fried. We ate so many I'm sure the snack staff was constantly reordering their pirogi stock.

Many of our friends would find their way to Milford Park during the same week. It was always a joy to renew old acquaintances.

I had my seven sermons ready to preach but I was wondering how Phil would do. We needed lots of songs because the same crowd would be at most of the services. Each night I would make a list of ten songs and bring them to Phil. He never hesitated to sing any of them.

One night, I stopped the service and explained to the crowd what an incredible job Phil was doing, but that tomorrow evening we wouldn't be giving him a list of the songs we would sing.

The next evening was a fun night. I began to choose songs that we hadn't sung for years. Phil took every song as a challenge. We couldn't stump him.

I finally thought of a song I was sure Phil didn't know. We had toured the country of Sweden and learned a song in Swedish, so I called out to Phil, "Lets sing, He The Pearly Gates Will Open, in Swedish!"

I knew we had him now, but much to my surprise, he started to play the introduction and, while Duane and I stared in disbelief, he started singing the first verse in Swedish. The crowd cheered and we finished the song together. That could never happen again in 100 years!

The six weeks went by without a hitch except for one song. Phil gave us the wrong key for an acapella song. Halfway through we had to change keys and when we reached for the next note, it was way too high. We had to stop singing; we laughed till we cried.

Neil's voice came back but it wasn't long until Duane was having the same problems.

We finally sent him to the doctor and found out that he, too, had a nodule on his vocal chord and had to have surgery.

We called Phil Armenia right away and asked him if he would fill in for Duane for six weeks. After looking at the itinerary and seeing a 40 day tour to the West coast coming up, Phil said that he didn't like being away from his family for 40 days.

We looked at our promotional manager, Paul Wislocky, and said, "You better get ready to travel. You have to take Duane's place for a few weeks." Paul had been singing one song with us at many of our concerts. This time we had to go through the torture of rehearsing. Paul worked hard to learn his part.

The first night Paul sang was an outdoor concert. Every single song that we rehearsed with Paul we sang in the first half. Intermission started and we were wondering what to do. Just then it started to rain and it poured "cats and dogs." The preacher came and said, "We have to cancel the rest of the evening, it's going to rain through the night." We quickly said, "Yes, we'd better cancel." We knew the rain wasn't the only problem we had. We didn't have any more songs to sing with Paul.

A Letter From Paul

Dear Dave,

I was thinking of you and the family today and prayed for you, also!

You have been a wonderful friend through the years and we both have so much to thank the Lord for. Both of us were born in western Pennsylvania and given a godly heritage by our parents. I still remember traveling to Central Bible College in your old green Plymouth, (remember how we had to keep adding oil?). I also remember taking a wrong turn in St. Louis which delayed our trip a little bit. You were kind and we had a lot of laughs on that trip. I remember the early Courier days at CBC and when you began your career as a gospel singer (how far you've come!).

I got to reminiscing about some of the great times of fellowship and ministry we've had together. God has been so good to both of us.

I have memories "to last a lifetime" of great youth camps, conventions, concerts and church services we shared together. There isn't anyone I'd rather share platform in ministry with than you; and I mean that for a lot of reasons.

You have always been a man of integrity, whose life has been commensurate with his calling. You have always been honorable in your dealing with others and have remained true to the fundamentals of the gospel. God has given you a unique ability in presenting the gospel in creative ways. I love the way your ministry is motivated by a passion for the lost, moved by a compassionate heart, and marked by dynamic preaching. It's no wonder God has blessed you and Judy with fruitful ministry.

I just wanted to write and tell you I believe in you and your family and am glad to be your colleague in the ministry. I'm looking forward to the next time we can get together for fellowship Let's make it soon!

Your good friend,

Paul Wislocky

Duane returned after six weeks. He was tired of whispering and writing his conversation on paper. His life was traveling and singing and he missed the road. He was anxious to see if he could sing again.

We needed Duane and his voice to make that old, familiar Courier sound complete.

It wasn't going to be as easy as we thought. Duane's voice didn't heal as fast as Neil's.

We had to go easy. We changed our program of songs to protect his voice. We didn't allow him to talk during the day so he could save his voice for the concert that evening.

The doctor requested that Duane start a running program. This would help control his breathing and strengthen his ability to hold the vocal chords together while singing the high notes.

On traveling days, Duane would get off the bus and we would drive two miles ahead and wait while he ran to catch us. He was putting everything it took into his recovery program, but nothing was working. He still couldn't hold on to the high notes, his voice cracked and he struggled through most concerts.

One of his vocal chords had stiffened in the healing process. Both vocal chords have to rub together and stay closed while singing. If one is stiff, air gets through and the voice cracks. It took great energy for Duane to sing a concert. He ended every night exhausted.

For the next twelve months we kept up our busy schedule but we made some changes in the program. Neil sang all of Duane's solos and I preached longer closings. Every night the crowd offered a prayer for Duane's healing.

We were just ten months away from our 25th year celebration. I was excited about our big anniversary but deep in my heart, I was troubled.

Every night at concert time I was frustrated. My stomach would knot and I didn't even want to sing. I was upset with the inability to sing with the old Courier gusto and at myself for the feelings I had toward God for not healing Duane. I wondered how long could I handle all this stress.

It was worse when I called preachers for a date. They would ask me if Duane's voice was any better. When I would say it was about the same they would say, "Dave, call me when Duane is better." That made my job as booking agent very tough.

We had started a new recording project to be finished in time for our 25th Anniversary Celebration. We had already sent $5,000 to get it started and now we were due to send the next $5,000. I didn't want to send it because I didn't think Duane was able to record.

In January, 1980, we were traveling from Brampton, Ontario, Canada, to St. Catherines discussing the recording business when I couldn't hold it anymore. I blurped out that maybe it was time for me to quit. I didn't think I could handle another year like the last one and we needed to talk about it.

We were pulling into the church parking lot when I made my statement and went immediately in to set up the P A system. I could see that Duane and Neil were crushed by my remark.

It was a difficult service with lots of tears. The crowd didn't know what was going on with The Couriers that day. Duane stayed at the altar after church that morning and wept uncontrollably. I hurried to my room in the bus. I sat on my bed and stared at the wall in silence.

I asked God a thousand times if I was right in leaving The Couriers. I begged Him for answers for my life. What would I do? Was there something else I was supposed to do? Was this God's way of getting me out of The Couriers to fulfill another task?

We arranged a special meeting at Neil's home on January 14th, 1980. This was only for the three of us to discuss our future.

The meeting was very quiet and, at times, none of us could believe what we were talking about. I said, "Even though we are getting ready to celebrate 25 years together I feel like I need to do something else with my life."

Duane and Neil expressed the feeling that they, too, did not want to replace me and that we should all quit together at the same time.

Well, how to quit was a major problem. Should we sing for two more weeks or just walk away from it or what? We decided to think about it and meet the next afternoon to decide what to do.

I looked at the date book and saw that our Spring Concert was set for April 19th. The next three months included our eighth Holy Land Tour, already planned, and a mission's trip to Kenya and Nigeria, Africa. I counted fifty-two concerts already scheduled from January 15th to April 19th. We could say good-bye to all of our friends and let everyone hear their favorite song one more time.

I presented this at the second meeting the next day and we were all in agreement. Our last song would be sung at the Forum in Harrisburg, Pennsylvania, on April 19th, 1980.

It was an overwhelming task to tell our families and staff about our decision. It came as a big shock to everyone and many of our friends called and tried to talk us out of quitting.

During the next three months we packed out the churches and concert halls. People came from everywhere. We completely sold out of all our records and tapes.

Someone said we should have quit for five years because of the crowds that came to hear us sing for the last time. It was wonderful, but very sad.

I would compare those final 52 concerts to 52 funerals. With tears in our eyes we said good-bye to friends who had faithfully supported us through the years.

My life with The Couriers was coming to a close. Everyday I wondered what my future held.

- Success Principle 27

TOUGH DECISIONS CREATE THE OPPORTUNITY FOR FUTURE SUCCESSES.

We are all faced with a series of great opportunities, brilliantly disguised as unsolvable problems! With every risk there is a season of uncertainty. Sometimes you have to go through a time of pain to create a future of gain. We struggle leaving the familiar. Taking a risk challenges our faith and pushes us past the tough decisions.

• • •

April 19, 1980. The Couriers' final night!

The Hopper Brothers and Connie and Danny Gaither Trio were already booked for our Spring Concert.

We sold enough tickets to fill two buildings. We scheduled a rotating shuttle from one building to the next throughout the evening. Every thing went as smooth as silk.

After our last song, we closed our 25 years together, with prayer. We hugged everyone and said our good-byes. It was over.

Long after my family went to bed I sat pondering, reflecting back on all the dreams we had and the goals we accomplished. I thought about our biggest goal through the years and that was to influence as many young men as we could to enter the ministry. We asked God to give us "A preacher a day."

And now, many years later as I travel across America I am ministering in churches whose pastors are the young men who came off the front rows in our Courier services.

I slept well that night knowing that my future was in God's hands and that tomorrow was the beginning of the rest of my life.

CHAPTER SEVENTEEN

DAVE KYLLONEN, THE FAMILY AFFAIR.

FOR MANY YEARS I HAD TRAVELED AND LEFT MY
family behind. Now I was given a golden opportunity to make an
investment in them first hand.

Judy, our three teenage daughters and I joined together to become
the **"Dave Kyllonen Family Affair."**

For the next two years we traveled all over America and Canada
having the times of our lives. We were finally, now, a full time family. We enjoyed being together.

We weren't the Couriers, that was for sure. I remember working
hard with the girls. I expected them to be able to do what I could do.
Just push their "Professional Button," and let it roll out automatically.

But they were only teenagers. When they talked, they talked like
teenagers. They sang like teenagers. They responded like teenagers,
and they attracted their own kind. We were reaching a different
crowd and I liked that.

When I finally relaxed and let the girls be themselves we began to
melt into a sweet family ministry. Our family got comfortable in our
services and we saw great results.

I remember the girls asking if we were going to do a missionary
project like The Couriers did. I said, "Yes, let's call Holmes Williams and see if we can do a crusade in Barbados."

Holmes was excited about our coming and extended us an invitation for the following February.

We arrived in Barbados in February, 1981, and started our crusade. A few nights went by and Holmes said, "Dave, your family is
doing a great job and our congregation has endeared themselves to
you. Is it possible you could come back and stay with us for a longer
time? I need you to help me pastor the church." I asked, "How long

are you talking about, Holmes?" He answered, "How about one whole year?"

I told him I would talk to God and my family and that maybe it could happen. He said we would talk about it again before the crusade was over.

• Success Principle 28

WE MUST ALWAYS BE READY TO RISK.

Nothing great ever happens
without risk. I am a great one
to risk. Money, time, effort
and energy were never considered
when God was calling.

• • •

What a conversation I had with Judy and the girls that night. Their reaction surprised me when they said, "Daddy, we can do it for one year. We're behind you one hundred percent."

I'm not sure if they really had "hard work" missions in mind. Was it the lure of tropical breezes blowing and the white sandy beaches? At any rate, we agreed to say "yes" if the subject came up again.

Several days went by and Holmes didn't bring up the subject. I told Judy, "Let's not talk about it either." Maybe Holmes was kidding and just got in over his head in our conversation.

Two weeks went by and we were down to the last service. When Holmes began to introduce us he said, "I want to make an announcement. Dave and Judy Kyllonen and their girls, are coming back to Barbados and Dave will be our new associate pastor for one year."

We were in shock! The crowd stood to their feet and began to clap their hands. I gave Holmes a great big hug and the deal was sealed.

I walked to the microphone and said, "We are honored at your invitation. We must go home and raise our support but we will return one year from today."

• Success Principle 29

DON'T KNOCK THE DOORS DOWN, BUT AS THEY OPEN, WALK THROUGH THEM.

Life is full of surprises. There is something wonderful about walking through unexpected open doors. God opens a door and greatness is gained by walking through it. We waste much time trying to open doors to our own desires.

• • •

After the service a businessman introduced himself. He said, "My name is Johnny Bourne. I'm an accountant and a bachelor and I live by myself in a three bedroom home. When you come back you can live with me for the whole year and there will be no charge." I found Holmes and asked him about Johnny Bourne and his offer. He said, "That's an answer to our prayer. Go tell him you accept the offer." God was sure working things out and confirming His will in our hearts.

• Success Principle 30

WHEN YOU TAKE ONE STEP, GOD TAKES TWO.

We never have all the answers but
we must first take a step that God
has asked us to take.
When we obey, God always comes thru!

• • •

We flew home the next day and immediately started preparing for our year of itinerating. We needed to raise our own support because Barbados had laws that would not allow the church to pay us a salary while we were there.

The first thing I did was call the Assemblies of God Missions Department in Springfield, Missouri, to see if we could open a missions account where churches could send their support. We were told that the mission's board would never accept us for a one year term and that we would need to raise our own support through our personal friends.

We had no idea how much money we would need for one year but guessed that $2,000 a month would cover our cost of living. Our goal was to find one hundred friends to send $25.00 a month.

We had one year to find them as we continued our schedule with the "Dave Kyllonen Family Affair." By the end of the year we had reached our goal of one hundred friends all signed up to start their support by March first. Praise the Lord!

Kristie and Robin, our two older daughters, would not be going with us. Kristie was getting married in June to Gregory Hollis from Kansas and Robin was going to Central Bible College in Springfield, Missouri, for the Fall term. It would be Judy and I and Connie, our youngest daughter.

We had two major problems to deal with. We needed to rent our home in Pennsylvania for a year and we needed to sell our fifth wheel camper and the pick-up truck we were traveling in.

Renting our house was easy. We found a pastor and his family who were moving into the area and needed a fully furnished home for one year.

Selling the camper and truck was a different story. Nobody wanted a two year old, 38 foot fifth wheel and a truck with 60,000 miles on it.

We advertised and talked to everybody we could. We were down to one week before we were to leave for Barbados and we still had not sold it.

It was then we received a phone call from Tulsa, Oklahoma. It was from an evangelist, Rev. Lowry, whom we had never met. He had heard through a friend of a friend of a friend that we were selling our unit and was asking if it was still available. He and his wife and four children desperately needed a fifth wheel camper and truck.

I said, "Boy, do I have a deal for you!"

There wasn't time for him to come to Pennsylvania to see our unit so he suggested I take Polaroid pictures of it and overnight them to him. I promised to take the pictures that afternoon.

This sure was a crazy way to sell a truck and camper, but maybe God was in it.

I looked out the window to see what shape the camper was in. It was in the side yard next to the house.

The day before we had a blizzard and I had piled all the snow from our driveway up against it. It was about a foot deep. Plus the camper was filthy from our last trip.

The truck was sitting in the driveway just as dirty. Why did I tell him I would take the pictures today? It sure looked impossible from the living room window.

What was I going to do? It was cold outside and the wind was blowing hard. The pictures needed to be sent in just a few hours. I had to do something, now!

Selling a camper with a picture to a man 1,500 miles away wasn't going to be easy. I decided to go for it. I got the snow blower out and hit the yard on the run. I sent snow flying everywhere. Then I got out the water hose that had been put away for winter and started washing the camper. It was so cold the water was freezing on the sides of the camper as I went along.

I knew my neighbors were looking out their windows, saying, "There's got to be something wrong with Dave Kyllonen. Can you believe he is washing his camper today?"

I not only washed the camper but I washed the truck, too. Then I backed the truck onto the fifth wheel and took about a dozen pictures of our shiny, spotlessly clean, camper unit sitting in a foot of snow. I guess the neighbors had a right to think what they thought! Judy and the girls were busy cleaning up the inside. I took another dozen pictures of the inside and we ran to get them in the mail.

The next evening Rev. Lowry called, excited. He had received the pictures and loved what he saw. He wanted to buy our truck and fifth wheel. Praise The Lord!

- Success Principle 31

GOD IS NEVER EARLY OR LATE, HE'S
ALWAYS RIGHT ON TIME.

*We have to learn patience in waiting
on God's perfect timing. When we forge
ahead in front of God we usually fail
to do what he has asked us to do.
"Wait for the Lord; be strong and take
heart and wait for the Lord." (Psalm 27:14)* NIV

However there was only one hitch. They were in an evangelistic meeting and couldn't possibly come for the unit for over a month. We were leaving for Barbados in five days. There was only one thing to do and that was to drive the truck and fifth wheel to them. Then I could fly back home just in time to leave for Barbados.

Arrangements were made with Rev. Lowry and I started out. It was 1,500 long miles to Tulsa, Oklahoma, but, I had to do it.

As I drove the Interstate toward Tulsa, I kept saying to myself, "There's more than one way to skin a cat, meaning, there's more than one way to sell a truck and fifth wheel!"

I drove for two solid days and arrived at the mall in Tulsa where I was to meet the Lowry family. I was right on time.

I saw an old pickup truck, with a family standing around it, in the mall parking lot. I knew it was the Lowrys. I quietly pulled up beside their truck.

I was eager to see their first reaction when they knew it was me and that this was their new home. The looks on their faces was worth a million dollars. Their mouths dropped open and they stared in disbelief. They were looking at a 38 foot fifth wheel that seemed monstrous in comparison to their small pickup truck.

And it was beautiful. Cream colored with brown and orange striping pulled by a matching truck, stripes and all.

I turned off the engine and jumping out said, "You must be the Lowrys. Welcome to your new home!"

They couldn't believe it was actually theirs. The children couldn't wait till I unlocked the door. You should have heard them scream when they got inside. "Mom," they yelled, "It has a kitchen, a living room and beds to sleep in.

I knew God had worked this out and that I had done the right thing. This family desperately needed our truck and fifth wheel.

I took a short walk while they looked it over. I looked back at the camper and I was proud of what I had brought. It still looked new and the matching paint on the truck made the whole unit outstanding.

It was a joy to hand over the keys and pray together that God would continue to bless their ministry.

I flew home having closed another chapter in the book of my life.

We were ready to be missionaries.

Going to the West Indies was another part of my heart that carried a challenging desire to work for God on foreign soil, on a full time basis. We would be there for a whole year and would have a chance to really know the people, live with them and understand their culture.

CHAPTER EIGHTEEN

BARBADOS, HERE I COME!

BOARDING THE PLANE THAT DAY WAS JUDY, Connie and myself. Kristie was now married to Gregory Hollis and would be living in Wichita, Kansas. Robin was enrolled in Central Bible College and would be living in Springfield, Missouri.

I can't describe the feelings in my heart when we disembarked from the plane in Barbados. Great anticipation to meet the challenge and, maybe, a little apprehension.

Our new Suzuki van was waiting for us at the airport. It was a little scary to spend $7,000 of our $25,000 budget the very first day, but we needed it.

I laughed when I first laid my eyes on it. It was so tiny I was almost too tall to get in. My knees bumped the windshield wiper button every time I changed gears and driving in Barbados required changing gears often. My legs were so long my feet had a hard time getting to the clutch and the brake. The steering wheel was on the opposite side. All of a sudden driving took on a new meaning.

We drove that little Suzuki van 60,000 miles before we left Barbados and hauled everything you could imagine in it. One day I would fill it with lumber, the next day sand, and the next day concrete. Plus a thousand other things too numerous to mention. It was the, "Kyllonen Speed The Light" vehicle and we definitely got our money's worth out of it.

Johnny Bourne, who had invited us to live with him for a year, was at the airport to greet us and to lead us home. We followed him up the steep hill to Rendezvous Ridge and our new residence. The house sat high on a bluff overlooking the ocean and provided a beautiful view from our back yard.

Johnny had bought a prefab home in Florida and had it shipped to Barbados. His three bedroom ranch was the only American house on the Island. He had just finished building it a few weeks before we arrived.

We put all of our stuff in the middle of the living room floor and sat down saying, "What did we do to deserve this?"

I went to the church office the next day and had my first staff meeting with Holmes.

First, he gave me my preaching schedule. There were six services every week and I would be preaching three of them. He asked me to take over the youth Sunday School class. There was a four minute radio broadcast everyday and I would be hosting many of them. I became the new emcee for a Gospel music program every Sunday night from 10 to 11 p.m. Holmes had a great radio ministry all over the West Indies with over one hundred broadcasts every week.

I walked out of Holmes' office shaking my head. I thought he would only use me to preach once a month. That was only twelve messages for the year so I didn't see the need to bring any study material for preaching. I thought I was coming to Barbados to help paint and repair things around the church. Holmes sure had other things in mind! The pressure was on!

On Sunday I stepped to the pulpit to preach my first message. Holmes asked me to be sure to preach an hour because it was being recorded for future radio broadcasts. I was to be aware that at 29 minutes into my message Holmes would stop the tape recorder and turn over the tape. I should then pause for two seconds and start again for the other 29 minutes left on the tape.

Well, I started my message and everything was going well. The people really got into the message and I got excited. They clapped and "amened" me and quoted the scriptures with me, out loud. They were an exciting crowd.

I preached everything I had prepared, twice, maybe even three times, and just as I was ready to wind it up I heard the tape recorder click. Holmes was just now turning over the tape. I was supposed to preach another 29 minutes. But tape, or no tape, radio broadcast or no radio broadcast, I was finished. I had preached everything I knew.

I was embarrassed and apologized to Holmes and told him it would never happen again.

At home in America, if I preached even 30 minutes people began looking at their watches. But not the Bajans. They loved church and they really challenged me. I went home and got on my knees to ask God to help me be a preacher that could preach for an hour. With God's help and the Bajan's enthusiasm, I am happy to report that I preached 326 messages in Barbados and they were all an hour long.

I loved it. I loved the preparation time and I loved sharing God's Word with people who loved hearing it.

Thanks, Holmes, for giving me that great opportunity.

I took a day and walked around the church making notes on what I thought needed to be done. The list ended up being quite long.

- The church needed to be painted, inside and outside.
- The roof on the Education building was leaking and needed to be repaired.
- There was a long row of open-air Sunday School classes built out of wood and chicken wire. The wood had rotted and needed to be replaced.
- The church needed a nursery.
- The church roof was caving in.
- The grounds needed grooming.
- The church offices needed to be updated and painted.

By the end of the first week the list had grown to 35 projects needing immediate attention.

The question was; where did we start? Well, one project at a time. One day at a time.

I went to work early and stayed late. I fell into bed every night totally exhausted. Some of the church members came to help and we had a wonderful time working together. The sun was hot and I was getting a great tan. Soon my white skin was nearly as brown as theirs.

I was picking up some unique Bajan lingo. When they like something they use the expression, "Cheese on bread!" So, when something we did turned out right I learned to say, "Cheese on bread." If it was something really outstanding they would say, "Cheesseessee on!"

My first water baptismal service was an unusual experience. On baptism Sunday the whole congregation made their way to the beach. They stood in the hot sun under a mass of umbrellas.

As Holmes and I waded into the sea, those that were to be baptized, and there were many, formed a long line in the water. The congregation sang wonderful worship choruses and old hymns of the church. One by one they came to be lowered into the water.

Much to my chagrin, I nearly lost the first candidate. Just as I lowered him into the water a huge wave rolled in and knocked us both flat. I got tickled and started to laugh. I had to force myself back into a serious mood. I learned very quickly how to prepare myself for the force of the next wave.

That same evening I approached Holmes with a brilliant plan. Why not let me build a baptismal tank in the side yard of the church property? He thought it was a great idea and I began my project.

Now you must understand I am a preacher not a construction worker. I couldn't remember ever building a bird-house let alone a baptismal tank before.

I designed a 5 ft. deep, 6 ft. X 12 ft. tank made of ceramic tiles. We built a wooden frame, like a box and lowered the huge bathtub tank into it. We built steps up one side and down the other.

Arlie, my friend, designed and cut a huge dove out of plywood. We attached that to the front of the frame and when it was all painted sparkling white, and the potted plants and flowers were placed around it, it was awesome. The People's Cathedral was proud to have their own baptismal tank.

The people cheered when it was announced that the following Sunday there would be a baptismal service at two o'clock in the afternoon at the church, not the sea.

Eighty people signed up to be baptized. Holmes was as excited as I. People were talking about bringing their families and friends for the service. It would be a big day for the church.

We decided we should start to fill the tank with water on Saturday evening and let it slowly run all night. Then it should be full by church time Sunday morning.

When I got to the church on Sunday morning, I ran to see how full the tank was. Much to my dismay it was only half full, even after running the water all night. I looked down at my feet and saw the reason. I was standing in water. The tank had sprung a leak. I couldn't believe it. After all that hard work.

Nothing could be done now. I was on my way to preach the two Sunday morning services and teach my Sunday school class in between. The church yard was starting to show little puddles of water here and there. I didn't dare turn off the water fearing the tank would be totally empty at the 2:00 hour. I would have to consider the problem after church.

Actually, there was nothing we could do. There wasn't enough time to fix the leak. If we were careful enough maybe there would be enough water to baptize the people.

A great crowd gathered early for the baptismal service. Many of the congregation had brought their dinner and just stayed on the grounds after church. The two morning services were packed with 1,500 people in each service. The side yard of the church was overflowing with the crowd and with water but no one knew of our dilemma. They were talking among themselves, "why all this water under our feet?"

This service was a first. It was one of a kind There had never been a baptismal service at the church. No one was going to miss this one!

The singing began with Ferdie, the song leader, at his best. So much enthusiasm and excitement. I love to hear the Bajan's sing and clap on the off beat.

Holmes and I both climbed into the baptismal tank together. I was to read the Scriptures and he was going to preach a short message. The tank was a little over half full. The water hose was still pouring water into the tank but I think the leak was getting worse. All eighty candidates were lined up and ready. Holmes and I would baptize every other one. Holmes would put them down and I would make sure they were totally under the water before he brought them up again.

After I baptized the first lady my eyes turned to the funniest sight I had ever seen at a water baptismal service. Several men of the church had formed a bucket brigade from a faucet, inside the church, all the way across the side yard to the baptismal tank. After each person was baptized a bucket or two of water was added to the tank.

One lady lost her wig when Holmes put her under. We had to quickly dive for her hair and I watched Holmes plop it back on her head like nothing ever happen. This was more than I could take. It was some time before I could regain my composure to continue on.

There were moments when I remembered the water baptismal services at home in America. They were quiet services with every-thing done in perfect order. There was always lots of warm water in a tank that was designed to fit the decor of the platform. Baptismal robes were worn by all the candidates. Dressing rooms were nearby for changing. Usually four or five people were being baptized. The service was over in a matter of minutes. I stood in this homemade tank wishing that every preacher in America could be here.

It was a special day! When the last person was baptized there wasn't too much water left in the tank.

After the service, Holmes and I were standing in the tank just re-laxing and watching the crowd. I reached over and hugged him and whispered in his ear, "Holmes, are you sure you want me to stay a whole year?"

The next day I began to ask questions about fiberglass. I took all the tiles off the tank and replaced them with fiberglass. It wasn't anything professional, that's for sure, but it never leaked again and we baptized hundreds of people in the following months.

In the tenth month of our year in Barbados, Holmes said, "Dave, you and your family have had an amazing effect on this church. I don't think you should leave us two months from now, so I'm asking you to stay another year."

I said, "Holmes, we're having fun and we still have many more projects to finish. We'll be happy to stay another year."

My Sunday School class with the teens was growing every week. When we got to two hundred young people we had run out of space.

I got another brilliant idea. At the right time I went to Holmes' office. I said, "I need more room and I think a big tent for my Sunday

School class would be just the thing. We could put it up in the side yard of the church and it could be used for many other church activities, too. I know we don't have the money to buy a tent but listen to my plan."

- Success Principle 32

CRUNCH BRINGS CREATIVITY!

Obstacles generate ideas. I went to
Barbados to do a work for the
kingdom, not just to sit on the beach
and take a year's vacation in the sun.
While I was hard at work, I was always
looking for other things I could do.
Our brain stops growing if we do
the same routine everyday.
Look left and right, maybe up and
down and get a new idea. Don't live
with, "That's impossible!" Shape your
life by trying the impossible.

• • •

A missionary builder from Canada, Harold Skovmand, had been helping us fix the church and he had an airplane. I suggested that Harold and I fly to the States and visit some churches and raise enough money for the trip and a new tent. We could buy a 50 ft. by 100 ft. tent in Valdosta, Georgia, and fly it home in Harold's plane."

Holmes loved the idea, so we ordered the tent and I booked the tour in churches in the States.

Flying a one engine, Cherokee Six, from Barbados to the United States and back again would be a new experience for me. Harold and I had become good friends so this would be a delightful trip.

- Success Principle 33

GOD'S PEOPLE MUST HAVE A LOVE FOR ADVENTURE.

I grew up in the state of Pennsylvania and never traveled out of the state until college days. When I saw how big the world was I became adventurous. There isn't a day that goes by without looking forward to some new adventure.

"The people who know their God shall be strong, and carry out great exploits." (Dan.11:32) NKJV

• • •

It took 19 hours to get to Kansas for our first meeting. I finally got comfortable with the plane and Harold's flying skills.

Within three weeks we raised $10,000 to buy the tent. God had given us favor with the churches and we were grateful for their generosity.

Now it was time to head for Georgia to pick up the tent and fly back to Barbados.

They were waiting for us at the Valdosta Tent Company. Our new tent was sitting in several huge canvas bags in the middle of the work area. After taking one look I thought, there's no way that tent will fit into our small plane. We had even taken all the seats out except for two for Harold and me.

Then I saw all the chains that came with it and I knew for sure we were in trouble. I heard Harold ask the salesman how much the tent weighed. His answer floored me when he said, "With the chains, about 1,500 pounds."

Harold and I had talked about the weight of the tent back at the beginning of our trip. He limited me as to what I could bring with me and I wasn't allowed to buy anything to take back because our load limit was 1,350 pounds. And that included the two of us, our stuff and the tent.

I was good at math and quickly calculated that we were going to be at least 500 pounds overweight. When I ask Harold about it he just said, "We'll have to pray and ask God to help us."

I was beginning to think that I should fly home on a commercial jet. I was getting the, "heebie j'eebies." Harold would hear nothing of it. He said to me, "Dave, you are going with me and the tent, no matter what."

We loaded the company truck with all the heavy canvas tent bags. The chains were put in boxes and stacked on top and off we headed for the airport.

Everyone from the tent company jumped into their cars and were following us. They weren't going to miss this take-off for anything in the world.

When we got to the airport and pulled up beside the plane it really got funny. The tent people were talking among themselves. "That plane? Why it's way too small! Only one engine? The tent will never fit!"

Every statement was making me more nervous. I knew we had bought too big a tent for so small a plane. Harold didn't like it when people referred to his airplane as small, so, I never said a word.

We lifted, squeezed, pushed, and tugged until our strength was gone. Slowly, but surely, each bag was jammed into the plane. It took us a couple of hours but finally we pushed the door shut. It all fit.

However, my seat was pulled up as close to the dashboard as possible. With my long legs I wasn't sure I could even get in. Two thousand miles to Barbados was going to be tough on my body. How was I going to relax being hunched over with that heavy unmoveable canvas pushing at my head? Too late to think about that now.

It was time to take off and all the tent people were still there. In fact, a bigger crowd had gathered.

We thanked them all for their help and climbed into the plane. Harold had a big grin on his face but I could tell he was concerned.

He and I prayed before he started the engine. "Oh God, we acknowledge our need of you. Please help us to get this plane off the ground and fly it to Barbados. Amen!"

At the turn of the key the engine roared and we waved good-bye as we taxied toward the runway. Harold called the tower and asked if he could use the whole length of the runway. I'm sure the man in the tower didn't know why our little plane needed all that room to take off but he granted permission.

Harold said, "Are you ready?" and I yelled, "Ready, Captain, go for it!" My heart was in my mouth. My knuckles were white from holding on. My mouth was dry. The engine's warm-up was vibrating the whole plane. The tower gave us the OK and we started down the runway.

I wasn't looking to see the crowd but I knew they were there. I could feel their eyes watching us.

The front end of the plane came up quicker than Harold had anticipated and with the wheels still on the runway we began to weave from left to right and back again.

I watched Harold to see his reaction. He was a great pilot and had flown over 10,000 hours in this plane. His expertise began to show as his steady hand kept everything under control.

The lift off was slow and difficult. We climbed to 2,000 feet very slowly. Finally, we reached 2,500 feet and Harold leveled off. He said, "We better stay at this height for a while, the engine is working hard." So at 2,500 feet, we flew to Fort Lauderdale, Florida, and landed safely.

After fueling the plane we taxied out for our second take off. This one was a breeze. Harold knew what to do this time and soon we were flying toward Puerto Rico.

I had the rare privilege of flying 2,000 miles over the ocean at 3,000 feet. That's very different from flying in a commercial jet at 35,000 ft.

The water was so clear I could see the ocean bottom. It was a beautiful aqua color. Harold's flying skills gave me confidence and soon I relaxed and enjoyed the most beautiful trip I had ever had in the air.

When we saw the Barbados airport and called for clearance to land we noticed something very strange.

We were told that war in Grenada had started and that the Barbados airport had become headquarters for the United States Air Force.

Planes and helicopters were lined up and down the runway. I counted at least 50 helicopters. Were we allowed to land? Was there any room for us?

Harold eased our plane down onto the runway in another great landing and I clapped my hands in appreciation of a great landing and a great trip.

We were both very happy the trip was over and that we had made it safely home.

I had never seen so much activity at the Barbados airport. Harold taxied around all the military planes and found a space to park next to a massive C-130. It made Harold's plane look like a tinker toy.

I thanked God for giving us a safe trip. Now we faced another big problem. Customs!

Holmes and I had discussed that subject before we left and I knew about the duty we would have to pay for bringing in the tent. I asked Holmes to be at the airport when we arrived back in Barbados.

When we walked into the customs office I didn't see Holmes but I will never forget what I heard. The Customs officer said to Harold and me, "What are you doing in here? Don't you know we're in a war and can't you see how busy we are? Please leave at once. Get back in your plane and move it to the parking area at the other end of the airport."

We made the quickest exit you ever saw. I grabbed Harold and gave him a great big hug. I said, "Harold, thanks for a great trip in your **BIG** plane. I love you and would fly anywhere in the world with you but let's not take a tent with us the next time."

After another ten months Holmes came for another talk. He said, "Dave, you and Judy have endeared yourselves to our church. You are working hard and project after project is being finished. We need you here and don't want you to go home at the end of your two years. Would you please stay for the third year?"

We felt good about our ministry here so we said, "We're having so much fun and God is continuing to bless us. We'll be happy to stay for our third year!"

• Success Principle 34

FRIENDSHIPS REQUIRE AN
INVESTMENT OF OUR LIFE.

Usually, an investment pays dividends.
A friendship investment comes through
in times of discouragement,
sickness, heartache and old age. To
have a friend one must be a friend.

•   •   •

Holmes owned a small 14 foot fishing boat that he kept anchored in a cove near my house. Three people in the boat was comfortable, four or five was a crowd and six was plain dangerous.

Some days the ocean was calm but on other days the waves were big and scary. Often we would take the boat out just for a pleasure ride but have to turn around and come back because the sea was so rough, the waves were coming into the boat.

Finally, we got smart. Holmes would call and ask me to look out at the ocean to see if there were any white caps. If there were no white caps we could go for a ride. White caps meant the waves were too big for our little boat and we'd better stay home.

I inquired about the strange looking wire cages I saw on the beaches in the areas where fishing boats were being repaired. They told me they were called "fish pots."

They are wire cages about four feet square and two feet deep. They have a funnel shaped hole that fish would enter and not be able to get back out. They were baited with bread, lettuce - anything green. Then they were dropped to the ocean floor about 50 ft. in depth.

Every other day the cages were brought back up and the fish taken out. In restaurants, pot fish was a specialty dish.

This seemed like an intriguing adventure so Holmes and I decided to get our own fish pots. There was an old fisherman in our church who was an expert fish pot maker. Brother Meiers went to work and made two for us.

Holmes and I loaded the two new fish pots into my little Suzuki van and headed for the boat. We were a sight to behold. The cages were so big the doors wouldn't close. It didn't matter. We were the two happiest guys in Barbados going to do something we had never done before.

The boat, like the van, wasn't big enough either. Holmes squeezed into the back of the boat so he could steer our little outboard engine. I squeezed into the front. It was my job to hold onto the cages to make sure they didn't fall out.

The ocean was a little rough but that wasn't going to stop us today. Brother Meiers had given us a 100 ft. rope with a large, heavy hook on the end. He also gave us a small, square, glass bottomed box. He told us to put the glass bottom under the water a few inches and by looking thru the glass we could see the ocean floor. After we thought we were far enough out Holmes stopped the engine and I took the special glass bottom box and held it three inches down in the water. Now I was ready for my first look at the ocean floor.

I had to lean out, over the side of the boat, and bend way down to get my head in the box. The waves were making the boat roll from side to side. Water was splashing all over me. I was holding on to the boat for dear life with one hand while the other hand held the precious box. My stomach was taking a beating as it scraped against the side of the boat. In that precarious position I found myself getting seasick.

What I saw under the water was incredible! It was like a movie produced by National Geographic. I was fascinated with the beautiful, bright colored fish. I remarked to Holmes, "You must have a look." That little glass bottom box was an ingenious invention.

When we lowered our fish pots 50 ft., to the ocean floor, we dared not release the rope until we "marked the spot." Out in the vast ocean we needed to know how to find them again. Our old fisherman friend had taught us the secret. We should line up, in our visual view, the old lighthouse on the shoreline to the right of us with a tall palm tree straight ahead of us. This would mark our imaginary X.

Two days later, with great anticipation, we piloted the little boat toward the X. We lined up the lighthouse in our view and turned to line up the palm tree. We looked for the palm tree, but to our utter amazement, there were over a hundred palm trees that all looked alike. "Which one?" I yelled to Holmes. He looked more confused than I. I picked what I thought was the right tree and bent down over the side of the boat with my trusty little glass bottom box. Holding on with my other hand I put my head in the box and looked for the wire fish pot. It wasn't anywhere in sight.

Holmes told me to stay over the side of the boat, with my head in the box, and he would guide the boat up the coast line. After a mile of looking at the whole ocean floor I was tired. The waves were rough and water was splashing everywhere. For the second time, my stomach was getting skinned up. My knees were hurting and I was getting seasick again.

Holmes said, "Are we having fun, yet?" The ocean, boats and fishing had never been a part of my life. I said, "There must be a better way. If we ever find those fish pots again we better learn how to mark, that's for sure."

After an hour of searching we wondered if we would ever find the fish pots again. But we didn't want to quit because we had too much invested. To tell everyone that we lost our fish pots in the ocean because we didn't know how to mark them was embarrassing. I said, "Holmes, you keep steering the boat up and down the coast line and I'll look for the pots, even if it takes all day."

I had to hold the box with two hands now. The boat was going faster and one hand wasn't strong enough to hold it against the current. Holmes was laughing because I wasn't holding on anymore and was being braver than ever. When he would hit a big wave I'd go tumbling.

After three hours I spotted the fish pots. I screamed at Holmes, "I can see them just ahead. Go slow and a little left. More left, more, easy now, back right a foot."

I reached for the rope with the big hook on it. I dropped it over the side while holding on to the other end. Now I had to get my head back in the box and hold the rope in place to catch the side of the cage as we passed by. Holmes had moved too far to the right and, by the time he moved over, we had gone by the pots.

Now we had to swing by again. This wasn't going to be as easy as I thought. I guided Holmes with my voice, even though I was over the side of the boat with my head in the box. "Slow, Holmes, slower. Looks good this time! Just a little left, that's it! We're only ten feet away! STOP! STOP! I've hooked it!" You would have thought we had found a million dollars. Holmes stopped the engine and we both started pulling in the rope. What had we caught? "Oh, yes," I said, "This is real fishing!" We pulled the cages up out of the water and into the boat. The smiles on our faces was worth everything. In our fish pot were five fish. Success at last!

- Success Principle 35

SATISFACTION IS SOMETIMES

FOUND IN THE LITTLE THINGS
OF LIFE.

*Don't overlook the seemingly
insignificant things in life.
True satisfaction can be found
in those often unnoticed
treasures.*

•   •   •

We learned to mark the fish pots so well that I would sit in the
boat and never look over the side until Holmes would stop the engine
and say, "OK, Dave, they're right underneath us. Just throw the rope
over the side and bring up the pots." Sure enough, there they were,
right underneath the boat.

• Success Principle 36

PRACTICE MAKES PERFECT.

*If at first you don't succeed,
try, try again. Golf pros
practice hitting 300 balls
every day. I have been
playing golf for over 40
years and I can't remember
ever hitting 300 balls in one
day. I guess that's why I
still play in the 90's.*

•   •   •

One day we pulled up the fish pot and found six big eels in it.
They are a long, slippery, snake like fish. They were each about
three feet long and three inches thick. They had sharp teeth and
looked dangerous.

They were wiggling all over the cage trying to get out. They were trying to get at us.

I never saw Holmes so frightened. His eyes were intense on the cage. He yelled at me to stay back. "Don't get close. They will take a huge hunk out of your arm if they get close enough."

It would have been bad to catch just one but we had six. I wanted to open the back door of the cage and let them fall back into the ocean but Holmes wouldn't hear of it. If one of them got out and stayed in the boat we would be in big trouble.

We got a big stick and tried to put it through the wire to smash their heads but we only got them more upset. They were after us.

We finally decided to take the fish pot to the shore and get out on the beach to let them go. At least we could run if we had to.

We beached our boat and carefully put the cage down on the sand. We were already drawing a crowd and three men asked us if we were giving the eels away. We said, "If you can get them out of the cage, they're all yours." They took over and had them out in a flash. They said it was the best eating fish in Barbados. Holmes and I said, "No thanks, they look too much like a snake."

We caught lots of fish through the years and ate our own "pot fish" every Saturday.

Judy and I were never issued a visa while we were living in Barbados. We had to leave the island every six weeks and come back in as tourists for another six weeks.

During these "off the island" times we held crusades in many of the other islands of the West Indies. We visited St. Lucia, St. Vincent, St. Maarten, the Dominican Republic, Haiti, Trinidad and even Guyana, South America. What great memories!

One visit to Haiti was filled with adventure. Holmes and I went for a week's crusade in the city of Port-au-Prince. We arrived early and helped with getting the soccer field ready for the crusade. A platform had to be built. The electricians were installing special lighting and PA system.

The day before the opening of our crusade, Holmes said, "We need to go and see our rivalry before we start our crusade." I wasn't sure what he was talking about, so I asked, "Holmes, who is our competition?" He shocked me with his answer when he said, "We need to attend a voodoo service!"

My first response was, "Never! Count me out!" I thought he was joking, but he was as serious as he could be. I finally told him, "If you're not afraid then I'm not either. Let's go."

We arrived early and met the priest in charge. He answered some of our questions and tried to prepare us for what was going to happen.

He told us the drummers would start beating their drums first. It would take about thirty minutes for the spirits to come from Africa. Then we could expect amazing things to happen. We found a seat close to the front. We didn't want to miss a thing.

Out came three drummers. They had some old drum sets at one end of the stage. They beat their drums while six or seven girls in white dresses danced and sang songs in a language I didn't understand.

It all started very slowly, but before long, the beat of the drums became fast and intense. These men knew how to beat the drums. What a performance!

At the end of thirty minutes the sound was overwhelming and the girls were swaying and singing like nothing I had ever seen. I had both eyes open and both of my ears were listening hard to what was going on.

Three men brought in a live goat. I couldn't believe my eyes, but right there in front of us they killed the goat. It's throat was slit open and all of it's blood was caught in a huge basin. Several men joined the girls on the stage and they all took a drink of the blood. What happened next was unbelievable!

Suddenly they had special powers. Some were beginning to eat glass. They were biting a drinking glass and chewing the pieces and swallowing it. This was more than I could handle.

Then I noticed hot coals were being uncovered in the center of the stage. They stirred them up and made them red hot. It looked like a big grill ready for a steak fry.

Now the men walked on the red hot coals in their bare feet. They weren't burned and it seemed as if they didn't feel a thing.

As the ceremony proceeded and they performed their feat they would pass out and fall on the stage floor. They were carried out to a special room for their recovery.

When it was over I looked at Holmes and said, "Holmes, I am leaving, now! I came with you today but let me assure you I will never come again."

Out in the parking lot I recognized two of the men who had performed. I asked one who had eaten glass if he swallowed glass in all of the services. He told me that he had been doing it for a long time and never had any ill effects.

The other man had not eaten the glass and I asked him why. He said he wasn't willing to give his whole life, in surrender, to the power of the spirit. Maybe, someday soon, he would. My whole system was so upset over what I had experienced that I couldn't eat for three days. I had seen the devil at work. I witnessed his imitation of the power of Christ. I felt sorry for those under his control. The devil is real and that day I got closer to him than I ever wanted to be.

- Success Principle 37

NEVER UNDERESTIMATE
THE POWER OF THE ENEMY.

*"Be sober, be vigilant; because
your adversary the devil walks
about like a roaring lion,
seeking whom he may devour."*
(1 Peter 5:8) NKJV

• • •

Holmes and I held another crusade in Guyana, South America. The meeting was held in the huge stadium in Georgetown. The crowds were big and exciting. I loved the people of Guyana. They were so responsive to our singing and preaching.

The crusade was almost over when I began to inquire about the cult leader, Jim Jones and his followers. I wanted to know if it was possible for me to go and see what was left of Jonestown, the cult's community, where so many of Jim Jones' followers committed suicide. I learned that Jonestown was 250 miles away and I could go there if I rented a small plane. Then I was told the following story:

Jonestown was taken over by the Guyana police department. That property worth millions of dollars was now going to be their new headquarters. Everything had been cleaned up and the police department was thrilled with their new facility.

However, strange noises were heard in the night hours. The police heard people screaming; loud talking every night - eerie sounds from another world. Finally, everyone refused to work there so the facility had been closed.

The entire place is now covered with weeds that have grown so high you can't see the buildings anymore. It isn't even a tourist attraction. It has become a ghost town. People stay as far away as possible.

Again, I was reminded that the devil is real. Jonestown was not for me.

One Sunday morning I was sitting on the platform of the People's Cathedral in Barbados while Holmes was preaching. I noticed that the ceiling was sagging. We talked about it after church and decided to watch the ceiling for the next few weeks to see if it was getting worse.

It definitely got worse. So Harold Skovmand, a construction engineer, and I climbed up into the space above the ceiling with our flashlights to take a look.

The trusses were 50 feet long and every one of them was sagging in the middle. Harold was upset. He said the whole roof could come crashing down at any time. We needed to fix it immediately.

Harold was going to give me a lesson in what roof trusses are all about. We went to the lumber yard and picked up a hundred two by sixes. We had to beef up the present trusses by adding these long, heavy two by sixes to each truss.

We rented some "come alongs" to help lift the sagging trusses into place. I had never seen this kind of equipment before. These were huge, heavy jacks with heavy chains that wrapped around the truss and lifted it back into place.

We had to get the 20 foot boards up into the cramped crawl space. The roof was made of sheets of galvanized steel. Each sheet was two feet wide and ten feet long. We had to remove a section to give us room to get the boards in place.

My six foot five inch body did not fit into the rafter area. I had to walk on my knees to get from one place to another. I was continually bumping my head as I tried to get my jack into place.

With three jacks on the same truss we worked together and lifted the truss till all the sag was gone. Then we nailed the 20 foot boards on to the trusses. It worked!

Then on to the second truss. Only 49 more to go.

Pounding the nails into the boards was a fierce job. There just wasn't enough room.

The sun was beating down on the galvanized steel roof. It was very warm and we were about to "hot to death." The ladies came every few minutes to keep a cold drink in our hands.

It was many days later that the final board was lifted and nailed into place. We were tired but happy with the results. The ceiling looked safe again.

Harold needed to go to St.Lucia, so we thanked him for his labor of love and took him to the airport.

The very next morning I went to the church and walked into the sanctuary to look at our finished job. I took one look and couldn't believe my eyes. The roof was sagging worse than before.

I ran and got my flashlight and ladder and made my way up through the ceiling. One truss was broken at the top and others were cracked.

I came down as fast as I could and ran for the phone to call Harold in St. Lucia. I was praying that he would be there. He answered the phone. I said, "Harold, the roof is sagging worse than before! What should we do?" Harold asked me if I had gone up to see the trusses. I said, "Harold, one truss has already broken and the others are cracking." He said, "Get out of the church and don't do anything till I get there. I'm on my way to the airport and will be there as quick as possible."

Harold rushed to the church from the airport and checked out the situation. I knew from the look on his face that things were very bad and very dangerous.

We went immediately up the ladder and looked again at the trusses. It seems we had added thousands of pounds to the already sagging trusses with all those 20 foot 2 X 6's we had nailed on.

Harold studied the situation and finally came with the bad news. Each of the 50 foot trusses had been made wrong and they all had to be taken down and rebuilt.

He said we would take one truss at a time, lift it out of it's place, and bring it down to the ground. Then we would take it apart and rebuild it and lift it back up into it's place. It was a big job and we needed to have lots of help to handle the weight of each 50 foot truss.

It took thousands of nails to put each truss plate in place. Many of the ladies came to pound the nails. We were rebuilding two at a time.

In order to get the trusses out we had to remove sections of the roof, six feet at a time. When we finished a truss we would lift it up in place and then take out another. It was a slow, tedious job but we all had fun working together.

Taking off sections of the roof was a major job because we had to be careful not to destroy the piece of metal roofing taking out the nails. We had to put it right back on after the new truss was put in place.

One day so many men showed up to help we put them to work removing the sections of roof. But they didn't just remove 6 feet. They took off 20 feet.

Things didn't go well that day and we got way behind. The trusses wouldn't come loose and we couldn't get them out. At 4:00 p.m. everyone started to leave and I looked up to see that massive 20 ft. hole in the roof. If it rained we would be in trouble and it usually rained during the night.

There we were just four of us left to put the roof back on before quitting. It was after midnight when we finished. We had worked 17 hours and we promised each other that we would never allow that to happen again.

It took us over a month to fix the roof and when the final truss was lifted into place we had a celebration. It was the biggest job we tackled while in Barbados but we saved the church thousands of dollars by doing it ourselves. We were proud of our work and ready to move on to something else.

Judy and I were nearing the end of our third year in Barbados. We had touched every inch of the People's Cathedral. Holmes came with a new verbal contract. "Please stay. Let's make it for twenty-five years this time. You and Judy never have to leave Barbados."

What a comforting statement that was, but I said to God in my prayer, "I'm ready to stay or go. If You don't call I'll spend the rest of my life here and know it's Your will. But, if You need me anywhere in the world, please call me and I'll know it's time to move on."

It wasn't long until the phone began to ring. Four different calls came the very next week.

The first call came from Westside Assembly of God in Davenport, Iowa. Pastor Ron Stevens was resigning and was saying, "Dave, I can't get you out of my mind. Would you consider being the new pastor at Westside?" I asked him for 24 hours to pray about it and to call the next evening.

I hung up the phone and called for Judy so I could tell her the big news. We got out the "Pentecostal Evangel" magazine that had listed the top 100 churches in the Assemblies of God in America. We looked down the list for Davenport, Iowa. We found Westside Assembly in 14th place. Attendance 2,150. WOW! What a phone call that was!

I called my mother and told her about Westside. She had the same magazine in her hand and said, "Son, are you sure you can handle that big church since you have never pastored before? Dad and I will be praying for you." One thing for sure my Dad and Mom knew how to pray!

In the meantime, Rev. Don Raymer and Rev. Cornelius were visiting with us. They had come for a couple of days from the Canadian Assemblies of God headquarters in Toronto, Canada. I thought they had come to see our Canadian missionary friend, Harold Skovmand. They needed a place to stay so we opened our home to them.

I wasn't sure if I should tell Judy in front of them but it was such big news I couldn't wait. I told Judy and the two preachers about being invited to be the new pastor at Westside in Davenport, Iowa.

Before Judy could respond, Don Raymer jumped up and said, "Hold it, Dave. We are here to invite you to Toronto to head a new department dealing with Family Life for the Pentecostal Assemblies of Canada. We didn't call you but flew to Barbados to talk to you in person. We need you to come to Toronto for an interview." I said, "But Don, Davenport called first so we must give them first consideration."

What a conversation we had for the next two hours. Don said that because they came in person that was better than a phone call so we should give our first consideration to Toronto.

Our third call came from First Assembly of God in Lancaster, Pennsylvania. Lancaster had a special place in my heart because The Couriers had been on television in that city on channel 8 for 14 years. To pastor a church in Lancaster was of great interest to me because of all the friends I had made through the years.

Our fourth call came from St. Maarten, another island in the West Indies. In fact, it is my favorite island next to Barbados.

Charles Vlahn, a wealthy business man and former Governor of St. Maarten, asked us to start a new church there. He was willing to build a new church and wanted me to be the new pastor.

I had been in St. Maarten for a Full Gospel Businessmen's breakfast and Charles had been to Barbados to speak in the People's Cathedral. He always told me that St. Maarten would be my next place of ministry.

I had been in Barbados for 3 years and had not received a call to go anywhere else. All of a sudden, in one week's time, I received four invitations.

What a choice! Two invitations by phone, two men who came in person with their invitation to Canada, and Charles Vlahn from St. Maarten.

I needed to pray. I needed help with my decision. Where did God want me?

I decided to visit each place in the order they came. If things didn't work out in Davenport, Iowa, I would fly to Toronto, Ontario, Canada next. Lancaster, Pennsylvania was third and St. Maarten was fourth.

Then came one of the toughest days of my life! I had to tell Holmes about the four calls and that I needed to fly to Davenport, Iowa, the very next week.

I sat at home pondering what I would say to Holmes, my best friend. Why should I leave Barbados? Things were going great. We were having five services on Sunday to handle the crowd. Life was really at it's best. I seemed to be at a peak in my ministry.

- Success Principle 38

WHEN YOU REACH THE PEAK
GET READY FOR CHANGE.

There's always another peak to climb
and, maybe, a greater challenge. As
soon as I finished one task the next
one always seemed to be more
important.

•　　　•　　　•

Holmes would never understand. He would think I was deserting him.

I went to the church and found Holmes in his office. I sat down in one of his comfortable chairs and took a deep breath. We had shared many conversations in his office but none of them felt like what I was feeling now. I was looking across the desk at a man whom I loved and highly respected. We had been all over the West Indies together. Every crusade we shared was etched in my memory forever. We had laughed and cried together. Holmes was a very caring man. I always had to be cautious about the things I needed because if Holmes heard me talk about something I wanted he would drop whatever he was doing and try to get it for me. I would rather have taken a beating than tell him I was leaving.

I finally closed my eyes and blurped it out. I waited with my eyes shut for his reply.

I heard his voice, almost in a quiet whisper, say "Dave, if God is talking to you and if He is asking you to make a change in your ministry, I would never want to stand in the way. Take a few weeks and go see if that's what you want to do. If nothing happens, we still need you here."

What an answer. What a friend!

A Reflection From Holmes Williams

During the three years of Dave Kyllonen's ministry at The Peoples' Cathedral, the outstanding qualities which contributed to the success of his ministry were those of humility and perseverance. Dave was always willing to be involved, not only with the big projects, but even with the humblest of jobs. No task was too small and insignificant as long as it was to help build the Kingdom.

He was constantly inspired with new ideas for the improvement and enhancement of the facilities, and never gave up until these ideas became reality. The Webster Dictionary defines perseverance as, "The steady pursuit of an objective." This quality of perseverance involves courage, patience and endurance in spite of obstacles and difficult situations. Sir Winston Churchill was once invited to his old school to address an auditorium full of school boys. The boys were encouraged to take notes of one of the greatest speeches they would ever hear. As he stood behind the podium he said, "NEVER give up!" After a minute's pause he continued more boldly, "Never give up." After another lengthy pause, pounding on the podium, he shouted at the top of his lungs, "Never, NEver, NEVer, NEVEr, NEVER give up!!!" That was the sum total of his speech that day.

Perseverance was a remarkable quality exhibited by Dave during his years of ministry at The People's Cathedral. A quality which made his ministry successful. Today, as we look around the church premises, we can see lasting results of his perseverance and ingenuity; beautiful landscaped gardens, nursery facilities and new office facilities.

Dave not only stood tall in stature, but tall in his example of hard work and perseverance.

> Rev. Holmes Williams
> Pastor, People's Cathedral
> Bridgetown, Barbados
> West Indies

CHAPTER NINETEEN

PASTORAL CANDIDATE.

JUDY AND I ARRIVED AT WESTSIDE ASSEMBLY OF GOD
in Davenport, Iowa, for the weekend. We met the staff and the offi-
cial board on Friday and Saturday but we would meet the church
congrgation on Sunday.

I was frustrated at first with some of the negative things that were
being said. Such as,

"This is his first church to be senior pastor?"

"I hear he's only a Gospel singer, not a preacher."

"If he is a friend of the existing pastor he'll never make it. We're
not going to have a friend dumped on us."

"We do not like long winded preachers. If his message is a long
one, our vote will be no!"

- Success Principle 39

IT'S NOT WHAT OTHERS SAY ABOUT
YOU THAT REALLY MATTERS IN LIFE.

*At first it affected me, but then
I realized that I had to be
myself and be confident with who
I was.*

GOD DEALS IN ABSOLUTES, NOT IN
COMPARISONS.

• • •

On the way to church Sunday morning I took a moment to talk to
Judy. I said, "Sweetheart, it doesn't look like we'll be moving to
Davenport. We'll never get the vote with all the negative things
we've heard so let's just relax and be who God wants us to be. To-

morrow we can move on to Toronto,'" We agreed just to have a great day. I would preach with all my might and not worry about anything else.

I preached an hour-long message, every time I preached in The People's Cathedral in Barbados. There was no way I was going to preach a brief message.now. I was at ease.

Judy was sitting with the rest of our family who had come in for the day. Greg and Kristie from Wichita, Kansas, Robin and Connie from Minneapolis, Minnesota. I was glad they were there. I felt their support.

Before leaving Barbados I picked a dozen messages I thought were my finest and put them in my suitcase. Surely, one of these would work for my "try out" sermon.

When I went to Davenport I couldn't decide which to preach. Nothing seemed to fit for Sunday's message. I had been preaching a series of messages from the book of Mark in Barbados. One message from each chapter. The last message was from chapter 13. The only thing I felt comfortable with was to go on with my series in Mark and prepare a new message from chapter 14. I would continue on like I was still in Barbados preaching my series from Mark's Gospel.

I approached the pulpit, read my text, prayed, paused for a brief second, and then jumped in with both feet.

This congregation was not only listening to my message, they were looking at me with great intensity. I thought, "Are my shoes shined? Is my hair combed to their liking? Do I have on the right suit? Does my tie match? Will they vote for or against me?'"

Those thoughts should have given me tons of pressure but, since I didn't have a chance of being elected anyway, I didn't have any pressure and enjoyed God's sweet anointing on the message.

When it was over, I felt good. I ministered to and prayed with the people at the altar.

Everyone was shaking my hand and telling me how much they enjoyed my message. It was a friendly church and they made Judy and me feel very comfortable.

On the way to the restaurant for lunch I thought, Dave, not everyone is going to vote no. Maybe God does have plans for me to be here after all. Then I silently added another line, "Oh God, I'm free to go anywhere in the world, why Iowa?"

On the way to church Sunday evening I decided to tell my family how I felt about the vote that would come after the service. I said, "I feel good about pastoring this church but you must understand that the vote will have to be 90% or more or I will not accept the position. They all agreed and would understand my decision after the vote was taken.

After the song service I invited my family to the platform to give special testimonies. I wanted the congregation to hear from all of us.

I preached a message entitled, "Without a Vision the People Perish!"

After spending some time in prayer at the conclusion of my message, my family and I were taken to the pastor's office while the congregation voted.

We all sat quietly in the office just looking at each other. They kept glancing at me to see how I was handling the situation. This was a big moment for our family!

The office door opened and in walked the present pastor, Ron Stevens, and the church deacon board. They were smiling and quickly began to congratulate me on being their new pastor. I paused for a moment and asked about the percent of the vote. Ron, in an excited voice said, "It was a great vote! 89%!"

My family looked at me and waited for my answer. I told them it had to be 90%. I knew my family so well I could hear their thoughts. "Is Dad going to cheat? Is 1% point close enough?"

- Success Principle 40

LET YOUR YEA BE YEA
AND YOUR NAY, NAY.

Our "word" is very important.
In 25 years, The Couriers never
signed a contract. Our word
was always accepted. We lived
according to our word.

• • •

I faced all of them and said, "I'm sorry, gentlemen, but I cannot accept the position. I needed a 90% vote, not 89%."

They all looked at me like I was crazy. Pastor Ron yelled out, "Dave, that's a great vote! Jesus himself wouldn't have gotten anymore! Come on, the congregation is waiting for your acceptance speech!"

I asked everyone to leave the office. I needed a moment by myself. I didn't want to hurt Ron Stevens, and I didn't want to appear cocky to the congregation. I knew the answer would be "No," but I needed some time to be able to say it right to the congregation.

Just then Jan Styre, a board member, came back to the office to see what was taking so long. I told him about the 89% vote and that I could not accept the position.

He then reached into his pocket and pulled out all the absentee ballots and said, "I knew the vote was so good that I never counted these." When they were counted and added up the vote totaled 90%, right on the money.

I jumped up and said, "I'm your new pastor. Let's go tell the congregation!"

CHAPTER TWENTY

WONDERFUL WESTSIDE.

THERE WAS GREAT EXCITEMENT IN MY HEART! I was finally a senior pastor.

My mind went back to the 7,000 churches I had visited in my years with The Couriers. In each one I had stood behind the pulpit and asked myself, "Could I pastor this church?" And, now, as I stood behind the pulpit of Westside Assembly of God I was saying, "Oh God, with your help, I can pastor this church."

Gregory, and Kristie were in Barbados when we got the original call from Pastor Stevens. They had finished with their mission's stint on the island of Trinidad and were taking a few days of vacation with us before going back to the States. I asked them then, if they would be interested in being our associate pastors at Westside. They said they would be a part of our "try out" day to see if that was the way God was leading them.

After the vote was in, their answer was, "Yes, we'll come and be your associate pastors."

Now there was double excitement in my heart. I was comfortable with Gregory. I deeply respected his understanding of the ministry. His convictions were very much like mine and his dedication to God and this ministry would allow us to work together smoothly.

While Judy and I flew back to Barbados to say good-bye and get our things, Gregory and Kristie moved from Wichita, Kansas, to Davenport, Iowa.

It was a quick trip back to Barbados. I preached three more times. Just enough to finish my series in Mark, chapters 14, 15, and 16.

It was hard to say good-bye to Holmes and Rosie and the congregation at the People's Cathedral. The final service was filled with lots of tears and many hugs.

When our plane lifted off the runway I looked down one more time at that little nation, only 14 by 21 miles, and thanked God for three great years of ministry to some of the sweetest people on earth.

We flew to Harrisburg, Pennsylvania, to put our house up for sale and pick up the rest of our furniture. We packed a U-Haul truck and headed for Davenport, Iowa.

We arrived on December 16, 1984, and it was bitter cold. In Barbados the temperature never got below 70 degrees, so our blood had thinned out and we were freezing. We had given most of winter clothing away so we needed to go to the mall and buy coats and boots. But that was OK because we had not been in a mall for three years.

We arrived Saturday in Davenport and Sunday was the starting of the annual Singing Christmas Tree. We got in on the final rehearsal.

We had big crowds all eight nights. Excitement was in the air. We were meeting many new friends. We were off to a good start. 1985 looked like it was going to be an incredible year.

I met Rev. and Mrs. Oscar Hamilton. They had been working on staff two years as the senior citizen's pastors and, they told me later, they were afraid I was going to replace them with someone else. I put my arms around them and told them how I admired them for their more than 50 years of ministry. I told them I was proud to have them on my staff and that they could stay as long as they wished. The expressions on their faces and the smiles of relief were priceless. I loved them dearly.

- Success Principle 41

ALWAYS APPRECIATE THE WORK OF THOSE
WHO HAVE GONE BEFORE YOU.

"For in this case the saying is true,

> *One sows, and another reaps.*
> *I sent you to reap that for which you*
> *have not labored; others have*
> *labored, and you have entered into*
> *their labor."* (John 4:37,38) NASB

•   •   •

That was a real tough winter for us. We couldn't seem to get warm. I caught a terrible cold and Judy got pneumonia. But we survived.

Spring came, and with it came warmth and new energy. I decided to walk around the church and make my list of things I thought needed immediate attention.

The carpet was worn out, even threadbare, in many places. The upholstery on the pews was spotted and dirty and children had even pulled out the padding in many places. The ceiling and walls needed paint. The gymnasium was painted a dark brown and looked like a dungeon. Some of the tiles had come up from the gym floor so it was dangerous to play basketball. The bathrooms were too small and the men's room had a terrible odor that needed immediate attention.

Then I walked out to the bus garage. There were 16 purple buses sitting all in a row. They were old and looked like they needed attention too. When I got closer they really looked bad. I walked around them for a few minutes while Jim Curtis, our bus mechanic, gave me the list of repairs needed to keep them on the road. He said, "Every bus needs new tires, batteries, brakes, heaters, and a tune-up." He also said, "The State inspector is coming at the end of the month and will probably ground all the buses."

Our bus budget was sparse but we did manage to repair eight buses and buy new tires for them. They barely passed the inspection. The inspector said next year he would be tough on us. He had let some things go this year; but next year would be different.

And that wasn't the only problem. At the end of my first year as pastor, our insurance company called to say they were canceling our insurance on all the buses. I got on the phone and said, "Please, you have to help me. I've only been here a year and I need these buses running next Sunday. Don't cancel us now. We need a little more time." Then the insurance agent said to me, "Pastor Dave, do you know how many accidents your buses have had through the years?" I said, "No sir, I don't." He said, "My records show me that you have reported 252 accidents. On one Sunday alone, you reported 8 accidents. I quietly accepted the cancellation and hung up the phone in disbelief.

The price tag for insurance from any other company would be exorbitant. Nobody was insuring buses older than 1977. All of ours were from the 60's.

I made the announcement to our congregation the next Sunday, "The bus ministry is over for now, but we will start it back up again when we are able to buy newer buses." God had prepared me years before for making tough decisions. The congregation understood and accepted the news graciously. The very next day we sold all the old buses to a man who wanted to buy them for parts. He paid us $3,600 for the whole lot.

My walk through the Educational Building which housed the Christian School and Day Care, the youth auditorium and children's church was also discouraging. The building had never been air conditioned and Iowa is as hot in the summer as it is cold in the winter.

The first maintenance project we tackled was to refurbish the platform. We extended the platform to make room for a bigger choir and orchestra. When it was finished and carpeted it looked good.

Sooner or later, I knew I had to tackle the restrooms. I was embarrassed when I thought of guests and visitors going into either the ladies' or the men's rooms.

Herman, the maintenance man, assured me that with the help of several men from the church, he could fix, repair and refurbish both restrooms for half of what it would cost a professional. I said, "Herman, we'll start tomorrow morning."

The next morning Herman and I got two sledge hammers and went to work on the men's room. I said, "Herman, we've got to find out why this restroom has such a bad smell."

We knocked out the walls and discovered a pipe that should have been connected to one of the urinals, but wasn't. The floor behind the wall was two inches deep with urine.

That was a day to remember. Sometimes a pastor's job includes doing something that he never studied in Bible College.

- Success Principle 42

   NEVER OVERLOOK A JOB THAT
   NEEDS TO BE DONE, EVEN IF
   IT'S ONE YOU DON'T LIKE.

   "Poor is he who works with a negligent hand, But the hand of the diligent makes rich." (Proverbs 10:4) NASB

   "The soul of the sluggard craves and gets nothing, but the soul of the diligent is made fat." (Proverbs 13:4) NASB

• • •

Some of the projects I worked on in Barbados were exactly the things that needed to be fixed in Davenport. The Lord had prepared me for this task. During the seven years I pastored at Westside we refurbished every inch of our facility.

- Success Principle 43

GOD IS CONSTANTLY PREPARING US
FOR WHAT HE HAS IN STORE FOR US
AT A LATER TIME.

The Bible says that God prepared
David for every task that he
would do. First he killed a lion,
then a bear, then he met Goliath,
the Philistine, and finally he
was made king of Israel. Each
experience enabled him for what
was coming next. (see 1 Samuel 17:36)

•　　•　　•

From the beginning, Gregory and I shared the pulpit. One Sunday I would preach in the morning service and he in the evening service. The next Sunday he would preach in the morning and I would preach at night. When he preached, I would lead the worship and when I preached, he would lead the worship. I would preach in the sanctuary on Wednesday evening while he preached in the youth service. This "team effort" was a great success.

I always believed that the young men in ministry would never learn how to preach by sitting and watching. They need to get up and stand behind the pulpit and learn by doing.

- Success Principle 44

GIVE A MAN A FISH AND FEED HIM
FOR A DAY. TEACH HIM HOW TO
FISH AND FEED HIM FOR A LIFETIME.

Hands-on experience is the most
thorough method of learning.
I learned that singing in the
practice room was easy, but in
front of people it was hard.
Preaching in the woods by myself
was a different story than
standing in the pulpit with a
congregation waiting on each word.

•   •   •

In one of our early conversations I said to Gregory, "If I ever hear anyone come into church and say, Oh no, the associate is preaching, you'll be finished and I'll do all the preaching."

There were times when I wondered if people were coming in on Sunday morning saying, "Oh no, the senior pastor is preaching today."

No one ever told me how to conduct a wedding, funeral, or baby dedication. I had always watched but never paid too much attention to what was being said or done. I learned by trial and error and ended up loving to do all three. They were highlights in my ministry. I worked hard to make them special days for the members of my congregation.

During my seven years as pastor of Westside assembly of God we lived some incredible days. We had many weddings, baby dedications and funerals.

One month I preached eleven funeral services. Runge's Funeral home wanted to put my name on one of their office doors, especially when I had three funerals in one day.

I remember one wedding in particular. A couple who didn't attend our church wanted to renew their wedding vows after 25 years of marriage. They didn't want a big to do. Just a short ceremony in my office would be fine. They expected two or three of their friends to be there.

I suggested that it might be more meaningful if we did the ceremony in the main sanctuary. Sacred vows needed to be said at the altar, if possible. They liked the idea and the time was set.

There was no need for a rehearsal. We would just meet in the altar area of the church for the brief ceremony on Saturday at 1:00 p.m.

I arrived at the church on Saturday about an hour early. The building was empty except for our custodian, Alta Tinder, who was making sure everything was ready for Sunday. I told her about the couple that was coming to renew their wedding vows, but not to worry, we would only be in the altar area for a few minutes.

At 12:45 there was not a soul in sight. I asked myself, "Are they coming? Did I have the right Saturday?" At 12:50 I looked out the window again and not one car had arrived. At 12:55, still no one in sight.

At 1:00 o'clock everything happened at once!

Cars, lots of them, came into the church parking lot. Many people were making their way into the church sanctuary. The bride came rushing up to me and whispered in my ear, "Pastor, where can I put on my wedding dress? I want it to be just like the first time. I can't let my husband see me until the music starts and I walk down the aisle."

I tried not to look surprised but I was thinking, "What music? Coming down what aisle? And who are all these people? Don't tell me she has changed her mind and now she wants a big church wedding. We hadn't even had a rehearsal!"

I sent her to a room near the gym and told her I'd be back to see her in a few minutes. I ran upstairs to the sound room. We were going to need music. I wasn't sure I knew how to run the sound system or even turn it on, but after pushing many buttons I got it working.

I found the cassette tape machine but I knew there wasn't any wedding music around so I finally chose, after listening to as many tapes as I had time for, a worship tape that sounded like something we could use in a wedding.

I ran to find Alta, the custodian, and said to her, "Alta, now they want the works. I need your help. Please come to the sound room so I can show you what to do."

She said, "Pastor, I have never been in the sound room and I don't know anything about it." I assured her that it was easy and I would show her very quickly what to do.

I said, "Alta, when I signal you from the platform, just push this button to start the music and here is the slider you push to arrive at the right volume. Only two things to remember. You can't go wrong. It's you and me, Alta. There isn't anyone else in the church that can help me. We are going to conduct a wedding together. You from the sound booth and me from the platform. Thanks for helping me, Alta."

I hurried to find the bride. She was dressed and ready to go. She had on the fanciest wedding gown money could buy. I remembered her telling me that this was to be a short ceremony in the front of the church and that she wouldn't be wearing a gown.

I gave her a few instructions about coming down the aisle and I told her about my signal to Alta to start the music and that she should wait till she heard the music before she started down the aisle.

Then my next step was to find the groom and the best man to tell them of our plans. Everything was set and, after we prayed, we walked out on the platform and took our places. Things were going well.

I signaled Alta to start the music. She pushed the cassette deck button but nothing happened. I remembered that the music didn't start for 20 seconds and that I had forgotten to set the tape to start right where the music started. Alta was shook up. She started pushing the slider for more volume. All she could hear was a hiss. When she had pushed the slider to the top, the hiss was very loud but still no music. I knew when it started the sound would be deafening. I was standing on the platform with the groom and the best man. How could I tell her to turn it back down?

Meanwhile, the bride got mixed up and started down the aisle when I signaled to Alta for the music to begin. She was walking down the aisle to the loudest hiss you ever could imagine. Just as she arrived at the front, the groom yelled out to her, "Go back, go back, you're not supposed to come until the music starts!"

Somewhere, between the bride going back up the aisle and the groom yelling, "Go back," the explosion of music happened!

I was hysterical!

It was a video moment and could only happen once in a lifetime.

"Dearly beloved" didn't come out easily that afternoon. But I told you that weddings were my specialty and this one was turning out to be very special.

The bride and groom and all the people left the church in a hurry after the ceremony. As I was leaving I said to Alta, "That wedding will go down in Westside's history as the funniest wedding ever. Too bad you and I were the only ones here to experience it!"

One morning I opened the door to the old choir room, which had become a cluttered storage room. "What a big room," I thought. "It must be 15 by 40 feet. This could be a great office for me." And the longer I looked at it the more I was convinced.

My office was small and the walls were paper thin. Counseling was difficult, especially, when someone would get emotional and yell at me or begin to cry out loud. Everyone on staff could hear what was going on and I hesitated to talk to anyone there.

I called all the staff and asked them to come to the old choir room. I told them that I would like to move my office to this room. I waited for all the reasons why I shouldn't but no one said a word. They all walked back to their offices like it was no big deal.

The very next morning I called for new paneling, paint and carpet. I made sure that insulation was put between the walls to make them sound proof. When it was finished it was beautiful. I had room for anything I ever wanted to put in an office.

And one thing I put in was a 160 gallon fish aquarium. I'm not sure if people made appointments with me to seek counseling or if they really came to see my fish.

"Chubby Cheeks" was my favorite. He was a big, fat Pacu whose face always seemed to be smiling. In fact, it was Chubby Cheeks who brought groups of children from the congregation into my office every Sunday morning before Sunday School. They would stand in the doorway and ask, "Can we see Chubby Cheeks, Pastor?" To be sure, those moments are a part of my cherished memories of pastoring at Westside.

However, there is one memory I have concerning that fish tank that I wouldn't mind forgetting.

One week day morning I came into my office and, as was my usual custom, I went immediately over to check on my fish. Lo and behold, all the fish were lying on their sides in about six inches of water trying desperately to stay alive. But the odd thing was the carpet around the tank was dry! Where did 150 gallons of water go?

Well, the little room directly under my office was the storage room where all the church records were kept and --- yes, you guessed it! A hose had become disconnected from the filter on my aquarium and was lying on the floor along the wall. All through the night that filter pumped water into the room below. What a mess!

The office girls should have been paid triple that week. They graciously helped me clean it up and were even willing to smile at me from time to time.

I loved to produce illustrated sermons. Three or four times a year I prepared an illustrated message that would be a surprise to everyone.

One of those "Surprise" messages was about the feeding of the 5,000. I asked Judy to bake five small loaves of bread and find two whole fish to bake but not destroy how they looked. She brought home two of the nicest trout, each about 10 inches long. I needed them to look like I had just pulled them from the stream that morning.

I headed for the church on Sunday morning with my message, my Bible and two baked fish and five loaves of freshly baked bread. It was all tucked away in a lunch basket.

I knew this was going to be a morning when no one would sleep during my message.

As I preached about the little boy bringing his lunch to Jesus I reached into the lunch basket and brought out five loaves of freshly baked bread. I offered a piece to the people sitting near the front of the church and everyone reached for his piece. The bread smelled so good and the taste was scrumptious. We all ate together while the rest of the congregation looked on.

I thought, <u>maybe next time more people will sit up front</u>.

Then it was time for the fish. I carefully pulled the two beautiful trout from the basket and held them up for everyone to see. They looked like they had just been caught.

Since everyone was so eager to take the bread I asked who wanted to help me eat the fish. No one raised their hand or reached for the fish. No one suspected that they had been cooked and were ready for eating.

While everyone was following me carefully with their eyes and listening intently, I took one of the fish and took a big bite!

Then we passed the fish along the row and as long as it lasted, others broke off their bite.

With such rapt attention I needed to preach this kind of sermon every Sunday.

- Success Principle 45

PREACHING IS 90% PERSPIRATION
AND 10% INSPIRATION.

*After you've poured your life
into prayer and study for your
sermon, you must not forget to
pour your physical energy into
it also. Be creative in
getting your point across.*

•　　•　　•

Another Sunday morning I didn't intend to preach an illustrated sermon but it turned into one anyway.

I was talking about how sometimes we put 60 cents in a coke machine and nothing comes out. I explained that in frustration, we give the machine a good kick hoping that the can will shake loose and fall.

I walked over to an imaginary coke machine on the platform and gave it a great big kick. Well, my shoe came off and flew into the congregation. I think it landed in about the sixth row.

This happened in the first service and as folks were leaving and I was shaking their hands, many said, "Pastor, if you're going to do that again, we're going to stay for the second service."

Then I'll never forget my illustrated "Lazarus" message.

On Saturday night I called Gary Patrick, one of our board members, to help me during the message in the morning. He would be the perfect Lazarus. Gary was 6 foot 7 inches and weighed about 225 pounds. He wanted to know what he would be doing but I told him it was a secret and that he should meet Judy in the gym during the worship part of the service.

I was excited! Only three people knew what was about to happen. Gary, Judy and myself.

I was preaching away and having the time of my life building up to the time of Lazarus coming down the aisle. I was glad we had kept it a secret. I was wondering how Gary would look. Then it was time. With great excitement and with a loud voice, I called out, "**Lazarus, come forth!**" Nothing happened, so I called again, "**Lazarus, come forth!**"

The door at the back of the sanctuary opened and there stood Gary. His huge frame was covered with white gauze. He had to walk stiff legged and his arms were straight out from his sides with gauze and white tape covering every inch of his body.

His head was the best part. There were two little slits so he could see and two little holes so he could breath. All the rest was covered with white gauze and tape. He was a great Lazarus!

But, it was amazing! Not one person turned around to see what was happening. So I pointed and shouted, "Look, there he is! There he is!" Still no one turned around to look. They just knew there wasn't anyone back there and they weren't going to be fooled.

Then Gary began his walk down the aisle to the platform. Row by row the people finally saw him. It was awesome! This giant stiff legged and stiff armed "Lazarus" was actually walking to the platform. No one knew who it was and Gary was playing his part to the hilt.

When he reached the front I said to the pastors sitting on the platform, "Loose him and let him go!" They began to unwind the tape and gauze from his head and when the people could see it was Gary they gave him a thunderous ovation.

"Lazarus, come forth," will never be forgotten at Westside. I'm still enjoying the memory and the surprised look on each person's face.

Richie and Patty Karl invited Judy and me out to dinner one evening. We had had brief conversations with them at church but this would be our first time to really get to know them. Little did we realize that night what special friends they would become for the rest of our lives.

Richie really surprised me when he said he was a golf pro and had won the 1976 B.C. Open in Endicott, New York. Because I am a golfer, too, we set a day to play together.

Playing with a pro is not the easiest thing to do. When I hit the ball as far as I could Richie would step up and hit his ball fifty yards or more beyond mine.

We played nine holes and stopped for a hot dog and a coke. I said, "Am I doing anything wrong?" I nearly choked on my hot dog when he said, "Pastor, you aren't doing anything right."

So, over the next few years Richie totally revamped my golf swing. He gave me a new driver for Christmas and a new golf bag for my birthday. However, my score didn't seem to get any lower.

Every year he gave me tickets to the Hardee's Golf Classic at the Oakwood Country Club in Moline, Illinois. I followed him during those tournaments and felt so proud to be a personal friend of Richie Karl's.

I liked Richie because he had the ability to talk to me on a level that few laymen can. He would fascinate me with his ability to ask questions that sometimes only preachers are willing to ask. He seemed to understand the ministry. I enjoyed every moment I could be with him.

One day Richie's wife, Patty, called and asked for an appointment. I was surprised because she seemed to have everything under control and I wondered why she needed counseling.

Patty is a beautiful person, attractive, classy, with great poise and the vice-president of Home Interiors whose headquarters are in Dallas, Texas.

When she came into my office I knew something was wrong. She sat down in a chair and struggled to get started.

She cried as she told me Richie was an alcoholic. It had been a problem in their marriage from the start. Now it was about to wreck their home and their marriage. Richie desperately needed help. Since I was his pastor and good friend, surely, there was something I could do to help Richie save his life and save their marriage.

I set an appointment the next day for Patty and Richie to meet me in my office. After a few minutes of small talk, Richie began to tell me his story.

All through his army life he had hit the bottle. While on the Pro Golf PGA Tour he would play Thursday and Friday and miss the cut. So, he would get drunk to forget the putts he missed. Now the drinking was out of control and he was desperate for help.

I had heard about the A A program but had never seen their book. I said that I would get a copy of the program and that I would meet with him and Patty in my office at 1:00 p.m. everyday for the next 28 days. I would give them two hours every afternoon and we would go through the program together.

On the day the A A book talked about a "Higher Power," I put the book aside and brought out the Bible. It was time for Richie to hear God's Word and respond to a call for salvation. He had to understand that his "Higher power" had to be Jesus Christ. Nothing else could be substituted. We prayed the sinner's prayer and ended the session.

Richie and Patty came to church the next Sunday morning and, after my message, Richie responded quickly to the altar call and fell on his knees at the altar. I remember it like it was yesterday. I saw Dr. Herb Wood, a chiropractor and long time member of the church, move quickly to pray with Richie. He prayed for him with great emotion. I knew a miracle was taking place in Richie's life. He was becoming a new creature in Christ Jesus.

When he got up I could see a difference on Richie's face. He told me it was as if his feet were glued to the floor and he couldn't move once he got to the altar and he felt as if a hose had been put in his head and totally washed him out.

Our A A program would continue, but Richie won the victory over alcohol at the altar that Sunday morning. Praise the Lord!

Today, eight years later, Richie still has not had another drink of alcohol. He is one of the pro instructors at the famous Eagle Ridge Golf Course in Galena, Illinois, and plays in some of the tournaments on the Senior's PGA circuit.

In a recent telephone conversation he told me, "Pastor, the next big tournament I win, I'm going to send you a check!"

"Oh, Lord, let him win!"

Pastoring has it's good days and it's bad days. It's like riding a roller coaster. Some days you go slowly up the hill and the next week the church moves at such a fast pace you just sit back and hold on for dear life.

It's climbing up the slow, steep hill when discouragement drags you down and you want to quit.

There was a time when our church was trying to reach the top of the hill but nothing was working and it seemed like we were stuck. We couldn't get moving no matter what we did.

One morning Gregory and Kristie called and said they were coming over to the house for a visit. I hung up the phone and said to Judy, "The kids are coming over for a visit and I think I know what it's all about. I think they are coming to tell us they are leaving." We had quite a conversation while we waited for them to come.

It seemed like an eternity before their blue van pulled into the driveway. There was such an odd feeling about this visit. It sure wasn't the norm for them to visit us in the middle of the day.

Gregory had four big, helium filled balloons in his hands. He and Kristie came smiling into the living room and sat down. I thought, "Boy, I never heard of bringing balloons to a meeting when you are going to resign. Maybe I missed something along the way."

Gregory began his speech as Judy, Kristie and I listened. He said, "Kristie and I have come to encourage you today. You and Judy are carrying a heavy load and we are beginning to worry about you. A lot of the things you are carrying you have to let God carry for you. So, today, we have brought each of us a balloon and a magic marker pen. We are each going to write on our own balloon everything that is bothering us and after we write all of our burdens on the balloon we are going to go outside and let them go up to God."

What a relief came over both Judy and me. This was turning out to be a very special meeting. Much different than I had expected.

I wrote about thirty things on my balloon. It was covered. Everyone was busy writing. When we finished we went to the front yard. We had a prayer time and asked God to take care of all these things. We were tired of carrying them and now we were sending them up to the heavens for Him to carry.

We let our balloons go at the same time and watched them for several minutes as they traveled high and away and finally out of sight.

The feeling was exhilarating. I was lifted in my spirit as new energy rushed into my life at that very instant. We hugged each other and went back into the house for some lunch.

The neighbors must have thought we were crazy but that moment changed our lives. We worked and preached with such freedom after that. Every time the devil brought up a problem I reminded him of, "The day of the balloons." God took care of the rest.

- Success Principle 46

**GOD IS BIGGER THAN YOUR
BIGGEST PROBLEM!**
*"Casting all your anxiety on Him because
he cares for you."* (1 Peter 5:7) NIV

• • •

Frank Carillo and his girlfriend, Sheila, began to attend our church and after the service one Wednesday evening they asked me if I could marry them on Saturday. "Oh no," I said, "I don't know you very well and I need a few weeks to counsel with you and learn more about you. Sacred vows are just that, Sacred." Then they told me their story.

They were living together but knew it was wrong and wanted to make it right. I gave them a proposal that night. I said, "Frank, you must move out of Sheila's house and live in your own apartment. Both of you must come to the services every week and you must pay your tithe faithfully every month. If you do this successfully, for one year, I'll be willing to marry you one year from today.

I never expected to marry Frank and Sheila but they did exactly what I said they should do. They never missed a service and faithfully paid their tithes. I married them, in the church, one year later. They were two of the most loyal people I ever pastored and are still attending the church today.

- Success Principle 47

**HIGH STANDARDS WILL PRODUCE
A HIGH LEVEL OF ACHIEVEMENT.**

*Don't be afraid to set a high
standard. Don't sell people
short. Everyone needs a
personal challenge.*

•   •   •

One of the biggest, most challenging, and, definitely, most spectacular projects I ever tackled was Westside's **Christmas Tree Lane**.

We turned our nine acres into a drive-thru Christmas wonderland
with over 40,000 lights and 200 freshly cut Christmas trees added to
the many trees and shrubbery already on the property.

We divided the property into sections. As cars entered through
the huge Christmas wreath at the beginning of the Lane they first
passed through Chrildren's Village.

Here we had life size displays on both sides of the lane of all the
familiar cartoon characters like Donald Duck and Huey, Dewey and
Louie. A 10 foot. Frosty the Snowman was there to delight the children. And to really spread Christmas cheer we had members of our
congregation dressed in Walt Disney costumes (the kind with the big
heads) to wave and pass out candy.

Turning the corner you sat and watched, for a moment, an ani-
mated light show which portrayed Noah sending the dove out of the
ark to see if the flood water had receded.

Then you found yourself driving down Old Fashioned Main Street
where shoppers in their long, old fashioned dresses and bonnets
called out a cheery, "Merry Christmas."

You drove past a little church with a live congregation listening to
the message from the parson. You passed the general store, the bank,
and the candy store, arrived at the train station where the conductor
was calling, "All aboard."

And, of course, a small town from yesteryear was not be complete without it's water tower and blacksmith shop. So we had ours, complete with live ponies and a live smithy pounding away at his anvil.

Traveling on down the lane between beautiful lighted Christmas trees you passed through the gates into the little town of Bethlehem. You drove past the shepherds' field where shepherds were tending their sheep and warming themselves around the fire.

At the Bethlehem Inn you felt sorry for Joseph and Mary, who was sitting on a donkey, as the Innkeeper emphatically shook his head from side to side to say, "There is no room here for you."

Then you felt relief when you arrived at the manger scene and saw Mary and Joseph and baby Jesus, all cozy and warm, snuggled in the hay. Sheep, donkeys and soft, brown cows who, with their eyes, bid you, "farewell," as they placidly watched you drive on.

Next you drove through a section that depicted the Life of Christ. You past one scene after another with live characters displaying the miracles Christ performed. It was a great witness to unchurched people about the "Mighty God" we serve.

As you made the last turn you were face to face with our grand finale. Thirteen men, twelve disciples and Jesus, dramatizing Leonardo De Vinci's, "Last Supper."

We actually built a room, that was a replica from the Bible era, on a flat-bed truck and placed in it a long table covered with white table cloths. The table was loaded with food. Cheese, crackers, grapes, apples, nuts, cookies, donuts, hot chocolate, coffee and Frank's famous bean dip. It kept everyone warm for sure.

The whole "Living Lord's Supper" scene was framed in a beautifully carved picture frame, extending out 3 feet, and painted gold. The scene was 30 feet long and 20 feet high.

Car after car would stop and look carefully at all the disciples sitting with Jesus and wonder if they were real people. After holding a certain position for about 20 seconds, the men would change to another pose and hold that for about 20 seconds.

It was the highlight of our entire "**Christmas Tree Lane.**" People told us how special it was and the special feeling that surrounded the whole scene.

I had the best job of all. I got to stand at the exit and receive everyone's kind comments. I then had the privilege of inviting them to church and giving them a packet containing promotional material.

It was a lot of work to set everything up before December 10th and many days it was very, very cold outside. But on opening night everyone forgot all the work and jumped into their costumes and ran to their set before 6:00 and took their places for the first hour and a half. Then back to the gym for hot chocolate while the second shift took their places.

To look down the road and see the cars lined up for a couple of miles was exciting. Over the next ten days, 30,000 people would drive through our parking lot and enjoying the incredible feeling that all of us helped to make. The lights, the Christmas music and our whole church congregation turned our town into a great celebration.

- Success Principle 48

PERSPIRATION ON THE BROW IS
A TRUE MEASURE OF UNITY.

A successful project is *all based
on pulling together as a team.
It unified our church.
A successful family must all work
together toward common goals.*

There was a young couple who had just moved to Davenport from Pennsylvania and decided to visit our church on a Sunday evening.

It just happened to be in the middle of our drive through **Christmas Tree Lane** presentation.

When they arrived at the church a few minutes before six o'clock, they got the surprise of their lives. Policemen were controlling traffic. There was a long line of cars to get into the church parking lot. They followed the waving arm of the policeman and got in line.

Moving slowly they made their way to the church. Now they were really interested in our church. This had to be some kind of a special church to have cars lined up for two miles trying to get in the parking lot.

After forty five minutes of following the cars in front of them they arrived at the entrance. Nobody else was getting out of their cars so they just kept following the cars in front of them. They drove through Christmas Tree Lane and decided this was the church for them. They could hardly wait to attend the service. If the preliminaries were this spectacular what must the services be like!

I was passing out our church literature at the exit when they stopped their car and accepted our packet of information and asked me, "When does your evening service begin? Where do we park? Which building is the main sanctuary?" Their story was quite funny and the next Sunday morning the congregation enjoyed their testimony of coming to our church for the first time.

Christmas Tree Lane was definitely the greatest ministry outreach the Quad Cities had ever seen. Over 30,000 people drove through with thousands of pieces of literature placed in their hands. They even listed this event in the Book of Tourism for places of interest to visit in the state of Iowa.

Many nights huge tour buses drove through the lane. I enjoyed driving through on the buses and talking with the people. When I told them I was the pastor they all had to shake my hand and thank me for making their Christmas extra special.

I'll always remember the people who worked with me on staff. Gregory Hollis, John Spurling, Ron Mooberry, Oscar Hamilton, Tim Taylor, Rod Solomon, Jeff Diltz, Mark Garber and Rod Anderson.

There are so many stories, but not room enough to tell them all.

Gregory and I did most of the preaching at Westside, but John Spurling was known as our "Specialty" speaker. I asked John to preach on Super Bowl Sunday night. He was eager to preach and accepted the opportunity even though the crowd was slim.

He did such a good job that I asked him if he wanted to preach on Memorial Day weekend and he gladly accepted the opportunity. Then came the 4th of July and on to Labor Day. The church began to expect John to preach on all the odd weekends of the year.

I would love to preach in the church John now pastors but I'm sure he would say, "Dave, how about Super Bowl Sunday or Labor Day?"

Jo Lummer, my secretary, was a big help especially since Westside was my first pastorate. She got me through a lot of hard places the first few months. She handled any job I gave her with expertise. But I wish you could have seen her face when I announced I would be gone for a few days and she would have to take care of my fish. She didn't like to see "Chubby Cheeks" gobble a gold fish or handle long slimy night crawlers.

A church staff is as awesome gang. Someone has described them so well.

- Pastor

Able to leap tall buildings in a single bound. More powerful than a locomotive. Faster than a speeding bullet. Walks on water. Gives policies to God.

- Associate

Able to leap short buildings in a single bound. As powerful as a switch engine. Just as fast as a speeding bullet. Walks on water if the sea is calm. Talks with God.

- Minister of Education

Leaps short buildings with a running start. Almost as powerful as a switch engine. Faster than a speeding BB. Walks on water if he knows where the stumps are. Talks with God if special request is approved.

- Minister of Music

Clears a quonset hut. Loses race with locomotive. Can fire a speeding bullet. Swims well. Is occasionally addressed by God.

- Minister of youth

Runs into small buildings. Recognizes locomotives 2 out of 3 times. Uses a squirt gun. Knows how to use the water fountain. Mumbles to himself.

- Church secretary

Lifts buildings to walk under them. Kicks locomotives off the track.
Catches speeding bullets with her teeth. Freezes water with a single
glance. When God speaks she asks, "May I ask who is calling?"

CHAPTER TWENTY ONE

ON THE ROAD AGAIN!

IN JULY OF 1991, I RECEIVED A TELEPHONE CALL
from my good friend, Glenn Pyles, that would change the destiny of
my life!

I met Glenn and Margaret Pyles after a Courier's concert in Peoria,
Illinois. He introduced himself to us and told us he owned a trucking
business in Goodfield, Illinois. He invited us to bring our bus to his
garage for a free fill up. I told him our fuel tank held 140 gallons but
Glenn said it didn't matter, he would fill it up.

We went there the next day and Glenn filled the tank. He said,
"Hey guys, anytime you're in the area come on in and let me fill your
tank, on the house."

Over the years we managed to find Glenn's place often, especially
when the fuel gauge said, "Empty." His gift of thousands of gallons
of fuel was a tremendous help to The Couriers.

I picked up the phone and said, "Good morning, Glenn, it's good to
hear from you. What can I do for you?" He gave his usual greeting
and then got right to the point.

Seven years ago he had taken a trip to the country of Panama to
visit friends. They took him to a small church of less than 100 people
on Sunday. The church building and parts of the church had never
been finished during their building program.

God began to speak to him about sending money to finish the
church and help with the pastor's salary. He started sending monthly
support to the small church.

He visited Panama twice a year and found 23 other little churches
that were badly in need of repairs. They were pastored by men who
received little or no salaries. Glenn felt impressed to support these
little churches.

None of the pastors had been to Bible School. They needed teaching on how to preach, what to preach, how to give an altar call, how to conduct church business and dozens of other church related functions.

Then Glenn said, "Dave, I need you to fly to Panama to conduct seminars for 10 days for all the pastors and their wives. You could preach at night in the different churches and show them how to preach and give an altar call.

What he was really asking was that I give them a four year education in just ten days!

I said, "Glenn, I'm pastoring this big church and it's taking all my time. I couldn't possibly go to Panama now. You'll have to find someone else to go for you."

There was a long pause on the phone then Glenn said, "Dave, you owe me."

Then I remembered all the gallons of fuel he gave us. I said, "Glenn, I'll go. I'll get the money and I'll take the time." It was amazing how fast our conversation changed!

I gathered some friends together including Rev. Richard Arrowwood, Rev. Ron Mooberry, Dr. Lyss and Denny Gray. We flew into Panama City and met all the pastors and their wives. We started immediately into our all-day teaching seminars. We had services each evening in a different church. I was having a good time with all my new friends.

I was extremely fascinated by an American couple from Kokomo, Indiana who attended the seminars. They were missionaries to the Darien Jungle and had come to Panama City for a few days of rest and to attend the seminars. The Darien Jungle was 150 miles from Panama City near the Columbian border.

Dennis Cook and his wife had brought their five children to Panama to evangelize the twelve villages in the Darien Jungle. The more they told me about their work the more interested I was.

I told Dennis that I was a man of adventure and would love to visit the Darien Jungle. He said, "Dave, why not come after your ten days of teaching and preaching are over."

We went to the airport and in a few minutes my ticket was changed to give me two extra days to visit the villages in the Darien Jungle.

I left with Dennis to travel 150 miles to his home in the jungle. It was a smooth ride for about 20 miles, then the pavement abruptly stopped. Dennis slowed his 4 wheel drive Bronco to ten miles an hour. There must have been a million pot holes. I bounced all over that vehicle and held on for dear life.

When I was totally exhausted from all the bouncing, I asked Dennis how much farther we had to go. I nearly fell out of the car when he said, "Dave, we're almost halfway there."

Somehow I held on and we finally reached Dennis' house after a long ten hour trip.

The last half mile was the hardest. Getting to his house from the road was thick mud over a foot deep. Thank goodness we were in a 4 wheel-drive vehicle or we would have never made it.

I was finally in the Darien Jungle. Dennis' house had no lights and no running water. When the sun went down he brought out his propane tank with a long metal stem coming out of the top and at the end of that there was a light bulb. Dennis lit the bulb and put it in the middle of the house. This was our only source of light, except for a candle or two.

We had supper and I was all ready to relax after our long drive when Dennis said that we should go to the village and have a service. I wondered how we could do that, unannounced, but he said all we had to do was "ring the pipe" and everyone would come to the church.

We headed for the village carrying the propane light. All the huts were built on stilts, even the little church. We rang the pipe and waited for the people to come.

The little church filled up. I counted a hundred people inside and many were standing around the outside.

Dennis asked me to sing and preach and he would be the interpreter. I was so tall in comparison to them they called me "The giant." My bass voice really scared them. In fact, some of them ran from the service when I started singing.

Then it was time to preach. I wasn't sure what to say to these totally uncivilized people. They didn't live with any modern conveniences; no electricity, no bathrooms, no stoves, no cars or bicycles.

I told them the simple story of the Gospel. How they could bring their burdens to God and how God loved them so much He gave His only Son to die for them. It came from deep within my heart. No matter where you are in the world the Gospel message is still the same. It never changes!

After I finished my message and prayed for them, they wanted to sing for me.

I cannot describe to you how moved I was. I have heard the finest in the Gospel music world. I have heard Dove Award winning talent that brought people to their feet amidst roaring applause. I have heard unbelievable harmonies and rhythms coming from our nation's best choirs, but nothing has moved me like the choir I heard that night when those Panamanian Indian's sang for me in a dimly lit thatched roof hut.

What a night we had. No one wanted to leave. They shared their love with me and I felt at home.

Before we left the village that night they performed a native dance for us in the middle of the village. Dennis explained this was a rare thing. It meant they had accepted me and I felt good about my first night in the Darien Jungle.

Dennis and I stayed up most of the night talking about his work. He was teaching the villagers how to plant trees, plants and crops, besides teaching them the Word of God.

He said that God called him to reach all twelve villages in the Darien Jungle with the Gospel. The last village was so deep in the jungle it took him eight hours to walk one way to have church. He tried to visit all twelve villages twice a week, every week.

He said he would never be finished with his task and he would die with his boots on in the Darien Jungle and never come back to America to live again.

As the night passed, Dennis got very big in the flickering light and I got very small. I felt I hadn't done anything with my life. Something oozed out of Dennis' life in the early hours of the morning and came across the room and oozed into my life. From then on I would never be the same man.

I arrived back home and went to the pulpit on Sunday morning to preach my missions message. Before I ever spoke a word I just stood and looked at our church.

We had just finished putting in new carpet and new pews. The church sanctuary had been painted and I knew the church had never looked better.

Yet, at that moment, I could only picture Dennis Cook 150 miles from civilization in the Darien Jungle, preaching his message in that dirty, little, thatched roof hut in the middle of the village surrounded by thick mud.

And he wasn't getting paid. He was doing it for free.

I said a prayer to God in those first few seconds that no one in the congregation could hear, "Oh God, why am I preaching here this morning? Look at me. I have it all. A wonderful home, a new van, and a paycheck every week. All the luxuries of life are mine. Please, God, if you need me anywhere in this world I want you to know I'm willing to go, even if it's for free."

- Success Principle 49

TO FOLLOW GOD, SOMETIMES YOU MUST
BE WILLING TO LAY IT ALL ON THE ALTAR!

• • •

I preached my message that morning without knowing that God did have a major job for me to do and that I might even be doing it for free.

The rest of July went by quickly and in August Judy and I were visiting in a city hundreds of miles away. I found myself sitting in a deacon's home talking about becoming the new pastor of their church. I shared this with Judy and the rest of our family. It seemed like our girls called everyother day to talk about it and ask if we were going to make a change.

I promised God when I went to Westside that I would stay seven years and I never gave leaving a minute's thought during those seven years. Now those years were coming to a close and I was feeling transition in my heart.

Around that same time I was visited by a deacon from another church who came to my office and asked me if I would consider leaving Westside to pastor their church. I told him I would call him in a few days.

I knew transition was coming. Panama had done something special to me and I was still praying, "Oh God, I don't know what you have in store for my life, but remember, I'm willing to go anywhere in the world."

Now it was September. Paul Eschbach asked if he could marry our daughter, Robin. I gave him a big "Yes," and their wedding date was set for **September 20, 1991**.

This was all happening right in the middle of all the talk about making a change and pastoring another church.

One month later, on October 21, Gregory and Kristie invited us to their house for supper. Gregory asked me if I was still considering leaving Westside and I said, "I don't know where I'm going or when but I am definitely looking to make a change."

He said, "Would you consider going on the road as singing evangelists?" He brought up the call from Mark Fox, a singing evangelist from Nashville, Tennessee, who came to our church for a weekend. We had sung as a trio on Sunday evening. It went over so well Mark asked us if we would like to sing full time.

I told Gregory that we would have to leave the girls behind and maybe that wasn't a good idea.

I reminded him that I had traveled over two million miles with The Couriers and wasn't interested in that life style again. But I suggested an idea that I thought would get me off the hook.

I said, "I will consider going back on the road again if the whole family will go. That means Mike and Connie, Paul and Robin, you and Kristie, Elijah, Isaiah and your new baby due in January, and Judy and me. There would be magic in all of us going together."

Gregory, Kristie and Judy couldn't believe what I had just said. They made me say it again. After a few minutes Gregory said, "I think I know where Mike and Connie are ministering. They are in Neilsville, Wisconsin, in a four day meeting and I'm going to find out which hotel they're staying in and call them right now."

What a conversation we had for the next hour. Mike and Connie had transition in their hearts, too, and asked, "All of us? Together? Had we talked to Paul and Robin, yet?"

Questions and more questions. Both Mike and Connie thought it was a great idea and that we could count on them if everyone else said, "yes."

I never saw such excitement in Gregory and Kristie. Even Judy was talking a mile a minute.

We called Paul and Robin. They had only been married one month, so this call would be very interesting. It was getting late and I thought maybe we should wait till the next day to call, but I was over-ruled.

Sure enough, they had already gone to bed. It was their first month's anniversary. What could we be calling about at this late hour?

I talked to them first. I told them the whole story and asked them about the possibility of them joining the rest of us in a ministry on the road. They listened to the plan and said they would call back in the morning.

We didn't know Paul well, as yet, and wondered what his reaction would be. He did say he'd always heard newlyweds should not live near their in-laws the first year of marriage.

Judy and I went home late that night. We had a feeling in our hearts like we never had before. I was excited about the possibilities. Maybe God had plans for us that we didn't know about as yet.

The next day Paul and Robin called with excited voices. They couldn't sleep and had talked all night about their future and were calling to give us their "yes." They wanted to go on the road with all of us. My whole body was shaking with excitement. It was really happening.

We arranged to meet near Minneapolis, Minnesota, the following Monday. This would be an all day meeting and we should come ready to pray and talk about our future.

Not another soul knew about that meeting. We met and talked all day. Everything was positive. No one was talking about the negatives and I didn't either. I knew that I could travel on the road but I wasn't sure about the rest of my family.

What would we travel in? I only knew about buses.

I called a bus company that day and asked if they had any used buses for sale. The salesman told me there were at least six or seven available. I told him we'd be there within the hour.

The girls asked some big questions. Where is the bathroom...? the shower...? hot water...? washer and dryer...? and 1,000 other things they said they needed.

I told them that it all had to be built in. This looked impossible to them. The money it would cost to fix these buses would be something we could never afford.

The salesman gave his final price at $40,000 a bus. It would take over $200,000 to refurbish them and still they would be old buses that no one wanted anymore.

We knew that day that buses were not going to be a part of our lives.

We started looking at RV's to see if they had what we needed. We checked out every motor home, every fifth wheel and every travel trailer on the market.

There was a lot of excitement building in our hearts; anticipating a new adventure.

We had several meetings in the next two weeks, and finally decided on a date for all of us to resign our present ministry positions.

January 5, 1992, would be resignation day.

We planned to start our new ministry on February 23, 1992.

The Couriers were having a big reunion in November in Harrisburg, Pennsylvania, and my whole family decided to go. We didn't know if we could travel together. A long trip with ten people squeezed into two vans would surely prove our patience, our temperament and our flexibility.

I called my brother Paul, who was pastoring a church in Chambersburg, Pennsylvania, and ask him if we could have a service in his church Wednesday evening before the reunion concert. My whole family would come and we'd sing a few songs.

When that day arrived, no one was aware that this was our very first service together. The secret we were carrying just between us was exciting.

When you know that you know that you know something is right it feels good. We were beaming from ear to ear. It was going to work!

Our decision to travel was sealed. With our commitment, determination, hard work, and God's help, we knew we could be a ministering family.

Christmas was just around the corner. The more we talked about our future and what it would cost we all decided we could not afford to buy even one gift that year.

So we came up with a plan. We would write letters of encouragement to each other instead of buy gifts. This meant I had nine letters to write. A letter to Judy, my mom and dad, my three girls and each of my sons-in-law.

It took me a long time to write my letters. I labored hard to put on paper my thoughts and feelings about my family. Writing letters to my sons-in-law wasn't the easiest thing to do. It was always easy to talk to them, but putting my feelings on paper was the hardest task I had encountered in a long time.

It would have been much easier to go to Dillards Department Store and buy each one a gift.

We decorated our Christmas tree as usual, and put up all the decorations around the house. But something was missing. There were no gifts under the tree. I was asking myself, "Are we doing the right thing?" But we had all agreed to write letters, so we would stay with the plan.

Christmas morning came and everyone was arriving at our house. They had their stacks of letters to put on the tree. After a few minutes the tree took on a whole new look. It's branches were holding a hundred white envelopes.

It was family time and we were all together talking and dreaming about the next years of our lives. It wasn't just one member of the family changing his life, brother, it was all of us.

For weeks we had to be careful not to mention to anyone that we were resigning. Today, we felt relieved that only family were in the house and we could talk, talk, talk.

We sang some Christmas carols. I read the Christmas story from Luke, chapter two, and we prayed. All three things were done with more intensity than ever before. We knew in eleven days we would be resigning and starting our new family ministry and we were the only ones that knew. The atmosphere was extremely intense and my family was enjoying the moment together.

Now it was time to open our unusual gifts!

The letters were taken off the tree one by one and passed to each of us. I held my letters in my hands and counted them to see if I had gotten a letter from every family member.

No one knew for sure what to do next. We sat in a big circle and stared at each other. Should we open our letters now? "Yes," I said, "Let's read our letters to ourselves."

I opened my mom's letter first. What did she think about me, her oldest child, starting a brand new ministry at this time of my life?

Mom's letter was priceless! My mother told me again that she loved me very much and with great tenderness wrote, "We're behind you, Son, with our prayers and support. God will go with you and help you minister to millions of hurting families!"

I reflected back to the story my mother had told me years before.

When she was just a young girl, she had a strong desire to be in youth work or to be a missionary. As the years rolled on she never had an opportunity to fulfill these tasks.   Now she was pregnant with me so she poured her desires into me.

She wanted me to be a strong child so she walked one mile, every day, until the day I was born. She read the entire Bible through during the nine months and memorized many Scriptures so that I would love God's word. She painted, stenciled, and decorated for the whole nine months and hoped that I would be creative.

She prayed for three things to happen to me. One, that I would have a strong voice. Two, that I would be a missionary. Three, that I would love young people and motivate them toward Godliness.

All of those traits she poured into me before I was born are in my life today.

She didn't tell me until all of them had come to pass. She never preached to me about doing them, she just prayed that they would come to pass. How interesting.

I didn't read but two or three lines until tears welled up in my eyes. I was trying not to cry but, finally, I gave in and let the tears run. I looked around the room to see if anyone was watching me. I was so blessed when I saw everyone else crying, too.

- Success Principle 50

HAVE THE ABILITY TO SHOW AND SHARE YOUR INNER EMOTIONS WITH YOUR FAMILY.

*This was not the time to push down
emotions; this was the time to
let them surface. I was getting
involved with my feelings.
Judy always told me that I was a
better husband and dad when I shared
my deep emotions - from my heart.*

"Pleasant words are a honeycomb,
sweet to the soul and healing to
the bones." (Proverbs 16:24) NIV

• • •

We were having the greatest hour of our lives. All of us were involved with our feelings and the tears were flowing freely.

Every letter was precious and built us up for the new challenge ahead. As I read my last letter I knew I was ready to travel around the world with my family.

- Success Principle 51

MONEY CANNOT BUY WHAT A FAMILY CAN GIVE.

Someday the man with the money
will look at the man with the
family and say, "I'd sell it all
to have what you have!"
It makes you feel good to give
your family love, appreciation,
character and time. It's the
simple things in life that
bring the most happiness.

• • •

We couldn't do anything about our new ministry until January 6th. We couldn't call pastors about having us in their churches. We couldn't send out letters announcing a new ministry available for services. We couldn't even talk about what was happening because no one knew we were resigning. We had kept the secret, even from our families, for 52 days.

The new year, 1992, started and I was preparing my message and my resignation letter. The 5th of January was going to be a tough, emotional day. Saying "Good-bye" to the congregation I had cared for, laughed and cried with for seven years wasn't going to be easy.

Sunday morning finally came. The news would be out in a few hours. Fifty- two days of secrets were now going to be known by all.

I worked all week on my message for this special morning. I entitled it, "God's Distinguished People."

While I was preaching, I realized that the message was for me. God had given me a message for myself.

Only three points but they all spoke to me.

1. **Unready, but employed by God.**
2. **Unwilling, but enabled by God.**
3. **Unusable, but exalted by God.**

I used David's life story and, since my name is David, every time I said "David" in my message, I knew it was me that God was talking to and about. What an encouraging message God gave me for my resignation Sunday.

After delivering the message I began to read the following letter.

To the congregation at Westside.

In the last seven years I've had to do a lot of things for the first time. I've learned about baby dedications, weddings, funerals, counseling and board meetings, just to name a few. Today I must learn how to resign.

Gregory and Kristie Hollis and Judy and I hereby resign from our pastoral positions effective February 23, 1992.

Books tell me that's all I have to say, but, when I see you today and think about who you are I must say more.

We will not forget all our treasured moments among you while we have been here at Westside.

No amount of pride, recognition or church growth is sufficient for me to make a final judgment on the success of my ministry here.

The ministry is like farming. There is planting, cultivating, fertilizing and watering. Waiting for the harvest can sometimes be long. The proof is in the crop. I must wait till the end for final judgment. Paul said, "Judge nothing before it's time."

We are not leaving because of trouble or frustration but we are leaving knowing that we gave our best for seven years. The church is on a high, not a low, and the physical condition of the church is fabulous. I feel we are handing the next pastor a piece of gold.

This new year, 1992, opens up days of opportunity for all of us. But please remember there is difficulty in every opportunity but opportunity in every difficulty.

This congregation will enjoy new leadership, new methods, new ideas and new voices.

We are not leaving you for a better church. All three of our daughters and their husbands are joining Judy and me to birth a new ministry called "Homefire." We will minister to hurting families all across America.

The task is incredible, awesome and unbelievable but, "If God be for us who can be against us."

This will be the biggest undertaking my family has ever dreamed of or hoped to do but the future is in God's hands.

We are risking everything, so we ask for your prayers. By the way, our houses, our cars and our stuff is all for sale.

Thanks for all your kindness to me and my family. I'll always appreciate your loyal support.

God bless you for allowing me to fit in a great chapter of my life with you.

We love you very much.

Pastor Dave Kyllonen and his wife, Judy.

Pastor Gregory and Kristie Hollis and their two boys, Elijah and Isaiah.

PS. If I could ask for anything from this church on my final day, I would ask to have a copy of all 700 messages I have preached from this pulpit during the last 7 years.

Thanks a million!

It was over. Everyone sat stunned for a few moments. Then some turned to others and quietly spoke to one another saying, "Can you believe it? They're leaving." Others were crying and some even sobbed out loud.

I slowly walked to my office and sat down at my desk in silence.

CHAPTER TWENTY TWO

©HERGIE

FATHER OF THE BRIDE.

I THOUGHT RESIGNING MY CHURCH WAS EMOTIONAL
but the next day, when all the kids came back home, now that was
emotional.

Judy and I had been living by ourselves for the last nine years.
The quietness of the empty nest was wonderful. Things were going
to be different now. All of us on the road in two RV's. There was
going to be lots of noise and activity.

Gregory and I put our houses up for sale immediately. Because of
that, we couldn't have our kids, with all their stuff, filling every nook
and cranny. Prospective buyers may not appreciate our piles.

So, Paul and Robin moved in with Grandma and Grandpap Kyllonen.

Our good friends, Bob and Kerry Walker were away on vacation
and offered their house to Mike and Connie.

However, we spent everyday, all day, at our house. We had one
long continuous family meeting as we discussed our future together.

We were still looking for two RV's to travel in and trying to figure
out how we'd pay for them when we did find them. We also ordered
a new P A system. Letterhead and stationery was being printed. I
was on the phone booking dates for the year. Practice was three
times a day; morning, afternoon and evening.

Kristie was only three weeks away from having her third child.
"What a time to have a baby," I said to Judy. "How can we handle all
these things at the same time?"

We learned to live one day at a time.

It seemed as though we were giving up everything we had worked
for. Security of a home, a weekly paycheck, cars, all our stuff we

thought was so important... just the routine of life we were comfortable with. The empty nest had felt good.

But something inside kept telling me there was something out there worth risking it all for. After living in a "get" society all my life, now God was asking me to bring it all back to the altar.

In the hub-bub of all this activity I couldn't help thinking back to the girls' growing up days.

Sitting in the family room in my big, over-stuffed arm-chair, I let my mind drift.....I had missed many of those precious days being gone with The Couriers. Maybe now God was giving me another chance.

There were many times when they didn't understand why we made certain decisions concerning their activities or why we would not allow them to date early or establish relationships that were a high risk.

Now they were going to be a part of our ministry. Judy and I saw such balance in their lives. They were trustworthy and supportive, willing to work hard; they were classy in their appearance along with an inward beauty. Their spiritual lives were pure and giving and full of compassion. They were organized, talented, thrifty and wise.

We valued their desire to want to be involved in ministry with us.

I found that daughters have an infinite capacity of love for their dads.

It seems like yesterday I was walking them down the aisle at their weddings.

Kristie was the first to get married.

She called from Central Bible College in Springfield, Missouri, and said, "Daddy, I've found Mr. Wonderful! His name is Gregory Hollis from Wichita, Kansas. His dad is Jonathan Hollis, pastor of the Colonial Heights Assembly of God Church, who went to Bible School with you. Gregory asked me to marry him and, Daddy, I love him very much. I know this is the man I want to live with for the rest of my life."

Gregory and Kristie came home to talk about wedding plans. Our new little church, Christian Life, in Camp Hill, Pennsylvania, was meeting in a warehouse. It was decorated nicely like a church but it was small and it was still in a warehouse building. Kristie said, "Daddy, I have a good idea. Let's have the wedding in our back yard."

So the wedding date was set. June 6, 1981.

It was a great day. We worked on the yard for several weeks before the big day. We trimmed every bush and every tree. We had planted all white flowers for the wedding but it was still a little early and they were not in full bloom.

But, my Mom came to our rescue. She found a whole garbage bag full of artificial flowers in the church dumpster. She dipped them in a bucket of white paint and set them in the flower beds among the natural flowers. We all stepped back and said, "It is good."

The gnats were having a big year and our yard had millions flying around. What could we do about getting rid of them for our big day?

Our friends, Dick and Jo Garber, who came to the wedding from Peoria, Illinois, solved our problem. Dick is in the "yard" business and knew exactly what to do. He rented a chemical fog machine and sprayed our yard all morning. By wedding time the gnats were gone.

One big tree in the yard was in bloom with little white blossoms and during the ceremony, when the wind blew, the little white blossoms floated down over the congregation as though angels were throwing confetti from heaven.

Jonathan Hollis and I would share the duties of the wedding. Jonathan would introduce the wedding party as they came down the aisle. I would escort Kristie down the aisle. He would perform the ceremony and I would sing and preach a special message.

My heart was pounding as the organ played and music filled the whole block. I stayed in the house with Kristie until it was time to walk her down the long, white runner that led to the altar.

We stood there for a moment and I said to her, "Kristie, this is a wonderful day for you, but if you have any reservations about marrying Gregory today and want to stop the wedding, I'll back you up all the way no matter how bad the embarrassment.

She looked up at me with the sweetest smile and took my arm and said, "Daddy, this is right. I love Gregory and want to marry him. Let's go."

I felt happy in my heart as we walked together down the aisle to stand in the shade of the two, giant 30 foot trees that spread their branches over the wedding party. Kristie had chosen right and I knew she would be happy for the rest of her life.

We met Gregory at the end of the aisle and I gently kissed Kristie and gave her hand to Gregory. Tall and handsome, he looked great in his white tuxedo. He began to sing to Kristie and I realized that God had brought into our family a man whom we could respect because he would love, cherish and care for our daughter. He lives by Godly principles and his submission to God makes him a strong husband and father.

I didn't tell anyone about my message because I wanted it to be a surprise. I entitled it, "TOGETHERNESS."

T --- Time management
O --- Ownership
G --- Gentleness
E --- Endearment
T --- Trust and obey
H --- Happiness that's real
E --- Emotional support

Obviously, a twelve point message was too long. Right between point seven and point eight Connie fainted. Judy, my mom and some of the wedding party were rushing to assist her. There was nothing I could do but stop the wedding. I, too, ran to help her and discovered that nothing was seriously wrong other than common wedding day jitters and not eating properly. In a few minutes she was back on her feet and I continued my message.

R --- Relatives, watch out!
N --- Nice, keep the honeymoon going!
E --- Eternity, these vows are forever!
S --- Sweethearts, always!
S --- Success is loving what you do.

As a part of the decorations in the altar area we tied 150 helium filled balloons, 75 in each cluster, to the plant stands that held the big white chrysanthemum bouquets. Each balloon was the size of a basketball so that, when we cut the strings to let them go as an act of celebration, they literally filled the sky above our yard as they floated off into the clouds. The congregation clapped and cheered.

Along with our family, everyone sensed that truly this was, "A match made in heaven."

From My Daughter, Kristie

The missionary was finished speaking, it was time for the offering. I opened my wallet and all I had was the same $20.00 I was to use to buy Greg's new Bible. Oh, he wanted it so bad. Do I give or do I buy the Bible? Of course, I give. The Bible will have to come later. After church the owner of the bookstore came to Greg and said, "The Lord told me I should give you this," Then he gave him the very Bible he had in his hands that afternoon. Things like this happen to me all the time. Why? I'll tell you.

As little girls we would hear these words, "Kristie, Robin, Connie, come in now, it's family meeting time." We would all sit down on the couch and Daddy would begin. He would tell us what he wanted us to be as a family and as individuals. One of the biggest things he wanted in us was a giving heart.

We would discuss what we wanted to give to this need and to that need. A family needed groceries or they needed a baby-sitter and they didn't have money to pay. As a young girl I began to feel the needs of others. Tears became a part of my life. I cry at the thought of someone in need.

Daddy is one of the most generous men I know. For a father who had nothing as a boy, in the way of goods, he gave us girls all we wanted but also taught us how to give it away. I look at his life and I am amazed over and over again. Giving is just a part of his daily life.

I guess I can say the biggest thing he gives is his life. He gives his life to Jesus to use everyday. He taught us girls that this was to be our #1 goal in life. He would say, "What have you given to Jesus this week?" That changes the way you live your life and you begin to look for opportunities to help others.

I wake up every day loving life. Loving the fact that I'm giving it all to Jesus. Daddy told us to marry men who were giving. He said, "Marry a stingy man and your marriage will struggle." All three of us wanted a man just like our Dad. I found mine. Greg helps me with balance or else I would give everything away. Many days in our home we are making piles and lists of things we are giving away. We are raising our three children with the same principles. We, as a family, are learning how to give it all.

I thank the Lord He gave me a dad who taught me that giving is happiness. It's the way God uses us.

Daddy, I gave you away to all the people who loved The Couriers but, really, you were giving yourself away to the Lord. He is blessing us now as we are giving ourselves to Him every day. Best of all, now we are doing it together.

God always pays back one hundred fold. For the first 18 years of my life you were gone, traveling here and there ministering for the Lord. Now we wake up everyday only a few feet from each other. Starting each day with a touch, a look, and a smile. I love the way God does things; you never loose by giving to God.

Thanks, Daddy, for giving to me all you have and most of all, all you are.

I love you!
Your #1
Kristie

A Letter From My Son-in-Law, Gregory

It's always a tough day when you meet your future Father-in-law for the first time.

Kristie said, "Make sure your car is clean, because Daddy says, `If he's willing to drive a dirty car - he's probably wearing dirty under-wear!' Dave Kyllonen - out of the ordinary! What an unusual man and what an interesting life!

Dave, there are three things I see in your life. First of all you have always been a laborer. Prov. 16:26 says, "The laborer's appetite works <u>for</u> him; his hunger <u>drives him on</u>." You are definitely a driven man! I've seen your hunger for souls. I've watched your unwillingness to live with the status quo. You are a laborer who is worthy of his hire.

Secondly, I've observed you as a leader. Your example as a leader has proven to be very effective. "To this day their children and grandchildren continue to do as their fathers did." II Kings 17: 42. You have led your family by your indelible example. Our children usually reveal what kind of leader we <u>really</u> are, and yours have truly shown you.

Finally, you are a man who has left a legacy! The legacy you have given your family and friends is an eternal one! II Cor. 4:18 states, "So we fix our eyes not on what is seen, but on what is unseen. For what is seen is temporary, but what is unseen is <u>eternal</u>."

Eternity has always been your view. I've watched as you have given it all up for eternal rewards. That is a legacy worth leaving!

Dave, thanks for letting me be a small part of your OUT OF THE ORDINARY LIFE! I am richer because of your LABOR, your LEADERSHIP and your LEGACY.

Your son-in-law & friend,
Gregory

Connie was our third daughter but she was the second to get married. Before I tell you about her wedding, let me take you back to how it all began.

During the school year of 1988, at North Central Bible College, Connie began to share her dream with me. She said, "Dad, God has touched my heart for missions and I have a desire to put together a ministry team and travel overseas. Do you think I could organize a world trip like The Couriers have done?"

My heart welled up within me, so proud that my number three daughter wanted to follow in my footsteps.

She was only 23 and single but confident that this was God's will for her. I knew that whatever she set out to do she would accomplish. Through the years, as a Courier kid, she had listened, observed and caught on to our unusual ministry.

I assured her with a resounding, "Yes." She could put together her own team and travel overseas.

- Success Principle 52

THERE'S A TIME FOR BEING
A DREAMER AND THEN
THERE IS A TIME TO BE
A DREAM BUILDER.

*Give your children more than an
education - give them a dream!*

•   •   •

It wasn't long until Connie called to say, "I've got my team, Dad. It's Dene' Beard, Mike Hammer and me. We're calling our group, "Press On."

They discovered that they could visit twelve nations of the world by following the Pan Am Airline's world tour schedule. The total cost would be $15,000.

Connie called again, with disappointment in her voice, to say," I don't think we can raise $15,000 for the tour in such a short time."

I said, "Connie, don't give up your dream. Let's think about it. I'll call you in a few days."

The following week I encouraged Connie to book fifteen churches. Maybe each of them would give $1,000 toward the trip. It wouldn't take long to raise the money they needed. I also gave her a date for our church at Westside and told her we would give the first $1,000.

Her voice raised in excitement! She already had $1,000 support raised. I could tell she was dreaming again.

"Press On" came to our church in a few weeks and sang and presented their vision to our congregation. Everyone responded and the offering totaled $1,650. They were on their way.

By the time they traveled to California they had raised all the money they needed.

"Press On's World Tour, January 12th to July 12th, 1989."

Australia, Philippines, Hong Kong, Singapore, Malaysia, Thailand, Germany, Austria, Poland, Switzerland and England. This trip would change their lives forever.

They called home every month and I always asked Connie, "Is there anything going on between you and Mike?" The answer was always, "No Dad, Mike is not interested in me."

Toward the end of the tour Connie called with the news that she and Mike had fallen in love.

One day we got a package in the mail from Mike.

It was a video that Mike, himself, had made. He was in a cozy room with a fire in the fireplace and he sang a beautiful romantic song. When the song ended, he sat down on the couch and began to talk to us. He told us he was in love with Connie and wanted permission to marry her.

The video was priceless, to say the least.

The next evening Mike called and asked if we had received the tape. I said, "Yes, Mike, we've already looked at it."

"Well, what's your answer?" he quickly asked.

I told him he would receive our answer via video tape.

The next day we started to make a video tape for Mike with our answer on it. I made my office look like the President's office. I sat behind my desk and thanked Mike for sending us his tape. I was as serious as I could be as I told Mike what I expected out of a son-in-law. I told him how proud I was to state that our answer was a great big, "Yes."

I thought it would be fun to ask the whole congregation to vote whether they approved of Mike marrying Connie. We took the video camera to record their response. The crowd stood to their feet and clapped and threw offering envelopes in the air. They cheered and yelled in such a fashion that Mike would never doubt that Westside was in favor of the wedding. Then they sang, "Where He leads I'll Follow."

The next day Gregory and Kristie came to the house to add their, "yes," to the video. Dad and mom came over and they, too, wanted to say their, "Yes."

Robin called from Minneapolis and asked us to send her the tape so she could say her big "Yes," too. She walked around the campus of North Central Bible College and interviewed many of Mike and Connie's former classmates and faculty members and asked them the big question, "Should Mike be allowed to marry Connie?

We ended up sending Mike a 2 hour tape just to say, "Yes, Mike, you can marry Connie. We will cherish that tape forever!

After they returned home Connie came to me privately and said, "Dad, I am so anxious for you to share your message for Mike and me at the wedding. But you know Dad, sometimes you can be kind of long winded and I don't want to be one of those fainting brides, so I have an idea. We can bring our living room furniture into the church and set it up on the platform. Then the wedding party can sit down while you preach the wedding message."

Mike Hammer and Connie Kyllonen's wedding day. February 17, 1990, in Davenport, Iowa, at Westside Assembly of God.

After we decorated the church, we all agreed the living room scene was spectacular. We surrounded it with a dozen trees painted white and filled with white twinkle lights.

Excitement was in the air as Connie and I paused before going down the aisle. I said, "Connie, if this isn't right and you aren't sure about Mike being your husband, I'll help you handle all the embarrassment. We can still stop the wedding." She held on to my arm and squeezed tight as she said, "Dad, I love Mike and want to be his wife. He is waiting for me. Let's go!"

When it was time for my message I unveiled a painting I had asked Marge Coleman, an artist in our church, to paint. It depicted a narrow river with white water rapids going through the middle of the picture. On one side of the river a great storm was brewing and the sky was dark and cloudy but on the other side the sky was beautiful with all kinds of colors. Over the water she painted a wooden bridge made with 15 planks. Each plank represented a verse in I Corinthians, chapter 13.

♥ **God's description of perfect love.** ♥

Love is patient.
Love is kind.
It does not envy.
It does not boast.
It is not rude.
It is not proud.
It is not self-seeking.
It is not easily angered.
It keeps no record of wrongs.
Love does not delight in evil.
Love rejoices with the truth.
It always protects.
It always trusts.
It always hopes.
It always perseveres.

♥

Near the end of my message I went behind the platform and brought out a big, heavy, eight foot wooden plank. I suggested that it would fit under the picture as a mantle, somewhere in their house. I said that I was actually starting to build their bridge and through the years they would have to continue to lay the planks over their troubled times.

When Mike and Connie left on their honeymoon I knew Connie was in good hands. Mike was a great choice for a husband and father.

My Dad, Dave Kyllonen

I have always been proud of my Dad. He lived a very public life. I watched him always surrounded by people who appreciated him and, yet, I can never remember being pushed aside or sent to the background. Instead he always included us and was glad we were there.

It seemed everywhere we went people knew him. Because he was on TV in our hometown, even my school teachers and friends knew him. I'm glad he was always the same, at church or at home. I remember asking, "Mom, is our Dad famous?" She would say, "Yes, but that doesn't give you the right to go through life expecting special privileges."

He was the best singer and preacher in the world. I loved to listen to him tell about the places he had visited, the ministry that took place, and the people's reactions. I always said to myself that I was going to do that some day, too!

Dad brought home for me records of other singers and I would sit by the stereo for hours and practice singing just like them. Then I would call the family in for a concert, (as if they hadn't heard it already!). Dad was always challenging and encouraging. By challenging, I mean, he would ask me what the song meant. If my answer wasn't good enough he'd tell me I wasn't ready to sing it. That's how I learned that a song wasn't just a pretty melody but a message that, when believed, goes forth with power and anointing.

He's still my favorite singer. He has enthusiasm and enjoys himself to the full. He always gives 200%.

He's passed on to me a love for singing and travel. I absolutely love it when people tell me I remind them of my dad. After all, I've been working on it for 31 years now!!

Love, Connie

A Letter From My Son-in-Law, Mike

Dave Kyllonen, you are an "out of the ordinary" man in every way. From your name, to your tall frame, from your deep down voice, to your style extrordinaire. I've come to respect you greatly, not only as a father-in-law and ministry associate, but as a friend, too! You've been my mentor for ministry. This is what you've taught me:

-You possess a unique style of leadership. You lead more by presence than by proclamation. You seldom roar out the commands like a lion. You're like the bull in the barnyard. You don't say all that much, but everyone just knows you're in charge and can charge if necessary. You lead by your presence.

-You've demonstrated the reality that living an anointed life is just as important as preaching an anointed sermon.

-You've always challenged us to give our best no matter how small the crowd. Doing just enough to get by is not only heating the people, it's cheating yourself and God.

-You're the best when it comes to closing a service. You have the ability to take an insignificant thought and turn it into a piece of gold. You don't lean on clichés.

-You've always had a remarkable platform poise. The serv ice never seems out of control or awkward. When the service throws you a curve ball, you hit it out of the park everytime.

-You've taught me that you've got to dream dreams in life that are bigger than yourself. Life really starts when the dream begins.

Thanks, Dave, for the privilege of traveling with you. These are unforgettable gifts that will shape my life and ministry forever.

Love, Mike

Robin was the last to get married. She had so many boy friends I thought she would have been the first to get married.

She always said that she wanted to be involved in full ministry but the boys she brought home or dated had other desires for their future.

I cautioned Robin that happiness would come for a few years but, over the long haul, if she didn't do what she desired in her heart she would be a very sad woman someday and not be able to change.

After graduation from North Central Bible College, Robin was hired on staff as the Student Activities Coordinator for the school. A couple of years later she took a three month sabbatical to work in the Bible School in Argentina.

They were three great months for Robin. Her phone calls and letters were filled with excitement and happiness. She came back to her job at North Central ready to go on with life.

One afternoon, she got a call from Paul Eschbach, the associate pastor at Templo De Fe, the Hispanic church in St. Paul, Minnesota. He needed tickets for his youth group to attend a concert hosted by North Central. He asked Robin about her trip to Argentina and, before the phone call was over, he was asking her out to dinner so he could hear more about her trip.

Robin's call to me was one I will never forget. "Dad, I have found Mr. Right. His name is Paul Eschbach. He is a preacher and works full time in the church as the youth pastor. I've been attending the church and have enjoyed working with the Spanish people. I want to bring him home in the next couple of weeks. I know you'll like him."

When they arrived for the weekend, Judy and I spent quality time just sitting around talking with Paul and Robin. Paul talked about himself and we talked about our family. Our conversation was a very meaningful experience. Paul watched us and we watched him.

It was a time to be accepted and understood by each other and it was a time to express our feelings and become aware of each other's feelings. We tried hard to be ourselves and it worked.

We were happy about Paul and Robin's relationship. Robin had found the perfect man.

The wedding would be in September and I was glad about that because they were being married in the little Spanish church in St. Paul. Winter would not have yet arrived in Minnesota.

We found the church on the corner of Payne and Jessamine Streets and accomplished the task of decorating the church. We enjoyed the time of rehearsal and the dinner with the wedding party, family and friends.

I went to bed late that night at the hotel, after I put the final touch on my top secret message.

Paul Eschbach and Robin Kyllonen's wedding day was September 20, 1991.

The crowd gathered and everyone was in their place. Paul was at the altar waiting for Robin. I wanted to give Robin the same opportunity I gave Kristie and Connie so just before we took our first step I looked into Robin's eyes and said, "Robin, if this is all wrong and you're not sure about marrying Paul, we can still stop the wedding and I'll help you bear the embarrassment."

Robin looked up at me and said, "Dad, everything is right. I want this more than anything else. God gave me Paul and I love him with all my heart and I'm ready for this marriage. Let's go!"

After all the proper words and the I do, I do, I will and I will's were said, and Rev. Alex Cordero pastor of Templo De Fe, prayed, I began my message.

"The Greatest Merger in the World"
"Today You Two Become One!"

I read from Matthew, chapter 19 verses 4, 5, and 6.

In the beginning the Creator made them male and female and
said, "For this reason a man will leave his father and
mother and be united to his wife and the two will become one
flesh. So they are no longer two but one. Therefore, what
God has joined together let man not separate."

I talked about all the things that would become *one* today.

> *Two hearts.*
> *Two lives.*
> *Two wills.*
> *Two names.*
> *Two voices.*
> *Two hands.*
> *Two lovers.*

I used two giant ropes to illustrate my message as I literally, "*Tied*
the knot." Staying tied during one's life is important in ten different
areas.

> *Talking*
> *Laughing*
> *Playing*
> *Discovering*
> *Planning*
> *Disagreeing*
> *Misunderstanding*
> *Needing money*
> *In sickness*
> *In crisis of any kind.*

I brought out a beautiful decorative music box for the close. "When you're both upset and no one wants to give in and when the tension is overwhelming, and you're about to spend the night with your backs to each other staring into the darkness, open the lid and let the music fill the room. Let it remind you of this day and help you to forgive each other.

The wedding was over. The reception lasted late into the evening. I'll never forget when Paul came and asked me if it was OK for him and Robin to leave. I was startled that he felt he should ask but I said, "Paul, you've waited a long time for this moment. Robin is all yours. I love you both very much. Have a great honeymoon in Barbados."

When they drove away I couldn't have been more proud of Paul and Robin. They were leaving with the blessing of God on their lives. Their marriage was made in Heaven, but would be lived out on earth with much love.

My reverie ended abruptly when Judy asked, "Are you going to help us clean up or just sit there and stare into space?"

A Letter From My Daughter, Robin

It's interesting that I am the daughter most like you. People have often told me that I look like you. I enjoy this comment because, from a little girl on, I have always thought, "My Dad sure is good-looking."

I also have inherited your personality, your name and your "Kyllonen look." Dad, you always said to me, "Stand tall Robin, you're a Kyllonen."

Now my little daughter, Erica Joy, has that same "look" and I'm hoping she will have a child someday that will "look" like us.

I reflect back on my single years and am reminded of the many times you guided me away from compromise. Remember all those guys that I thought were so perfect for me but you said, "Robin, if you marry him you'll have to compromise the call of God on your life!"

I am in my thirties now, married to Paul, who is so perfect for me, and I am happy following my dreams. It's all because YOU WERE THERE FOR ME. Now my name is changed to "Eschbach" but in the deep of my heart I'll always be a "Kyllonen". Thanks for the heritage you gave me, Dad.

I love you, Robin

A Letter From My Son-in-Law, Paul

Dear Dave,

It seems like it was just yesterday that we shook hands for the first time in your kitchen in Davenport, Iowa. Though it wasn't long ago, a thousand experiences have passed between us that have made me laugh, cry and caused my admiration and respect for you to grow.

Your life and words have impacted me greatly. You have taught me about everything from a golf swing to a gentleman's manners. Church life, faith, sincerity, accepting people, patience and hard work are just a few of the others.

Of all these things you've modeled for me, there's still one greater. I have been deeply impacted, taught and impressed with the degree to which you have taken care of your Mom and Dad. I've seen you sacrifice your time and resources for their benefit though it was inconvenient. That's the kind of unconditional love and sincerity I want in my life. A love that's willing to be spent with no promise of something to be gained; a commitment that doesn't diminish with the passing of time.   Your treatment of Andy and Viola over the long haul has expanded my concept of love and given me something substantial to practice in my own life and family.

With Great Love and Respect,

Paul

CHAPTER TWENTY THREE

©HERGIE

FOLLOW YOUR DREAMS.

BUSY, BUSY, BUSY! WE WERE ALL TRYING TO GET things done. Every hour was important. Gregory and Kristie went to Wichita, Kansas, to record the background music for our new cassette tape. I couldn't imagine recording a record after being together for only six weeks.

Mike, Connie, Judy and I took a day to go to Elkhart, Indiana, to look at more RV's. We were now looking at 5th wheels instead of motor homes.

We called Gregory to find out how the recording was going and he told us that he and Kristie had just looked at a new 5th wheel called "Travel Supreme," and that the factory was in Wakarusa, Indiana, just eight miles south of Elkhart. We needed to go there and see how they were made and see if they would be willing to make us two special models.

We found the little town of Wakarusa and the Travel Supreme Headquarters. We met Jerry Ryman, one of the executives, and he arranged a tour of the factory for us.

We were impressed from the very beginning. Jerry said they could make us a 40 foot unit with two bedrooms and three slide outs. This meant that when parked 31 feet of the 40 could expand out, and give us an additional 3 feet of living space. The units were equipped with washers and dryers which brought smiles to the girls' faces.

We found a Travel Supreme dealer in Elkhart, and drove there to check the cost and how soon we could get them.

The first person we met was Ezra Schmucker, the salesman. We told Ezra our needs and asked him if there was anyway he could make us a special deal on two units. He finally came with numbers we couldn't believe. $89,000!

Gregory was still in Wichita working on our sound tracks but he took time out to check prices at the Travel Supreme dealer in Wichita. He couldn't beat Ezra's deal so, "Ezra, let's talk."

Then came the bad news. Ezra couldn't put the order in until the down payment money was in his hand. The factory wouldn't build our two units until we could prove we had a loan secured.

On top of all that news, we hadn't even looked at pickup trucks, yet. How much did they cost?

So we visited Eby's Ford Sales and Service. WOW! I couldn't fathom what they were telling us. $33,000! Each! Down Payment? Secured loan? No job? No income, yet?

It was the same story we had just heard from Ezra Schmucker at Travel Supreme.

We were learning the language of the business world. That language says, "We want to see numbers on the paper." They told us, "We don't deal with faith or hope or God's will. Numbers folks, only numbers."

On the way back to Davenport we added all the things we needed to the list to borrow money for.

√ Posters for advertising.
√ Pictures for the poster and newspaper ads.
√ PA system.
√ Advertising packets.
√ Recording studio costs.
√ Stationery and printing.

We were nearing the $200,000 mark that we needed right now.

I visited every bank in the Quad Cities and, after answering all the questions, our loan was refused by all.

Glenn Byers, our banker in Moline, Illinois, told me that his bank would never consider giving us a loan for several different reasons.

- I didn't have a job with a fixed salary.
- I was selling my home.
- We didn't have enough dates booked yet for the year.
- Our new ministry was a huge risk. Four families traveling around the country in 2 RVs seemed risky. Maybe impossible.

I felt like a fighter in the ring. I was knocked down for the count, but not out!

God was surely testing our faith and our willingness to answer His call, no matter what. There were days when circumstances looked impossible. But, "discouragement," was not a part of our vocabulary. We prayed and kept up our faith. Then I received letters like these:

To my good friend Dave,

Maybe it is the fact of my being the son of a minister, or having been involved in many ministries in my life that brings me to the heart of "Dave Kyllonen, out of the ordinary." Quite honestly, Dave, your book's title could not be any more correct. What is it that has set you apart from others?

I will never forget the first time I met you. Before me stood a person who had just given up all for a new calling God had put on his life. How many people in their fifty's have literally sold what they owned and invested it in a newly called ministry. How many people said, "You are nuts," or "It will never work!" I will never forget the time we were playing golf together and someone asked why you were doing this. "What about your house?" "What about your investments for retirement and for what reason would you give up those things for which you had worked so hard?"

Your attitude and obedience remind me of Paul's writings in Philippians saying:

"Not that I speak in regard to need, for I have learned to be content whatever the circumstances. I know what it is to be in need, and I know what it is to have plenty. I have learned the secret of being content in any and every situation, whether well fed or hungry, whether living in plenty or in want. I can do all things through Him who gives me strength." Phil. 4:11-13

Daily lives are being touched; not just stirred, but changed. I rarely have seen such an effective ministry.

Thank you for your integrity and uprightness. The one thing I remember most in talking to others who knew you before I, was your principles. Integrity and uprightness are words, and even more, actions, that receive little attention today. For all the times we have been together, thank you for being the one who stayed consistently right in your actions and words. You truly have been an unordinary individual.

Certainly not the least of what I have said, is that I can call you my friend. We have had some absolutely wonderful times together and I look forward, with great anticipation, to the future. Thank you for allowing me the heritage of your friendship. My prayer for you would be, "Lord, continue to keep Dave in the center of Your will in everything he does and be that constant guiding light unto the pathway of life."

Keep dreaming, my friend, for it is through those dreams the greatest of days are yet ahead.

God Bless You, Dave Whitcomb

Dear Dave,

I have heard of marriages made in heaven, but perhaps good friendships can be also. I remember the first time we met, Dave. It was at a concert of The Couriers at First Assembly of God in Pekin, Illinois. Since that night, God has allowed our families to enjoy many special times together.

Dave, you have not only been an inspiration to Joan and me, but also to our entire family. I suppose you could say that I have always looked up to you (of course I'm only 5'9'')! There is no one I admire more than you as a man after God's heart. I have seen you as a leader not only in ministry, but also as a leader in your own home. Your whole family exemplifies your Godly leadership.

Dave, I have said many times, "It would be wonderful if everyone could have a friend like you." They would be so blessed. Our prayers are that God will allow your ministry to continue until Jesus comes.

My love be with you in Christ Jesus,   Dick Garber

Then things started happening!

A bank in Orlando, Florida gave us the loan we needed! I guess they didn't ask the right questions or maybe not enough of them.

We got on the phone immediately and put in our order for two 5th wheels from Travel Supreme and two white Ford pickup trucks. All four were promised to be ready by March 11, 1992.

Now, excitement was running high. You can't believe the emotions we felt when we literally watched God's hand put the pieces in place. Preachers from across the country began calling us. Rev. John Palmer from Des Moines, Iowa, wanted us to come to his church for our first day of ministry. I remember saying, "John, you are on! Our first Sunday on the road will be with you. Thanks for believing in us!"

Sam Johnson, pastor of Crown Christian Center in Charlotte, North Carolina, asked us to come to his church. Assemblies of God District Superintendents from five states invited us to sing for their District Councils. Ohio, Pennsylvania, Iowa, Kansas, and West Virginia. George Edgerly from Springfield, Missouri, invited us to sing at the National Sunday School Convention for the Assemblies of God in Dallas, Texas.

Thank God the phone was ringing!

We worked hard during our rehearsals and our singing was getting better. It looked like we would be ready to record our first cassette on February 16th.

Right in the middle of all this busyness Kristie informed us that her baby was coming. "Oh No"! "Oh Yes"! "OK, everybody, let's take time out to have a baby." The whole family headed for the hospital.

This was a special time for me. I was there when my first two grandchildren, Elijah and Isaiah, were born. Now I would be there for the birth of my third one. I was miles from home and on tour with The Couriers when my own daughters were born. How things have changed.

Kristie is our "emotional" daughter and I'll never forget how loud she screamed when her baby was being born. I was sure she could be heard two blocks away. It sure scared me.

I was taking pictures with my video camera and got so shook up I never turned the sound on the camera and today, we have a lovely silent video.

Alexsondra Kabri Hollis was born at 2:30 p.m. in the St. Lukes hospital, Davenport, Iowa, on January 21, 1992.

I still can't understand how Kristie handled all the things we were into, had her baby right in the middle of it all, and survived.

Before she was born Alex had been to every practice session and heard every song over and over again. After she was born we propped her up on the couch while we rehearsed and she slept right through it all, no matter how loud we got.

And, believe me, with our new PA system, we did get loud.

We all made suggestions for a name for our group and Judy came up with the winner. "HomeFire."

It all started when Robin surprised Paul at their wedding reception by singing an old love song to him called, "Let Me Call You Sweetheart." The second verse says, "Keep the homefire burning in your heart each day." Judy sang that song for days after the wedding. It didn't take long for "Homefire" to be Judy's suggestion for our new name. We liked it and it stuck.

March 11th came and our traveling units were ready. And, of course, the whole family wanted to be there to pick them up. We all piled into my van and drove to Indiana.

We were like a bunch of little kids getting a new toy. I don't think they were ready when we pulled into Eby's Ford Sales. We jumped out and ran, screaming, toward our new trucks. Such commotion you have never heard.

There they were! Big, beautiful, white, crew cab trucks with painted stripes to match our new 5th wheels sitting right in front of the showroom windows.

All the doors were opened and we ran around each truck like it was Christmas. Mr. Eby, the owner, got a great look at our family, full of emotion, excited and very, very happy because God had performed a miracle for us.

But now, we were excited to pick up our new campers.

We pulled our new trucks into International RV World and saw two of the most beautiful, 40 foot, Travel Supreme 5th wheels we had ever laid eyes on.

Standing with Ezra were our friends, Dick and Jo Garber from Peoria, Illinois. They didn't want to miss this big day. They had been a part of many big days in the past and they knew this one was special.

Then the commotion began. "Ezra, unlock the doors. Let me in, I want to see, too! Look at this. Look at that." We were all yelling at the same time.

It took several hours for us to learn about our new homes. Not many of us had ever been involved with campers so we listened and asked a thousand questions about how everything worked.

It was long after dark when we hooked up the trucks and pulled away. When I pushed the gas pedal down nothing happened so I checked to see if the parking brake was on. It wasn't, so I tried again. This time we began to move very slowly. I couldn't believe how heavy our 5th wheel was and how hard our pickup truck was going to have to work.

Soon we were on the Interstate and actually got the speedometer to reach 50 mph. We were a happy family driving back to Davenport, Iowa.

I learned that God could do the impossible if we didn't lose our dream. So.... we "hit the road."

At the same time a wonderful thing happened. Sam Johnson the pastor of Crown Christian Center in Charlotte presented Homefire with a house to live in. Whenever we were tired and needed to go home we had this lovely four bedroom house to relax in. This gave us the assurance that God was going to provide for all of our needs.

Our first six months were amazing. We had chosen songs that spoke to families' needs. Our new family musicals, "Love Will Be Our Home" and "Let's Hear it for Love," were ministering to hundreds of families that had lost their peace and hope.

CHAPTER TWENTY FOUR

PANAMA
"DIOS LE BENDIGA"
"GOD BLESS YOU"

GLENN PYLES CALLED ME IN THE SUMMER OF OUR first year as HomeFire and said, "Dave, I hear you're on the road with your whole family and I need you all to go to Panama in January of next year. You can evangelize all those 24 little churches again and take your family to the Darien Jungle with Dennis Cook."

I paused for a moment and said, "Glenn, that sounds great but we don't have the money to do missions at this time. We are just getting started and we're struggling to make it here in the States."

He suggested we raise the money in our services; but I knew that would be impossible.

Glenn didn't give up easily and asked me to pray about it for a few days and call him back.

I checked the cost of flying to Panama with my family and then added transportation, food and lodging costs. Not to mention paying our bills here at home. I came up with a figure of $10,000 to do the trip and that didn't include any income for us.

I called Glenn and gave him the plan I had put together.

"Glenn, you host a banquet at the Holiday Inn in Peoria, Illinois. Homefire will come and give an hour of ministry and talk about our missions' outreach to Panama. At the end of the evening we'll ask the people for an offering to care for the expenses of the trip."

Then I made sure he understood that the offering had to be $10,000, that night, in cash or pledges. If it wasn't then we would not go to Panama in January. I reminded him again that we couldn't raise the money in our future services so, if the offering is short of $10,000 we would not go. Glenn said it all sounded good to him so the banquet date was set.

Tuesday, September 29th, we pulled our two 5th wheels into the parking lot at the Holiday Inn in Peoria, Illinois.

Judy and I were eating our prime rib dinner when I whispered to her, "I've counted the people and there are 88. I don't think that we would get $10,000 from them if we had a gun. I think they are here for the free meal. So baby, just relax. We'll never get the money and we won't go to Panama in January. Let's just have a nice evening without any pressure."

We presented our ministry and our desire to visit Panama to evangelize the 24 little churches and then it was time for the offering. I asked for $10,000 dollars to be given, that night, so my family could go to Panama. After the offering was taken the crowd was dismissed and everyone said their good-byes.

Someone brought the news that the offering was only $500.00. Dick Garber said he would give $1,000 tomorrow but that only totaled $1,500 so we were $8,500 short.

I stayed clear of Glenn and hurried to carry out the PA system. I didn't want to see his disappointment.

When almost everyone had left, a man walked up to me and said, "Dave, I never met you until tonight. I don't know Glenn Pyles or anything about all those churches in Panama but I was impressed with the whole evening. I don't know what the offering was but I am willing to make up the difference to see that your family goes to Panama in January."

I couldn't believe what I was hearing. Every bone in my body leaped with anticipation. We were going on our first missionary trip!

The next morning Glenn and I met to talk about the arrangements for the trip. I asked Glenn if the man knew how much we were short and if he knew that his contribution needed to be $8,500. Glenn said, "No, but we better call him before you leave town."

What a call that was! The man couldn't believe that we needed $8,500. He thought we would only need a thousand or two at the most.

I graciously said, "Hey, there's no obligation. Maybe we could do the trip some other year, in the future, and he could help us then."

He said, "Oh no, you need to go in January and I still want to help you get the $8,500 you need. Let me think of a plan and I'll call you in a few days.

A few days later he called and had a plan to get his share of the money.

During Christmas vacation I would fly to Peoria, Illinois, and meet with ten couples who were his best friends.

The plan was to share our need for our missions trip and hopefully each family would give a donation of at least $1,000 and everything would be cared for.

My main concern was how was I ever going to book January if I waited till Christmas and Panama didn't work out? Was this just a wild goose chase?

Well, after our final service in December my family took off for Christmas vacation and I flew to Peoria for a week.

After sharing with the ten couples, their combined offering was $1,000. We were discouraged.

Driving home after lunch Glenn said, "Stop right here, Dave. I know the man who owns that Firestone Tire store. We whipped the car into the parking lot and went to meet the owner. After a short visit, with me telling my story, the man wrote out a check for $200.

We got back in the car and decided that, maybe, God was showing us a way to get the other $7,300. So, down the street we drove stopping at various businesses along the way, telling our story and hoped we could get a contribution.

I could not believe what we were doing. I didn't like asking for money for my missions trip this way.

It was Friday and we still needed $3,000 to reach our goal. This was my last day in Peoria. We started early that morning to meet a businessman for breakfast at 7:00.

After I had given my talk about Panama and my family, I waited for his response. He said, "Dave, you don't know me, but I know you. My name is David Risinger. I have gone to every Gospel concert in this area since back in the 1960's, and The Couriers were my favorite group. My wife, Marilyn, and I have been blessed by your ministry for years. "Let me write you a check for $3,000 and your project for missions can be finished."

Praise the Lord!

On the way home we talked about our week.

I looked at Glenn and said, "This is the first time I have ever raised money for missions in this manner. And, Glenn, you can be sure it's the last time, too!"

We landed in Panama and began our tour of the 24 churches. Glenn drove us to each church in a rented van.

We were packed in like sardines but, occasionally, Glenn would say, "We have to stop and pick up the pastor." We'd say, "Glenn, there's no room." But we'd stop and not only did the pastor come but his wife and, usually, 2 or 3 little children.

The churches were very small and we struggled to fit on some of the platforms. People came from everywhere. Each church had standing room only crowds. Excitement was building and the Lord was doing a great work in the families of Panama.

The people cried when we arrived and cried when we left. They said that not many singers or evangelists ever came to their churches.

I was glad when we received the news that Dennis Cook was expecting us for three days in the Darien Jungle. I wanted to see how my family would handle driving down that 118 miles of dirt road filled with a million pot holes.

Out of the city we drove, and for awhile it was easy but when we had been driving for five hours and everyone was ready to be there Dennis said, "We're almost halfway there." I loved it!

Many times we had to get out of the car and walk because the ruts were so deep that the car was dragging on the frame.

We arrived at Dennis' home hot, bedraggled and exhausted. But guess what Dennis said? You're right! "We have a service tonight but we'll just go to the first village. It's not far from the house and it's easy to get to."

We sang and preached to our hearts' content, and once again it was an emotional experience. Especially for my family who, some for the first time, were experiencing ministry to uncivilized people. Somehow the sights, sounds, smells and the awareness of what we were doing in the jungle, brought new energy and excitement.

All of a sudden we were actually living out all the missionaries slides and pictures we had seen since we were young.

We awoke refreshed and ready to go again, when Dennis came with news that we were going to the second village. He said, "It's a nine mile walk one way, so we better get started or we might have to stay overnight in the village." We carried sleeping bags just in case.

The nine mile walk wasn't too hard because we were "psyched up" and it was mostly down hill. Walking back up that mountain would be the greatest challenge. We arrived late in the day and I knew we would have to stay in the village overnight. Where were we going to sleep? Well, we couldn't worry about that now. Dennis was ringing the pipe and church was about to happen.

I stood outside the little church and looked at the last few minutes of the sunset. I knew that in just a few minutes, it would be spooky dark.

Here we were, 150 miles from the city and civilization, and about to have a service with people who didn't know much about the world outside their own village.

We had church by using three flashlights. One on the speaker, one on the interpreter and one on the backdoor, so we could see who was coming or going.

At least, one time in their life, every person should be a part of a church service like we had. It's very, very special and an experience that will always be a part of one's memory.

I admire Dennis Cook and his dedication in helping these people hear the precious story of the Gospel. I look forward to the visit in the future when we'll have to walk eight hours to get to the last village. The adventure in the Darien Jungle isn't isn't over yet.

After the service we were taken to our home for the night. We were sharing a hut with one of the families in the village.

When I walked by the fire in the yard of the hut I paused long enough to open the lid of the big black pot sitting in the middle of the fire. I took one look and thought, I would never eat that! But in a few minutes it was served to us before going to bed. I pushed mine around on my plate to make it look like I was eating, but I noticed my sons-in-law gobbling it up like it was chocolate cake. The only thing to wash it down with was a cup of thick, black, home brewed, Panamanian, jungle coffee.

I didn't sleep much that night. I could see the stars through the holes in the thatched roof as I lay in my sleeping bag on the hard, filthy, wooden floor.

Every thirty minutes out hosts' little baby, who had the croup, had a major coughing attack and I was sure she wouldn't live till morning. I was finding out what it was like to depend totally on God. No doctor, no hospital emergency room, no pills, no running water, no refrigerator and no juice. Nothing that a very sick baby needed. All I could do was pray and ask God to touch her and heal her little body.

The Cooks had already given seven years of hard work in those villages. They said they would never leave the Darien Jungle and would die right there among the people whom they dearly loved.

The total population of the twelve villages numbered several thousand and, already, many had given their hearts to Christ and were taking Bible study courses. Dennis told me of his desire to build a church building in each of the twelve villages.

I kept trying to work it out in my mind how I could help. Where are the men that would carry bags of cement and block into the villages? How much concrete and how many blocks would it take to build a 30 by 40 foot church. What about the last village that is an eight hour walk, one way? Are there any men willing to carry one cement block for eight hours? That's what dreams are made of. Maybe someday I will be a part of making that dream come true.

Sometimes the task of fulfilling God's call to win the lost is not easy.

A reflection From Glenn

When I think of a friend and someone that has been as close as a brother, a special person that God has used to mean so much in my life, Dave fills that part.

What a privilege it is to be a small part in the life of a man and his family God has blessed and is using so greatly. Many feel, in their later years, that it is time to slow down But to see Dave keep going, preaching, singing, helping families, as well as his own, makes me feel blessed to have him as a friend.

Thinking of the many times we shared together, my mind goes to the first time I saw The Couriers. Here was a group that stood out above all others. There was something about their message, their appearance, the way they presented themselves, as well as their singing for the Lord. And there was that tall bass singer. It was not long until we became friends.

I remember a night after The Couriers came to our church. We had finished a few more services together. Dave said, "Glenn, whether you know it or not you are in the middle of this." That was the beginning of my helping The Couriers, and later helping each one of The Couriers in scheduling, and in other ways.

The vacations together, traveling, being a part of seeing God call him to pastor the church in Davenport, Iowa. Only by being a special friend can it mean this much.

When I started the ministry of Christian Alliance of Panama (C.A.P.) I could never have kept going without the encouragement from Dave. And then for him and his family to become a part of it was a great blessing. The ministry of C.A.P. in Panama could not have succeeded without their part. How little did I know that our time together in the jungle, in the churches, and even sleeping in the Indian hut, would soon change both of our lives so much.

Now, to be a part of HomeFire Ministries gives me great joy. Dave, I thank you from the bottom of my hear for what you have meant to me and my family. Only when we get to heaven will you know of the times your friendship pulled me through.

Thanks for being that special friend,

Glenn Pyles

CHAPTER TWENTY FIVE

THE ENEMY ATTACKS!

DR. RICHARD DOBBINS, PRESIDENT AND FOUNDER OF
"Emerge Ministries," in Akron, Ohio, and long time friend, came up
to my family after we had sung in one of the services at the Sunday
School Convention in Dallas, Texas. He complimented our ministry
and was very excited about our future and our goal to reach a million
hurting families.

But he stopped us dead in our tracks when he said, "Homefire, I
have a word from the Lord for you." We all stood like soldiers waiting for the next command.

Here was a man who was the Assemblies of God's Assistant District Superintendent of the state of Ohio, a pastor for over twenty five
years in Akron, with about 50 years of ministry experience.

We listened closely to what he had to say. He boldly stated, "You
are doing such an important task for the Lord the devil is going to
attack your family. Be ready and understand that it is only an attack."

We left Dallas and headed for Kansas. It was my turn to drive. I
remembered what Dick Dobbins had said and paid special attention
to my driving. I was carrying precious cargo and didn't know how
the devil would attack us.

We were conducting a three day meeting in Baxter Springs, Kansas, when I got up on Monday morning with aches and pains in every
one of my joints. By Tuesday evening I had a raging fever, but finished the service sitting down. The next morning I was worse, so
Mike took me to the emergency room of the hospital in Joplin, Missouri.

I thought I had the flu, but after examining me, the doctor said,
"Dave, you are a very sick man. You have a urinary tract infection
and it will be several days before you will be able to leave the hospital." I insisted that he just give me some antibiotics, and I'd be OK.

I had never been sick enough to be in the hospital in my life. For the first time I experienced nurses putting needles in my arms and taking blood every morning. My hospital stay was nine days.

We had services booked in Minnesota for the following Sunday. Judy stayed with me but the rest of the family needed to go on to Minnesota. After they left I said to Judy, "I think they were excited about doing the services on their own. Maybe we've lost our job."

It was then I realized this attack was from the devil. He was doing his best to destroy the ministry God had called us to.

After the kids had been in four services by themselves in Minnesota they called and said, "Dad, if you and Mom don't come back soon we will quit. We need you very much. Please, hurry and get well." When I hung up I said to Judy, "Well Baby, we still have our job!"

Physically, I went through many months of crazy, little things. I caught a cold that hung on for months. I suffered with the flu. I played in a softball game at Colonial Heights Assembly of God in Wichita and pulled a muscle in my left arm. Since I am left-handed, I really struggled. I couldn't even comb my hair without holding my left arm up with my right hand. That problem lasted about eight months.

I was checking one of our generators underneath the 5th wheel and twisted my knee and tore a ligament. I could barely manage getting to a church platform. I tried everybody's home remedies, exercises, ointments, braces and suggestions. After six weeks of limping around, I finally saw a doctor. I had to have surgery on my knee.

November 7,1993. We were in the Word of Life Church in Springfield, Virginia, for a four day meeting. I was deathly sick all day. We were finishing the Sunday evening service and I was bringing the service to a close. My brain told me I needed to go to the restroom but I had already wet my trousers in front of this big crowd.

I turned to Gregory and asked him to finish the service. We all knew the urinary tract infection had returned.

I hurried to my camper and changed my clothes. Then I just sat and stared into space waiting for my family to finish the service.

Associate pastor, Darrell Peterson, came with my family to take me to the hospital in Fairfax, Virginia. I said, "Can't we wait till morning?" My family emphatically answered, "Never, Dad, you are going now! This time we've got to find out what's causing this problem."

My hospital stay this time was five days.

The doctor told me I must see a Urologist as quickly as possible. Something was drastically wrong because the same problem was reoccurring too often. I dare not have another infection because, the next time, it could be damaging to my body.

While spending a few days in Charlotte, North Carolina, at Christmas time I made an appointment with Dr. John Kirkland. He gave me a PSA blood test and discovered my count was twelve. Anything over four is cause for concern.

He took a biopsy, which was routine procedure. He told me not to worry. My prostate was probably just enlarged and that could be fixed with medicine. He said I should call him in a few days to find out the results.

Judy came with the shattering news. "There is cancer in the prostate and you will need surgery."

I was surprised at my reaction. Only a quiet sigh.

In my heart I was thinking about Dr. Dobbin's word from the Lord. "The devil is going to attack your family. Be ready, and understand that it is only an attack." When I realized it was only an attack from the devil, it eased my mind and I knew I could go on and win the victory.

We tried to set a date for my surgery. We were going to the West Coast for the first 6 months of the year and then our summer was full of family camps in the Midwest.

I asked Dr. Kirkland if I could wait until the end of July to have the operation. He said, "Dave, if you were in Charlotte I would insist on the operation now. If we have to wait until July, then we have to wait."

We set the date for July 28, 1994.

The news leaked out that I had cancer and people started asking big questions. Finally, I started talking about it from the platform in all our services. It was good because we were building an army of prayer warriors in every town.

I was prayed for in every service and remember people telling me that I would know when healing came. They said a warm feeling would come over my body. There had been many, many prayers sent up to heaven for my healing, but I didn't feel that warmth!

We finished our last family camp of the season, Lost Valley Assembly of God Camp, in Gaylord, Michigan, on July 24th. Judy and I said our good-byes to the friends we had made and to our family and left for Charlotte, North Carolina.

At 5:00 a.m., on July 28, 1994, I entered Presbyterian Hospital. You can imagine how surprised I was to see my good friends, Dick and Jo Garber, all the way from Peoria, Illinois. In addition were Fred and Joyce Knop, also from Peoria, and my buddy, David Whitcomb. Pastor Sam Johnson was there to pray for me. Agreeing with him were friends all over the nation that said they would pray for me on July 28th. What a comfort that was for me.

I was taken down the long, dimly lighted corridor past the girls in white, to the operating room where I met Dr. Kirkland.

When I awoke in the recovery room I was very aware of the presence of God. It was then that I felt the warmth of His healing.

- Success Principle 53

TRUE SUCCESS IS DEPENDENCE
ON GOD.

*There are times that we can't do
anything about our situation, and
God proves to us how much we need
Him. His ways are higher than
our ways!*

• • •

I didn't understand, and still don't, why I had to have the surgery, but I was directed to a verse of scripture, Hebrews 12:15 that says,

"See to it that no one misses the grace of God and that no root of bitterness grows up to cause trouble and defile many."

I experienced that His grace was, and is, sufficient for me.

CHAPTER TWENTY SIX

AND THEY CALL ME, "PAPPY".

AS THE SONG SAYS, "WE'RE ON THE ROAD AGAIN." AS I sat in the driver's seat of my motorhome, I felt good. I was comfortable here. I reflected back over the last several years. I thought about the years that Judy and I shared our living space with Gregory and Kristie and their three children.

It was always a precious moment when little, two year old Alex knocked on my bedroom door and said, "Can I come into Pappyland?"

She came for her daily squirt of my Halston men's cologne. I teased her that someday she would be the only bride wearing men's cologne at her wedding.

I remembered an unforgettable moment that happened at Toys R Us. Isaiah, age 5, spotted a motorized motorcycle and just had to ride it up and down the aisles. He pleaded and begged his Dad to buy it for him. But it cost $300.00.

I waited to hear Gregory say, "No way, Isaiah. We don't have that kind of money, and never will, to spend on a motorcycle."

I was blessed by the wisdom Gregory used when he said, "Isaiah, when you save enough money to buy that motorcycle, you can have it." He didn't squelch a little boy's desire but instead, dropped a dream into his heart and mind.

Walking out of the store I asked Isaiah how much money he had. He grinned real big and said to me, "Pappy, I have $2.50. I'm gonna save $300.00 and buy that motorcycle. My Dad said I could."

Days later, we were ministering at a Couple's Retreat in Cincinnati, Ohio, Godly Principles for the Family. In order to illustrate a point Gregory told the story of Isaiah and the motorized motorcycle.

Well, Clyde Miller, the pastor, surprised us all when, at the close of our meeting, he took a love offering for Isaiah so he could buy his motorized motorcycle. I believe God honored a father's wisdom and a little boy's dream.

Many people have seen Isaiah riding around the church parking lot not knowing the real story. The other day he came to our camper with pictures of a huge motorcycle and said, "Pappy, look what I'm going to buy when I'm sixteen!" I said, "Why not, Isaiah, and you can do it when you save your money, right? Cause your Dad said so!"

I believe God honored a father's wisdom and a little boy's dream.

When Elijah, was nine and Isaiah was seven a family invited them to their house to spend some time with their boys.

During the afternoon they started watching a movie. When Elijah realized that the movie was rated PG 13 he had to make a major decision for his young life. Gregory and Kristie did not allow their children to watch anything but G rated movies.

Here was their chance to finally see what PG 13 was all about. This family had invited them over and Dad and Mom were not around. Why would one little movie be wrong? But instead, two little boys found the mother of the family in the kitchen and said to her, "We aren't allowed to watch this kind of movie. Is there anything else we can do for the next hour?"

That dad and mom came hurrying to church that evening and found Gregory and Kristie. They said, "Our family has learned a vital lesson today. If children are taught family values, they can obey under any circumstances. Congratulations, your boys absolutely stunned us with their ability to do the right thing, even at their age."

- Success Principle 54

TEACH YOUR CHILDREN FAMILY VALUES
SO THEY WILL OBEY UNDER ANY
CIRCUMSTANCE.

That's the day you reward your
children for obeying God and
parents. That's the day you
know you're on your way to raising
a real man, not a juvenile
delinquent.

IT IS BETTER TO BUILD CHILDREN THAN TO REPAIR MEN!

• • •

Just about the time we thought we had all the kinks worked out in our traveling ministry, Paul and Robin made the great announcement that they were expecting a baby.

They were asking all these new questions Where are we going to be in April of next year when the baby is due? Can we adjust our schedule? How about a doctor?

So many things to work out!

Three months later Mike and Connie told us their great news. Connie was pregnant and their baby was due in July.

Two daughters pregnant at the same time was wonderful!

I looked at Kristie and said, "Why don't all three of you have a baby at the same time?" She wasn't convinced that the Hollises should have four children. Three was enough.

Robin had a doctor and a hospital all lined up in Davenport, Iowa, so I scheduled the month of April, with the exception of a few days in Topeka, Kansas, all around Eastern Iowa.

I planned our schedule with some time off in April for Robin to have her baby in Davenport, Iowa.

Wouldn't you know the baby came four weeks early!

Erica Joy Eschbach was born, on March 27th, 1993, at 7:09 p.m.

From that day on I said to the girls, "Go ahead and have your babies but I'm not planning our schedule around your delivery dates. Wherever you get your first labor pain, that's where we will find the hospital and have your babies."

Rev. David Nelson, the Superintendent of the South Dakota District, invited us to be the special guests at the family camp near Rapid City, South Dakota.

Everyday we asked Connie, "Is the baby coming today?" She would always answer, "No, not yet." After the camp was over we had a few days break before heading for Lexington, Nebraska, and the Assemblies of God Family Camp with Rev. Robert Nazarenus.

So we decided to do a little sight-seeing. We got up early Wednesday morning to tour Mt. Rushmore and see the famous four faces. We were getting ready to leave when Mike said we wouldn't be going to see four old faces today but that we would be seeing one brand new face.

Victoria Michael Hammer was born July 14th, 1993, at 1:45 p.m. in Rapid City, South Dakota. Mike was overjoyed because he, too, was born in South Dakota.

Two new babies living together in a 40 foot camper was going to test the dedication and commitment of both the Hammers and the Eschbachs.

We were getting to be quite a family, learning how to live together. We sure had to practice what we preached each evening in our services.

CHAPTER TWENTY SEVEN

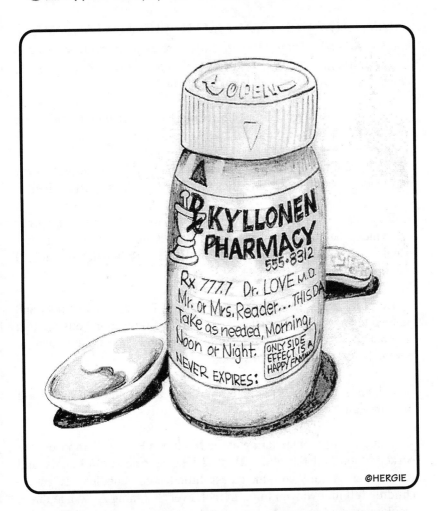

PRESCRIPTION FOR A HEALTHY FAMILY.

I HAVE ALWAYS BEEN A MAN WHO LOVES HOME. I enjoy yard work. I enjoy fixing. I enjoy relaxing in my easy chair. I enjoy sleeping in my seven foot bed. I enjoy a closet big enough to hang all my clothes without being squinched.

But, my "HomeFire" lifestyle requires me to live constantly, "on the road," in a 40 foot motor home.

No yard, no easy chair, no seven foot bed and no big closet. Judy and I share a small closet and she uses 3/4 of it. I'm still squinched!

Recently, while parked in a church parking lot, I was looking out the window and saw my son-in-law, Paul doing something very unusual. He was planting his garden in the back of his pickup truck. I couldn't believe my eyes.

He purchased, from the hardware store, five big flower pots and planted beans, onions, radishes and carrots. Pretty soon he lugged all five pots, up the ladder, to the top of his camper. He wanted them to get the benefit of the full sunshine.

I chuckled to myself realizing Paul was getting the best out of life even though the Homefire lifestyle is not always easy.

While we were ministering at the Michigan Family Camp we were parked among all the other RV's. Right next door to Gregory and Kristie was a family with the cutest, little tea-cup poodle. My grandchildren fell in love with him. In fact, every morning Alex, age three, would say good-bye to her mom and go next door to spend the day with the little poodle.

The poodle's owner mentioned to Kristie that there was one little puppy, from the same litter, that was still available.

When Rev. William Leach, District Superintendent of the state of Michigan, saw how much the Homefire children loved the dog he surprised us all by receiving an offering in the evening service for the kids. They all decided to buy a puppy with their offering. The campers were all excited because they had helped the dream of HomeFire's children's come true.

They named him, **Moses Jonathan David Hollis**. We call him Moses for short.

- Success Principle 55

WHEN ONE'S LIFESTYLE REQUIRES THE
UNUSUAL, WE MUST MAKE THE BEST OF
THE CIRCUMSTANCES.

Getting the best out of life is
learning how to, "Go with the flow."

• • •

Being on the road requires good health. Physical health, social health and spiritual health.

Developing social skills might be the most difficult for us. Especially, on a day when we are tired and exhausted from a long day of travel.

1. **We must learn to work together.**
2. **We cannot be selfish.**
3. **It is important for all of us to communicate our feelings.**
4. **We must strengthen our relationships with each other.**
5. **We must understand what is valuable and significant.**

When we have love, patience, understanding and the right attitude then we have the valuable qualities that keep a family socially healthy.

We have made a strong commitment to each other and to God. We are ministering in churches 250 times a year. No one sleeps in or stays in their camper during services. We all go. This takes lots of initiative, discipline and confidence.

We are <u>learning to discipline our desires</u>. We never say,
"If only I could live in a house."
"If only I made more money."
"If only I had a 9 to 5 job."

We have found comfort in our fate, courage in our fears, and have confidence in our faith.

We love it when we minister for four days in a church. Aside from the dramas and special presentations we do on Sunday and Wednesday, we are able to conduct teaching seminars for all members of the family on Monday and Tuesday nights.

Another highlight of our ministry is when we are invited to minister in the Family Camps during the summer.

One of these special times happened during the Family Camp in Big Prairie, Ohio. We really got to know the people and learned about the burdens they carry   I remembered how meaningful it was for me to write my burdens on a balloon and send them up to God while I was pastoring at Westside. Maybe it would be a great encouragement to our friends here at the camp in Ohio.

I remembered too the sight of the people writing on their helium filled balloons. Everyone was involved. After writing we all went outside the tabernacle and prayed. On the count of three, hundreds of balloons were sent floating up to the heavens. I remembered them filling the sky and singing as they drifted out of sight.

I thought of the couple who drove several hours four months later to share with us this story:

"At the balloon service four months earlier we wrote only one word on our balloon - "B A B Y."

We had been married for ten years and couldn't have a baby. This weighed very heavy in our hearts. HomeFire inspired us to ask God one more time, for a miracle. We came to tell you our balloon made it all the way to heaven. God gave us the miracle and I'm four months pregnant!"

It was just like Gregory penned in his song,

> "Dreams are forever,
> Don't let your dreams pass you by.
> If you would ever dream something big,
> Now is the time.
>
> Dreams are in God's plan,
> The miracle is in His hand.
> Don't let your dreams ever die.
>
> Your dreams might have been shattered,
> Broken and torn apart,
> Crushed by a circumstance
> That took away your heart.
> But now the Lord wants you to know,
> Your dreams can live again.
> Bring it to the Master's hand
> And let your miracle begin.

At the same time Robin announced, "I didn't write BABY on my balloon but I'm pregnant again."

Then Connie made her announcement, "I didn't write BABY on my balloon either but I'm pregnant, too."

I immediately calculated that there would be four little babies, under the age of two, and two sets of parents living together in one 40 foot camper.

"Oh, God, please help us now."

On April 18th, 1995, baby **Ellie Noel Eschbach** arrived in Harrisburg, Pennsylvania.

On July 23rd, 1995, baby **Tiffany Joann Hammer** arrived in Rice Lake, Wisconsin.

> *"Grandchildren are the crown of old men."*
> (Proverbs 17:6) NASV

HomeFire members now consists of fifteen. Four families traveling together continuing to answer God's call.

"This great caravan keeps on rolling along!"

What we think about Pappy!

To our Pappy.

When we go to the Mall or when we go to the store we always want to go with pappy. He always gets us a little treat.

We love him with all our hearts.

We race to sit by pappy at the restruant.

A man 6ft. 5inch. should be in bascketball.

Our grandfather knows more about the Lord than almost any person in the world.

He taught us to be a cheerful giver. He taught us that how much you give to God, He will give twice as much.

(We love you Pappy.)

Elijah, I said, Alex, Erica, Jory, Ellie and Tiffeny.

Written by: Elijah Hollis, 11 yrs.
#1 Grandchild

CHAPTER TWENTY EIGHT

YOU, TOO, CAN BE SUCCESSFUL!

THE NUMBER ONE QUESTION THAT PEOPLE ASK IS, "Tell me, Dave, how is it that your family is so successful? What is your secret?"

Success is getting the best out of life. I've taught my family that it doesn't matter how little or how much we have. We can still live happy lives and be fulfilled.

There are several ways for this to happen.

- Success Principle 56

YOU HAVE TO BE A DREAMER.

D	*Direction (which way?)*
R	*Risk (narrowing the percentage of failure)*
E	*Excitement (keeps the home from being gloomy)*
A	*Attitude (raises one's expectancy)*
M	*Motivation (eliminates boredom)*
E	*Effort (doesn't come easy)*
R	*Reach (everyone reaching together)*
S	*Seasons (dreams come and go)*

• • •

"Your future is only as big as your dream." Go to bed at night with a dream and wake up everyday to pursue that dream.

Our dreams for the future are huge, in fact, in the natural, they're impossible.

I know these "DREAMERS" principles work!

We dreamed of having four RV's one day. One for each family but we had no one to ask, "Will this work?" The risk was great. But we kept dreaming, waiting for God to work it out.

We looked at dozens of RV's on the market. We studied every brochure and floor plan. We flipped through our RV "Dream" books everyday.

It made for great conversation. We actually lived out our dreamer's list. Not one of the eight points was left out.

I'm so glad we allowed God to work out our dream. In His perfect timing he did something really wonderful for us.

We were holding a four day meeting in Walnut Grove, Pennsylvania, where our very good friends, Gerry and Carolyn Hindy, attend.

Gerry is a businessman in the Pittsburgh area and very knowledgeable about finances. Our debt load was overwhelming so we asked Gerry if he could spare an hour of his time to help us organize our finances.

His first suggestion was to pay off one of our trucks. He told us to make double or triple payments if we could. Whatever it would take to pay off one piece of our equipment.

We thanked him for his time and left. We wanted so much to be able to do that, but is seemed impossible. God was faithfully meeting our needs but there was never enough money in the budget to make a double payment, let alone a triple.

In a family meeting we discussed what we could sacrifice to make a double payment.

When we finished our four day meeting the pastor gave us the honorarium check from the church. Then he reached into his pocket and handed me an envelope. He said, "The Hindy's wanted me to give you this. They said you would know what to do with it."

Everyone in the family needed to be present when we opened the envelope so we called another family meeting. We rejoiced, we shouted, we laughed, and we cried, when we discovered the check was enough to pay off our truck!

Now we could make double payments on our second truck and lessen our debt load. We finally could see a light at the end of the tunnel.

Our `thank you' to Gerry and Carolyn and their four sweet daughters was a video we made. In the video we destroyed the payment book, sang a song, and prayed a prayer of thankfulness for the Hindy's.

On June 1, 1995, our dream came true.

We picked up two brand new RV's in Elkhart, Indiana. You should have heard the chatter on our CB's that day. There wasn't an ounce of gloom in our homes; excitement was running high.

"Break one time for that Green Dream." (that's me)

"You have the Green Dream here. C'mon?"

"Dad, slow that buggy down. We can't even see you anymore."

"OK, come on, Sound Man (that's Gregory), take the lead and I'll bring up the rear."

"How boutcha, Bachmobile? (that's Paul) Got your ears on?"

"Ten four. Truck's running good today. I'll fall in
second."

"This is Hammertime (that's Mike). How about me?
I'll squeeze in between the Bachmobile and the Green
Dream."

For the next several hours we kept the CB waves hot with conversation.

It took almost four years to see our dream come true but we never
lost hope.

- Success Principle 57

YOU HAVE TO BE A LEARNER.

*Families are limited by their
lack of knowledge.
Our libraries are full of good books.
Bookstores have information about
every subject we want to know about.
We must teach our children to be
learners.
It is within the family unit that a
person first learns how to interact
with others and how to work with
others. We learn to respect and
care for others by first learning
it in our families.*

• • •

The three basic values of trustworthiness, politeness and compassion are a must in the learning of every child. If these are not ac-
quired at home then it is quite possible they will go through life never
fully acquiring them.

Trustworthiness

To believe, to hope without misgivings, to have confidence, committed to caring and to be reliable. These are only six values that can be learned by every child growing up.

Politeness

We polish all the character traits in our children during the years they are still at home. They must learn how to be courteous, have good manners and refine the rough edges of life.

Compassion

Children must learn about suffering, pity and sympathy. These things need to taught in family meetings a little at a time. My prayer for America is that we as parents would develop our leadership and teaching skills so our children will be learners.

Judy and I raised our three girls in Harrisburg, Pennsylvania. Many good things happened during those years of our lives. One of those was that I met Charles (Tremendous) Jones, my new insurance agent. I remember going to his beautiful, executive office and finding it full of cardboard boxes. They were everywhere.

After signing the contract Mr. Jones said to me, "Dave, help yourself to a book out of each box. I love to give books away, so you can have one from every box."

Man, I selected a stack of books so high I wondered if I could carry them to the car. They were expensive books and full of helpful information that would teach me many things in the years to come.

Just before leaving he told me an intriguing story.

His son just had his 17th birthday and asked his dad for a new car. He wanted a new XKE Jaguar sports car. Mr. Jones told me that he could have bought the car for his son but wanted to help grow in character by making him work for it.

He offered his son a plan. "If you will read 100 books and give me a book report on each of them then I'll buy you the Jaguar."

"But there's just one little catch. I get to choose the books!" Mr. Jones purchased the finest books that money could buy.

His son read the books, made the book reports, and got the car.

He not only drove the car away, but he became the most intelligent young man in town. He was ready to face the world to be a great success.

That maroon Jaguar was worth all the effort, but, it's value never amounted to what the value of learning gave him in return.

I hurried home because I had a plan of my own. I called Judy and our three girls into the family room for a meeting.

I said, "Girls, I have a special deal for you. I will give you five dollars for every book you read and write a book report about."

Their eyes were wide with excitement and they said, "You mean, if we read a book every day this month, you will give us each $150.00." I said, "Yes, but there is one thing I forgot to mention. Your mother and I get to choose the books."

They thought the books were going to be little, fiction books with less than 100 pages. Boy, were they wrong. We were able to get our girls to read some of the greatest books about life, and autobiographies of great women and wonderful, character building virtues that they would never have learned any other way.

They thrive today because they learned early about honesty, self-sacrifice, personal responsibility and respect. It helped them learn about identity, belonging and discipline.

Our goal as parents, was to give our children a strong sense of identity, knowing who they are, so they were not easily persuaded by peer pressure.

Parents work hard to give their children things. Some even have two or three jobs. But everybody loses in the long run because when those children need their parents, they're not there.

The Gallop Poll states that children are growing up today without a scripture in their minds, a hymn in their hearts and a prayer in their homes.

Let's be families who continue to learn.

- Success Principle 58

BE A WORKER.

Triumph is made up of two words -
try and umph!

•　　•　　•

One of the lessons we wanted to teach our girls was the value of hardwork. I learned about it at an early day. I was 12 years old when I heard my mother complain that we didn't have a yard like other families.

Our house was built on the side of the hill and there wasn't one foot of level ground on either side of the house. She wanted a level yard with grass and lawn chairs to sit in and maybe even a swing.

Every time I heard my mom complain, I'd go up to my bedroom and look out the window at the hillside. I wished I could do something about it.

One day while looking out the window I saw our yard in a different light. I envisioned a terraced hillside that would give us three flat areas where we could plant grass and give Mom her dream.

Dad worked hard everyday and didn't have the time to change the hillside into a terraced yard. My three brothers were still too small to be of any help. So, I asked my mother if I could work on the yard by myself.

She said, "Why, that's too big a job for a 12-year-old. You'll never get it finished."

I searched our whole house over for tools. I found two old beat up shovels, one rusty pick, and a badly beat up old wheelbarrow.

Out to the hillside I went. I measured off 30 feet and started digging into the side of the hill. It was hot, and soon, sweat was pouring off my body. I was learning how to use the pick to loosen the dirt and then shovel it in the wheelbarrow and dump it over the hill.

It looked great from the very first foot that I leveled. My family encouraged me to continue. They brought me Kool Aid to drink and told me how proud Dad was going to be.

And, believe it or not, I was having fun. I was learning how to work. It was hard and at times I thought I would never finish, but I didn't give up. I worked at it the whole summer.

I got a great tan. My muscles were growing big. I learned what determination was and found out that I had lots of it. I slept well at night and loved it when I looked up at the window and saw Mom's smile. That was worth everything.

I proved to myself that I was a worker. The only pay I needed was my mother's smile and hug at the end of each day.

I still love yard work and hope to have a great yard of my own when I retire.

<u>Don't be lazy. Be a worker.</u>

- Success Principle 59

YOU MUST BELIEVE IN YOURSELF.

Oak trees don't grow overnight.

•　　•　　•

We never let our girls say, "No," to activities at church. We wanted them to have confidence if they were asked to participate in singing, drama, puppets, nursery work or teaching. My favorite line to them was, "No one will believe in you if you don't believe in yourself."

On Kristie's sixteenth birthday I told her my gift was special because she had obeyed God, her mother and me. So today I would make the down payment on the car of her choice. I told her to go and look at all the cars in town and when she found one she liked she could call me and I'd come and take her to the bank to arrange the loan.

Later that day she called and said she found the car. I said, "Kristie, you found a car already? Are you sure it's the one you want?" She said, "Yes, Daddy, I found my car. It's perfect! It's my size and the perfect color. Daddy, I'm not telling you anything else about the car. You have to come and see it for yourself. Please come as quickly as you can." I said, "I'll be there in fifteen minutes."

As I was driving to the car lot I tried to envision what kind of car Kristie had chosen. She didn't tell me the make or how much it cost. This should be interesting. I thought I knew my daughter pretty well. This would be the real proof.

When I drove to the address Kristie gave me it was a foreign car agency. I thought, <u>Oh no, I'm in trouble now</u>. Kristie came running to meet me. She was so excited.

I got out of my car and walked with her across the lot. There were cars everywhere. All shapes and sizes. I kept saying, "Which one is it?"

Then I saw it, sitting there all by itself. I couldn't believe my eyes. I finally said, "Oh, Kristie, what a car! It's so different from anything I thought you'd pick. It's great, but, I don't even know what it is. I've never seen one before."

Jumping up and down she said, "Daddy, it's a 1976 Triumph, TR 7! Don't you just love it?"

I slowly walked around the car and opened the door to get in. The car was so small I wasn't sure I even could get in. After trying to get in front ways and not succeeding, I turned around and decided to back in. My long legs finally made it. I was in.

It was so different from American cars with all its special buttons. The leather was soft and smelled wonderful. Then I noticed it was a stick shift. I said, "Kristie, you don't even know how to drive a stick shift." She said, "Oh, Daddy, that's no problem. You can teach me how to drive it tomorrow!"

I'll never forget what happened when we pulled out of the car lot. Kristie started to cry. Still she did her best to talk, and said, "Daddy, I love you very much. I still can't believe you trusted me enough to let me pick my own car. I will never forget this moment even if I live to be a hundred. Today, I went from a little girl to a grown up lady.

Thanks, for believing in me. I'm glad you're my dad! Let's go home and show Mom and the girls what we bought."

When Kristie got married and left home for good, she gave the car to me and I still have it. It's an antique.

When my first grandchild was four years old I said to him, "Elijah, on your 16th birthday I am going to give you the TR 7."

He had no idea then what I was offering him, but on the very day, of this writing, he turned 11 years old. He now understands all about cars.

He said to me at his birthday party, "Remember, Pappy, only five more years and the TR is mine."

And I said, "Remember, Elijah, there are two conditions."

1. You must be serving God with all your heart.

2. You can never sell the car. When you don't want
   it anymore you must give it to someone else in
   the family.

Elijah has had many years to live with a dream. It will come true someday because I always keep my promises.

I'm reminded of the time, when our girls were young. I was on tour to the West Coast and called home to see how my family was doing. Judy complained about the heat and mentioned that the girls were driving her crazy because they were about to "hot to death," as they put it.

I said, "Tell them, when I get home, we're going to put a swimming pool in our back yard."

The girls could hardly sleep at night dreaming about that swimming pool. When I finally arrived home they didn't even say, "Welcome home, Dad." They said, "Did you really mean what you said about the swimming pool? When are we gonna get it?" Thinking that a small kiddie pool would suffice I said, "We can have it in our backyard by tomorrow morning." So off to the swimming pool place we went.

Would you believe, the salesman convinced me that the kiddie pool would NEVER do. We left that store with our station wagon packed to the hilt with a pool kit containing a 16 by 32 foot, in the ground pool.

The salesman asked me if I could read. When I said, "Of course," he said, "Then you can put this pool in the ground yourself. Just read the directions." Well, just between you and me, it wasn't as easy as, "Just read the directions." My girls were elated. They said, "Boy, Dad, thanks for keeping your promise."

For 15 years that swimming pool not only blessed our family but all the girls' school friends, all the church kids, all the neighborhood kids and, sometimes, kids we didn't even know.

Don't put off accomplishing those great plans you've made for your family. Teach your children to believe in themselves.

- Success Principle 60

SET A GOAL WITH A TIME LIMIT.

Sometimes families establish a goal
but never get around to accomplishing
it. This creates a feeling of
mistrust in children's hearts. A
time limit takes away the phrase,
"Tomorrow son, we'll do it tomorrow."

Forty-one years later, I'm still quoting from Psalm 1 when I preach and I'm still telling the world that the blessed man is the happy man. It all started back in homiletics class in Central Bible College when I found that Scripture to be of great strength in my life. It now becomes my final success principle.

- Success Principle 61

SUCCESS IS MORE THAN HAVING MONEY
IN YOUR POCKET, IT'S BEING FULFILLED
IN YOUR HEART.

Happiness described in Psalm 1,
is a success principle that has
helped me everyday. I sleep
through the night with little money
on the night stand, but a smile
on my face, knowing in my heart
that I am doing my best to live
out God's call.

● ● ●

Happiness for me is driving down the highway in my motorhome with Judy, my wife of 38 years, following my children in their RVs and watching our seven grandchildren grow up as we travel.

Happiness for me is conducting services and seminars and performing dramas with my family.

Happiness for me is "Fighting the good fight, keeping the faith, running the race, and having the rare privilege of passing this HomeFire baton on to my children who, in turn, will pass it on to their children.

Happiness for me is having a twenty-two year old come up to me after the service with tears in his eyes and thank me for bringing my family to his church because at the altar his dad hugged him for the first time in his life.

Happiness for me is having a teenager thank me for coming to his church three months before when his parents were breaking up their home. He said that since our service they have fallen in love again and have put their family back together.

Happiness is hearing that a mother found forgiveness after having an abortion 16 years ago.

Happiness is knowing that many times things cannot be seen at the time of our service but hearing many months later how God did a great miracle for a family.

Happiness is living a life that is "OUT OF THE ORDINARY!"

Ju**D**y

Robin

Dav**E**

P**A**ul

Mike

Conni**E**

G**R**eg

Kri**S**tie

Our good friends Chuck and Vickie Fichtner designed this acrostic for us. HomeFire truly is a family of DREAMERS. There's no time like the present to start dreaming...

Sweet Dreams!

CHAPTER TWENTY NINE

I CAN TYPE.

AS THE AUTHOR, I TYPED EVERY WORD OF THIS BOOK. I must confess I didn't type at 90 words a minute and I made lots of mistakes!

CHAPTER THIRTY

©HERGIE

MY FINAL STATEMENT.

IT WAS EASIER TO LIVE MY LIFE THAN TO WRITE ABOUT IT!

"O God, Thou has taught me from my youth; And I still declare Thy wondrous deeds. And even when I am old and gray, O God, do not forsake me, until I declare Thy strength to this generation, Thy power to all who are to come." (Psalm 71:17,18) NASB

HomeFire Order Form

Music *All music available on cassette or CD!*
   Cassettes - $8.00 ea. or 5 for $25.00
   CD's - $12.00 ea.
- **Send The Fire • Peace Speaker • HomeFire**　　　　　_____
- **I Am Not Ashamed**　　*Mike and Connie Hammer*　　_____
- **The Kingdom Of The Lord**　　　*Gregory Hollis*　　_____
- **Deep Down**　　　　　*Dave Kyllonen*　　_____

Videos $10.00 ea.
- **Dreams Are Forever**　　*Musical Drama*　　_____
- **Let's Hear It For Love**　　*Musical Drama*　　_____
- **Love Will Be Our Home**　　*Musical Drama*　　_____
- **House Beautiful**　　*Practical Teaching*　　_____

HomeFire Seminar Series $15.00 ea. or two for $25.00
Seminar Series I - Leadership Skills In The Home -　　_____
   Following God's Lead - Who's The Boss
   A Vessel For Honor - Raising Your Children
   Before They *Raze* You - Forgiveness, Oil For
   The Family
Seminar Series II - D-R-E-A-M-E-R-S, A Family　　_____
   Meeting - Help! "I'm a Parent!" - The
   Coming Crisis For Families - Getting The
   Best Out Of Life - Passing The Baton

Family Resource Material
Developing Godly Character In Children - $20.00　　_____
   A practical handbook and resource guide for
   parents. *Identifies 93 Biblical character qualities*.
Coinciding Flashcards - $8.00 per set　　_____

Mail your order to: HomeFire Family Ministries
**　　　　　　　　　　　PO Box 3126**
**　　　　　　　　　　　Shiremanstown, PA 17070**

Please make checks payable to Homefire - add $3.00 postage.

NOW AVAILABLE! NEVER BEFORE OFFERED!

2 ALBUMS ON EACH CASSETTE OR CD!!!

- **OVATION**
(Live in Toledo)
The Inspirational Album of the Year!
Dove Award Winner!
Ovation is a double album!

- **NOTHING BUT THE GOSPEL TRUTH**
- **WE'VE GOTTA SING**
Here are the Warner Brothers albums!

- **STATUE OF LIBERTY**
- **TOWN AND COUNTRY**
"Statue of Liberty" - #1 song in gospel
music in 1976! My favorite albums!

After years of waiting, these releases can be yours! Order the best of The Couriers during their 25 year history, even the Warner Brothers albums on cassette or CD!!

Each double album set is only $10.00!
Buy all 3 sets for $25.00!!

(Please indicate if you would like your double album set on
CASSETTE OR **CD**!)

Send Orders To: HomeFire Family Ministries
PO Box 3126 Shiremanstown, PA. 17070

How **You** can
Join the Family
of HomeFire...

helping us reach hurting families in this great land and around the world!

As one complete family, spanning three generations, our mission is to equip families with Godly principles for life now, and life in the 21st century. All that we are and everything we own has been given to this cause of strengthening families.

Your monthly support is needed! Individuals and businesses can be strategically linked with us by making tax-deductible contributions. Your participation will help underwrite the rising costs of transportation and the expenses of developing the finest family resources available today. If you can help, please **JOIN THE FAMILY!**

For more details about **JOINING THE FAMILY**, please contact us at:

HomeFire Family Ministries
PO Box 3126
Shiremanstown, PA. 17070
Phone: (309) 699-3473